THE BOOK OF
THE POOR IN SPIRIT

THE BOOK
OF THE POOR
IN SPIRIT

BY A
FRIEND OF GOD
(Fourteenth Century)

A GUIDE TO
RHINELAND MYSTICISM

*Edited, Translated
and with an Introduction*

by

C. F. KELLEY
(Ph.D., Prag.)

Egil Grislis.

HARPER & BROTHERS
NEW YORK

PRINTED IN ENGLAND

To

D. S.
H. S.
A. S.
D. S.

" Blessed are the poor in spirit, for theirs is the kingdom of heaven."—Matthew 5.3.

CONTENTS

❋❋❋❋❋❋❋❋❋❋❋❋❋❋❋❋❋❋❋❋❋❋❋❋

ix

Part II

*GOD'S WORK AND MAN'S
CO-OPERATION*

Part III

*HOW A MAN SHALL ATTAIN TO A
PERFECT LIFE*

I. FOLLOWING CHRIST'S LIFE AND
   TEACHING

INTRODUCTION

✳✳✳✳✳✳✳✳✳✳✳✳✳✳✳✳✳✳✳✳✳✳✳✳✳

IT is an accepted maxim that the more a particular age
becomes secular and dead to religious truth, the more
marked becomes the line of demarcation between the
indifferent and the concerned. The concerned person finds
himself bound to abstain from occupations and pleasures
which, though not injurious in themselves, have become
corrupt. Furthermore, the perils of enthusiasm, the mistaking one's own natural emotions for divine influence, are
greatest when that influence, known by the concerned to be
real, is ignored, even denied by the world in general. Yet
the world in general always claims to be preoccupied with
truth.

When we counsel others: "Know the truth, and the truth
shall make you free," what kind of truth do we mean? How
often do we confuse truth with a collection of undigested
facts, a mere recording of events? We concern ourselves with
what has taken place but too frequently fail to ask why.
Because no "scientific proof" is possible we tend to ignore
real issues. We become indifferent to the realm of opinion
and speculation. But intellectuals without conviction are
little more than irresponsible disciples of objectivity, and
their disciples in turn become a clan of spectators, not actors.
For without real purpose there can be no real action.

The pursuit of truth is certainly not synonymous with
objective research. It is not an examination of the different
sides of a question and then refraining from adopting a conviction. It concerns itself with meaning and purpose, first
principles and ultimate reality. It also concerns itself with
belief and commitment. And belief and commitment imply

1   B

concerned action. The more a man commits himself to the
pursuit of God's truth, which is inseparable from His beauty
and goodness, the more receptive he becomes to the divine
influence.

The truly concerned man—one might even call him a
mystic—recognizes more in nature than mere natural pheno-
mena, more in the word of God than its verbal meaning.
Every person, thing or event is for him a vision from the
Unseen. Viewing God in all things and all things in God,
he lives in a world of parables full of spiritual meaning. And
though the presence of God is for him everywhere, he finds
it most where it is perceived through the eyes of faith. He
requires nothing mysterious to produce it, for it is already
there and everywhere. And when he turns to the Scriptures
he finds far more than the mere student of the letter. Regardless of all else that the Scriptures may contain, he also finds
in them the clearest recording of that which has been revealed
to man as indispensable for his soul's pursuit.

Certain members of the concerned have in each age
endeavoured to pass on to others what they have found to
be the spirit behind the letter of Scripture. Their exaltation
of eternal views, with a life centred in them, springs primarily
from a personal inward experience. Yet their findings are
most sound and most helpful to others when they are supported by philosophical common sense, the witness of other
concerned seekers as well as the revealed Word itself.

In presenting to English readers a modern edition of *The
Book of the Poor in Spirit* I am presenting what all who are
familiar with the text agree is one of the most " concerned "
works of Christian literature. Taking for his theme " Blessed
are the poor in spirit, for theirs is the kingdom of heaven,"[1]
this unknown fourteenth-century writer has composed a treatise
of such high spirituality and balanced intellectual power that
it ranks with the leading writings of the school of Rhineland
mysticism. When all sides of its teachings are considered,
it is seen to be perhaps most representative of those Friends
of God whose leaders were David von Augsburg, Meister

Eckhart, Nicholas von Strassburg, Johann Tauler, Heinrich Suso and Marcus von Lindau. Moreover, its author accomplished what some of his colleagues failed to accomplish— a preservation of their mystical doctrine, coupled with practical counselling, within the sound framework of scholastic thought and the authority of Christian tradition.

1

Until the latter half of the nineteenth century, *The Book of the Poor in Spirit* was thought to have been written by Johann Tauler. Many aspects of its doctrine are akin to the teachings of this great exponent of German spirituality. But only Tauler's *Sermons*, and not more than eighty per cent of these can, according to the critics, be said to be truly his.[2] Even those who now believe that Tauler could not have composed this book agree that it was written about 1350 by a Dominican Friend of God—one of that large group of concerned seekers who formed the nucleus of the Rhineland school of mysticism. Nevertheless, the author has taken pains, not only to conceal his own identity, but to construct a treatise (or set of four treatises) compact, complete and individual in itself, yet full of the basic teachings which guided the mystic spirit of that time. (See Addendum A, p. 287.)

It is a book which has had great influence on Christian thought since Marcus von Lindau, who died in 1392, quoted so extensively from it in his treatise on the *Ten Commandments*.[3] Those who admire it consider it not only an outstanding spiritual classic, but also a summary of the teachings of fourteenth-century German spirituality. In other words, here is what not a few have taken to calling the text-book of the Rhineland school, a compact instruction which is clearer and more precise than that to be found in the actual sermons of Eckhart, Nicholas von Strassburg or Tauler himself.

Surius, the famous Carthusian monk from Cologne, translated it into Latin in 1548 and through this translation it played a part in the rise of the Carmelite mystics in Spain;

it was on the shelves of St. François de Sales; both sides of the Quietest controversy referred to it; even the English Benedictine, Father Augustine Baker, had frequent access to it. All, of course, attributed it to Tauler and even regarded it as his most important work.

Since it is a religious book which is almost entirely free of any dogmatic and formal questions, it has always commended itself to a large number of Christians. Lutherans have praised it highly,[4] though some of its teachings, especially those placing a stress on charity, were naturally criticized by some followers of Melanchthon and the Calvinist Beza. When one learns about the influence the book exerted on Abbot Blosius, it is easy to understand how he confuted their objections.[5] For one of the features of the book is that its views are those shared not only with the orthodox Rhineland teachers, but with the most eminent saints and doctors of Christendom and the Plotinian thinkers of earlier times. Obviously influenced by the philosophical groundwork of St. Thomas Aquinas, the author moves on into the realm of pure spirituality and at once joins hands with Richard or St. Victor, St. Bernard, St. Augustine and the Pseudo-Dionysius.

As early as 1250 the Rhineland became a centre of interest for the Franciscan and Dominican Orders of the Church. It was they who were mostly instrumental in causing the sudden development of German prose, elevating it to a level equal to, if not above, the wonderful poetry of the old Minnesingers and Nibelungen-Lieder. The Franciscans and Dominicans more and more came to the front and soon proved, through their admirable treatises and sermons, that the German language of their time was adequate to cope with their most profound and lofty themes. Most of the Rhineland mystics came from these Orders and their impact throughout the Upper and Lower Rhine became so great that they have always been known as the fathers of German speculation.

It is in these men that the beginnings of German philosophy, the origins of well-known systems of Western thought,[6] and even the seeds of later spiritual movements may be traced.

Apart from the men mentioned above—the popular leaders—
there were a host of lesser known men and women, each
caught up in the rapid growth of this religious movement, a
movement, what is more, which lessened the gap between the
clergy and the laity. It was one of those wonderful yet strange
periods of spiritual flowering, perhaps one unequalled by any
other in Western tradition. How are we to account for such
a sudden bursting forth into the realms of mysticism and
speculative thought, a flower which bloomed for a few genera-
tions and then withered and died? More puzzling still is how
such a flower could bloom in the midst of the brambles of
fourteenth-century society. For it was a society which remained preoccupied with the unholy feuds of peasants, princes,
bishops and monks, a society which lay burdened by unbeliev-
able sufferings, plagues and wars. Or is it only a weak human
eye which creates this paradox?

Yet in times of religious, political and economic conflict—
in times like our own—the good people of this world always
cry out: "Stop this madness!" But how can we expect anything but a certain degree of insanity in this world of time and
space which by the very nature of its existence is schizoid—split
between hell and heaven, evil and good? It is then that our
mystics and saints tell the merely good people that love is
still the only virtue that counts, that the only real sin is not
to love. As our author says: "God prefers any kind of love
to no love at all" (Part IV, Chapter iv, Section 3).

But a period of crime and natural calamity does not alone
explain the rise of the Rhineland mystic spirit. There have
been other dark ages which failed to produce it. Furthermore,
that spirit has sometimes flourished, as in sixteenth-century
Spain, when the local culture was at its peak. Nor can
one say that Rhineland mysticism was merely a reaction
against the theological schools. After all, most of its leaders
were products of scholasticism and, in fact, incorporated
scholastic traditions into the very core of their teachings.
Neither Eckhart, Nicholas von Strassburg nor Tauler are ever
found in opposition to St. Thomas or Albertus Magnus in an

essential point of doctrine.[7]   For them theology was of the
utmost importance.

To say that the ascendancy of the Rhineland school was a
protest against institutional religion is at best a fragmentary
truth.   Here again it must be remembered that its leaders
were all members of the Church hierarchy.   These Friends of
God did not rebel against the established order of the Church
as it existed in those hectic days of the early fourteenth
century.   They were in their beginnings a result of the indifferent conditions of the times.   If some of their descendants
later went off on particular heretical tangents, that was certainly due to other causes and was in no way connected with
the origins of the movement.

Perhaps the most plausible explanation is that this sudden
development of the mystic spirit was due to the introduction
of scholastic philosophy to educated women in the convents.[8]
Continual wars and conflicts had killed many men and caused
a surplus of women.   Many unmarried women of the educated
class entered the cloistral life, and, as a result, religious houses,
especially those of the Dominicans, greatly increased in
number and importance.   The duty to administer these
nunneries and maintain their spiritual discipline fell, of
course, to the friars, and those chosen to undertake this
pastoral care were learned teachers.   Hence it happened that
in these religious houses of women there was an active intellectual life and many writings in prose and verse give evidence
of it.   Take, for example, Mechtild von Magdeburg, Margaret
and Kristina Ebner, Elsbeth von Begenhofen, Adelheid Lang-
mann, Elsbeth Stagel.

The task of the friars, then, was to express theological and
philosophical ideas in a guise that would make them understood by these women.   The result of all this was that many
of the finest spiritual writings were sermons, conferences or
treatises designed for nuns.   Most of Tauler's Sermons, the
Conferences of Nicholas von Strassburg and Heinrich von
Nördlingen, Suso's wonderful *Little Book of Eternal Wisdom*
and, perhaps *The Book of the Poor in Spirit* belong to this

category. Scholasticism provided a philosophy of mysticism. Sermons and treatises of a devotional nature were composed in the vernacular; and where technical terms suitable to the Latin were lacking, they had to be invented; abstract ideas were simplified and a more personal tone was introduced so that the true seeker became passionately aware of the immediate presence and accessibility of God. Thus the eloquence of these early Friends of God kindled a flame that long survived their death.

2

In the Rhineland of the fourteenth century, the Dominican Order held a position somewhat similar to that of the Society of Jesus three centuries later. It was the academy of great theologians, preachers and confessors. Originally bound together to combat heresy, these sons of St. Dominic soon realized the necessity of providing a teaching which could purify the streams of European thought at their source. In the first half of the thirteenth century they surmounted the opposition of University heads at Paris and succeeded in founding chairs of theology from which they challenged the paganizing philosophers of Christendom with their own weapons of reason. In St. Albertus Magnus of Cologne and St. Thomas Aquinas they in a sense reconquered philosophy for the Church and christianized Aristotle who soon took Plato's place as the Master of Philosophy.

Some of our Rhineland mystics had spent their student days at Paris, and most of them were thorough-going scholastics, that is, they thought it supremely important to give reason the noble respect due to it and to establish an intellectual expression for belief. Eckhart, Nicholas von Strassburg and Tauler, for instance, were reckoned among the most intellectual men of their day, but by the time they reached their prime, especially Tauler in the second quarter of the fourteenth century, many of the French Schoolmen had let themselves be taken prisoner by this wonderful gift of reason

which St. Thomas had found so liberating. As our author
says: "True wisdom is not studied in Paris but in the
Passion,"[9] which echoes St. Bonaventure who wrote: "The
divine Word teaches one more in real wisdom than all study,"[10]
a statement with which St. Thomas certainly agreed. Tauler
says in one of his sermons: "Those great teachers at Paris
read enormous books and turn over the pages with great
diligence, which is a very good thing. But spiritually enlightened men read the true living book, wherein all things
live. They turn over the pages of the heavens and the earth
and study the admirable wonders of God."[11]

Though recognizing the study of God's wonders to be the
best that a man can choose, Tauler and his colleagues always
hold that the study of philosophy is a "very good thing",
that reason, like form, like the body, is a good if not necessary vehicle to God. This sound position, however, was not
favoured by all. There were some people in the Rhine provinces who advocated the denial of reason and form, the
doctrine of absolute freedom of the spirit, the abolition of all
distinctions between the creature and the Creator. Called
Beghards and Brethren of the Free Spirit they were quite
energetic in their proselytizing work among the clergy as well
as the laity. In Cologne they were very numerous, and in
spite of—or because of?—frequent persecutions, they continued to grow. That some of the Rhineland mystics were
connected with them is certain, but they do not seem to have
exercised any influence on men like Eckhart, Tauler, Suso
or our author, who preached and wrote against them, and
whose position is clear enough: "The Free Spirits, striving
after a false freedom, and on the pretext of following
the interior light, follow only the inclination of their own
nature."[12]

The following selection of passages from Tauler is also worth
noting, for it furnishes a complete refutation of the charge of
these tendencies sometimes brought against his own sermons,
and it serves as a fitting prelude to *The Book of the Poor in
Spirit*:

From these two errors proceeds the third, which is the worst of all. The persons who are thus confused call themselves beholders of God. . . . They think that they are free from sin, united to God without any means whatsoever, and that they have risen above all subjection to the Holy Church, above the Commandments of God and above all works of virtue. For they believe this emptiness to be so noble a thing that it should in no way be hindered. Hence they remain empty of all subjection and do no works either toward them who are above or below them. They believe that if they work it hinders the work of God, and therefore they empty themselves of all virtue. And they would be so empty that they would not give praise or thanks to God nor pray, for they have already, as they suppose, all that they could pray for and think that they are without self-will. . . . For the sake of this emptiness of spirit they desire to be free, and obedient to none, neither the Pope, nor the Bishop, nor the Pastor; and though they seem outwardly to be so at times, yet they are inwardly obedient to none, neither in will nor action. . . . They believe themselves to be exalted above the angels, and above all human merit and faith, so that they can neither increase in virtue nor commit sin. For they live, as they suppose, without will, and possess their spirits in peace and emptiness, and have become nothing in themselves and one with God. They believe that they may do freely, without sin, whatsoever nature desires, because they have attained to the highest innocence, and there is no law or commandment for them, and therefore they follow all the lusts of the flesh in order that the emptiness of the spirit may remain unharmed. They care neither for fasts, nor feasts, nor precepts, because they live without conscience in all things. Let each man examine himself whether he be not one of these![13]

The fanatical Beghards were by no means the only promoters of heresy under the guise of mysticism. The Catharists, Waldenses, Albigenses, the Jochamists and a host of others were still making their presence felt. In fact, the fourteenth-century Rhinelanders were almost engulfed in religious anarchy. And little wonder! The whole German race was riddled with political dissension and warfare. These battles were in turn mixed up with the religious controversies then flourishing. Moreover, there was discord between the heads of the Church and its most diligent servants. Bishops clashed with the Pope, pastors with their bishops; Franciscans clashed with Dominicans and these with their Provincial Superiors.

On 25 November, 1314, at Aix-la-Chapelle, both Ludwig of Bavaria and Frederick of Austria were crowned head of the Holy Roman Empire. The result, of course, was a war which lasted until 1322. The whole Rhineland was divided between the rival Emperors and when Frederick marched up the great river in 1315 and entered Strasbourg, most of the burghers received him, not as their sovereign, but merely as a distinguished guest. The Bishop of Strasbourg and the clergy, on the other hand, gave him regal honours. When Ludwig heard of this he immediately confirmed the privileges and liberties of the city. Five years later when he arrived with his army and was offered the allegiance of the people in the great cathedral, he again confirmed their privileges. Public worship, however, had been suspended by the clerics who still recognized Frederick as Emperor and on whose side most of the nobles took their stand.

When Ludwig finally took Frederick prisoner, the hot war ceased, and when many of the noble families and some of the clergy came over to his side, it seemed that peace might be restored. But Pope John XXII, fearing that Ludwig's power, popularity and conceited temperament might make him too independent of the Papal Chair, decided to intervene in the affairs of the Empire. He refused to acknowledge Ludwig and placed all who did (this finally included whole cities!) under the famous interdict of 1324. Not only did this action create new and dreadful calamities throughout Europe, it stirred up the people to a resistance which was bound to weaken their reverence for the Holy See.

The clash between temporal and spiritual authority became more marked. Again Ludwig countered. He published a manifesto in which he refuted all the accusations brought against him and tried to prove that the Pope lacked authority to judge the Emperor. And to display his own sense of unchallengeable authority, he ordered that no one should observe the papal interdict. In fact he sentenced all who did, individuals, communities or cities, to be deprived of their citizen rights and privileges. In many places the churches had long been closed, and when the clergy did not obey the Emperor's edict to open them, the impatient citizens forced all priests who refused to perform services to leave.

This split the clergy into two parties. The larger number obeyed the Pope and removed themselves to other provinces. Some remained, particularly the Dominicans and Franciscans, who had availed themselves of the special privilege granted to their Orders of celebrating Mass during the time of the interdict. They did not cling to this out-dated privilege very long, however, for, as the Emperor continued in his open opposition to the Holy See, the fear of excommunication weighed more heavily upon them and all but a few left. In some places churches, monasteries and schools stood empty for nearly three years.

How this affected our author we do not know. But Johann Tauler was in the midst of it all and the question has often been raised as to the part he played. Most of the evidence indicates that he, along with the Dominican house at Strasbourg, submitted to the Holy See. If this meant the giving up of important duties in that city where he lived with the mystic Johann von Sterngassen and the theologian Johann von Dambach, it certainly increased his field of labour elsewhere. Most of the free cities from Cologne to Basle heard his sermons and lectures, and he became quite as well known as his teacher Eckhart of the preceding generation.

There was a time during the interdict when Tauler lived with his Carthusian friends at their monastery near Strasbourg. Neither Tauler in his sermons nor our author makes precise comments on current events or on political and religious problems; but the tone of their writings certainly evinces an utter disappointment in the conduct of their temporal and spiritual leaders. Tauler says: "Now the Apostle tells us to contend against princes and powers, and the rulers of the darkness of this world. This means the devils. But it also means the princes of this world, who ought to be the best of all, and are nevertheless the very horses on which the devils ride to sow discord and treason, and who torment their subjects by their pride and unjust tyranny and manifold oppressions, as we now see throughout the world."[14]

And to all these political and ecclesiastical disturbances even greater miseries were added. The upper Rhineland was successively laid waste by violent tempests, earthquakes and famine, culminating in the Black Death of 1348. In some places two-thirds of the population perished, causing a state of terror and the complete disruption of social bonds. Popular fanaticism frequently accused the Jews of causing the plague by poisoning the wells, and the furious mobs, setting fire to the ghettoes, burnt thousands of men and women and children in their homes. It was not uncommon to find among the masses a hope for a Messiah in the person of the great " priest-hater ", Frederick II, who was to rise from the dead, redeem the poorer classes, punish the priests, force nuns and monks to marry, and then crusade to the Holy Land and place his crown on the Mount of Olives. Nor was it uncommon to find people turning to another fanaticism, to the extravagant penance which developed into the ghastly processions of the Flagellants.

All these convulsions of the natural and social world struck terror in the depths of men's hearts. But, as often happens in an age of fierce violence and suffering, the fourteenth-century Rhineland culture was distinguished by restless and energetic productivity. A general level of excellence was not to be expected in a land so broken and disordered, but the soil of German human nature was nevertheless rich in capacities. From its confused and retarded vegetation, rare plants emerged —inventors, architects and craftsmen of great capabilities. These people, who were unable to produce a great statesman or a Dante, did put into use two implements which have done most to revolutionize Western society—gunpowder and the printing press. But more than this, it produced men like Eckhart, Suso and Tauler who, with the earnestness of profound conviction, began to discourse to the people in their native tongue on lofty philosophical and spiritual themes, till then only thought fit to be treated in Latin before learned assemblies. And because virtue has no publicity, it is unlikely that we shall ever discover how many saints it produced.

3

The need for a revival of the religion of the heart was, in the fourteenth-century Rhineland, quite obvious. But it was equally necessary that such a revival should preserve as well as respect the established order of religion, for there was no other social bond able to hold men together. Keeping this order intact when so many forces were tending towards schism was one of the secrets of the Dominicans and Franciscans.

Now, in spite of all the scandals of that age, most of the people were far from being " wicked ". In that age, as in ours, there were many men and women who possessed clean, calm and affectionate natures. Being schooled in conscientious habits, so many of their desires were for quite harmless or even good things that it was frequently difficult to see why or how they should be renounced. They were good people—just, kind, finding much of their personal happiness in the happiness of others. And for the most part they lived in pleasant relations with their neighbours and had little to trouble their conscience beyond the fear of neglecting the path upon which duty had called them.

But the dangers to which such people were exposed were more insidious (because less obvious) than those which faced others who were sorely tempted. Their greatest danger perhaps was their tendency to depend too much on the respect and affection which others gave them. They were in danger of measuring themselves according to a standard of virtue which had come to be, not one of spiritual combat, but one of placing intellectual clarity above moral strength and insight; of mistaking the comfort they felt in the performance of duty for submission to God's will; and perhaps most important, of recoiling from new perceptions of truth which might temporarily disorientate their faith and disturb the even-going pattern of their lives.

The spiritual welfare of such people as these (and we have seen that a great number of them were nuns) became the chief responsibility of the friars. In lifting a few of them out of their groove, they did not turn them into mystics or saints; but they filled them with a concern for truth and the spiritual life, and out of the concern mysticism and sanctity were the logical developments. Now when the concern is genuine it produces a genuine mysticism, not a magical pseudo-mysticism based on the assumption that demons, superhuman powers, angels, even God, can be compelled to do whatever the ego may want them to do. There is a pseudo-mysticism— all too natural and human—which seeks mastership over God; there is a genuine mysticism—supernatural and divine—which seeks friendship with God.

The term "Friend of God" is one which is frequently observed in the writings of the Rhineland mystics. It is a title which seems to have two different connections.[15] On the one hand it indicates those who habitually practise a spiritual, rather than a mere formalistic devotion. On the other hand, "Friends of God" denoted an actual group of individuals who formed more or less a nucleus to this religious revival. They differed widely from each other in station, opinion and vocation, counting among their members Franciscans and Dominicans, married and single tertiaries, nobles, craftsmen and servants, a great flock of nuns like Margaret and Kristina Ebner, many Beguines, a Queen like Agnes of Hungary, a banker like that strange and dubious Rulman Merswin, then Ludolf the Carthusian, Konrad von Kaiserheim, Deitrich von Köln—even the Flemish Ruysbroeck, even Johann von Schön-hofen of the Netherlands, for the *Pfaffengasse* or "Parson's alley", the highway of the Rhine which led to Rome, had its northern extension into the heart of the Low Countries.

The title *Gottesfreunde* or Friends of God, which also applied to many others less known, was undoubtedly used among them-selves to indicate those who gave evidence of being more truly concerned about the realities of religion than the great majority of their neighbours. In John 15:15, we read: "I will not now call you servants: for the servant knoweth not what his lord doeth. But I have called you friends: because all things, whatsoever I have heard of My Father, I have made known to you." It was an inevitable process that those filled with such common concerns should instinctively seek out each other. By clinging to and relying upon each other, an association without precise plans naturally developed. And if one reads the writings of men like Tauler, Suso and Ruysbroeck it would appear that the main distinction and bond of the *Gottesfreunde* was the sense of having entered into a personal co-operation with God. And this friendship with God was accompanied by a compassion for those who had fallen, either into wickedness or into mere respectable goodness, and a desire to assist them in their efforts to raise themselves to where the reality of God became more real than the realities of time and place.

The Friends of God did not form a sect. In fact they rejected any tendency in that direction. As Tauler himself says: "The prince of this world has in our time been sowing everywhere brambles among the roses so that the roses are frequently suffocated, or seriously torn by the brambles. Dear Children, there needs to be a flight or a distinction, some sort of divergence, whether within the cloisters or without, and that such friends of God should profess to be unlike the friends of the world does not make them into a sect."[16] And these friends of God became friends of the friars. Many of them were lay people, some continued with their professions, introducing into them a godlike direction. Others—women particularly, the famous Beguines—without entering any of the established Orders, withdrew from society and formed little communities. And though they lived together without monastic rules, they differed little from the regular religious. References to these communities are often found in the friars' sermons, and a great number of their members attached themselves to the leaders of this religious movement.

The Friends of God aimed at becoming saints and at giving

edification in Catholic devotion, not heterodox enthusiasm; at affective contemplation, not mystical brain-work. And that leaders like Tauler had full confidence in them is shown when he says: "For those who want to live for the truth, it is a great assistance to have a Friend of God who may guide them by the spirit of God. It would be well worth one's while to travel a hundred leagues to seek out an experienced Friend of God."[17] Similar affirmation can be found in Suso's *Briefbuchlein*.

As long as the *Gottesfreunde* remained under the guidance of men like Tauler and Suso, they were preserved from defect. In an age that was witnessing the sterility of scientific theology, Heinrich Suso was founding the Children of Mary. As his *Little Book of Eternal Wisdom* was composed for spiritual reading, so was his *The Book of Truth*[18] written to refute the errors of the Beghards. Nicholas von Strassburg, himself a great mystic, placed more emphasis on ascetical devotion than on metaphysical speculation. And Tauler, as we have seen, opposed the pseudo-mysticism of the Free Spirits and the schismatical tendencies of Ludwig of Bavaria while directing his followers towards a full co-operation with God's grace. But the glory of the Friends of God was not to last.

It is very easy to show that the leaders of Rhineland mysticism were orthodox in all their principal teachings and that their obedience to the Church was throughout irreproachable. But it must also be recognized that their mystical doctrine of the inner and outer life, of the spirit and the letter, gave lesser minds an excuse for a disregard of many aspects of Catholicism, so far as in their century and land it consisted largely in formalism and obedience to external rule. For instance, the influence of Meister Eckhart's boldness is strongly felt in Tauler and Suso, in the mysticism of Ruysbroeck, and later in the synthesis of Nicholas von Cues, in Thomas à Kempis and Angelus Selesius.[19] But it was also felt no less in persons not nearly as astute.

Professor J. M. Clark in his *The Great German Mystics*,[20] has been the first to point out to English readers how the unorthodox have often tried to claim Eckhart for their son, disregarding his overwhelmingly orthodox teachings and his unswerving fidelity to order and the Church. They endeavoured to establish their claim on a few exceptional passages which he later modified or corrected; but does not the exceptional always gain the most publicity? The Meister's occasional failure to clarify his views resulted in the condemnation of some of his statements. Though he recanted, the blow to mystical speculation was felt. And after his death in 1328, mysticism became more practical and less speculative. Of the three stages in the mystic way—purgative, illuminative and unitive, it was the first two, the preparatory stages, in which the will played the more decisive role, that received importance. No doubt the tragic fate of Eckhart opened the minds of men like Tauler and Suso to the dangers of discussing the profounder mysteries of theology in the presence of untrained minds. As Tauler says in one of his sermons:

> A well-loved Master [Eckhart] has written and preached to you concerning this mystic union with God and you did not understand him. He spoke in terms of eternity and you understood in terms of time. Dear Children, if I myself have talked too much about this, it is not too much for God, but you must forgive me; I will make amends gladly. This wonderful Master once spoke of that rare perception that knows no way or form. Many people seize upon this with their sensual minds and become sinful men, and for that reason it is a hundred times better that one should arrive at it by ways and forms.[21]

There is always a danger of institutionalism and of hardened systems of thought, whether scholastic or otherwise, in the touch of the living God on the heart of man. But Tauler, Suso and the other leaders did accomplish the unique task of upholding the law they were in duty bound to obey while at the same time speaking of the inner secrets of the soul, which became for them a profound reality. It meant the adoption of a *via media*, and as long as this middle course was kept, the Friends of God grew in spiritual and numerical strength. The association, however, did not long remain under the guidance of wise men.

One of the happy aspects of this movement was that it did

C

not confine itself to priests and nuns, and in one sense the merchant Rulman Merswin represented its lay genius. But Merswin, probably through ignorance and excessive zeal, played a large part in bringing the whole movement of Rhineland mysticism into disrepute. By founding a religious house which was to be a great centre for the Friends of God, and by writing a book about his alleged spiritual master—a mysterious layman of the upper Rhine (*Der Gottesfreund vom Oberland*),[22] he became very popular and after Tauler's (1361) and Suso's (1366) death, the favourite leader of the movement. It was then, and towards the turn of the fifteenth century, that certain exaggerated and erroneous doctrines began to creep into the Friends of God.[23] In a posthumous work, *The Book of the Nine Rocks*, Merswin ascribes to his unknown *Gottesfreund* (the Friend of God *par excellence*) counsellings in favour of violent discipline, all sorts of revelations, prophecies of impending chastisement and a divine mission to expurgate the Church. All of this is diametrically opposed to the teachings of Tauler, Suso and the author of *The Book of the Poor in Spirit*.

The story of Merswin and those who looked upon him as their spiritual leader is certainly one of the greatest puzzles of the fourteenth-century spiritual revival. Most of the critics have now concluded that his famous *Gottesfreund*, the anonymous spiritual director, was quite fictitious. Even in his own day the true descendants of Tauler and Suso refrained from association with these pseudo-Friends of God, and they gave still less attention to Nicholas von Basel who, upon Merswin's death, became the recognized leader of the heterodox wing. He, however, was eventually condemned as a Beghard and from 1410 the Friends of God, whether true or false, disappear. Either because of the general decline of the mystic spirit and the terminology connected with it, or because the term itself fell into disrepute as a result of Merswin and heretical associations, the word *Gottesfreund* fails to appear in the spiritual writings of the fifteenth century. Here, perhaps, is another example of how the death of true mysticism is the inevitable result of vicious attacks on the false mystics.

4

Not to know anything about mysticism is not to know anything about a most vital part of human nature. Yet there is
perhaps a greater need to realize what genuine mystics are not,
than what they are.   They are certainly not dreamers, nor
illuminists; they are not reactionaries nor maladjusted citizens.
Mysticism is neither a sect nor a religion. In fact the label
"mystic" is given to them by others; perhaps thousands of
the concerned believers have been and are mystics without
themselves being aware of the term. For mysticism is simply
the philosophy of religious experience. Mystics are, in other
words, the only religious empiricists, and is not the realm of
experience that which is most decisive of truth?

Genuine mysticism is not a disregard of the formal, of the
letter or the rite. It is that element in religion which is not
mere formalism. Although inseparable from the form, it is the
concern for the spirit within and is therefore not limited to any
one aspect of religion. Hence a contemplative monk, bowed
in meditation in his cell, may or may not be a mystic, no more
nor no less than a bus-driver, nurse or public accountant.
Nevertheless, the danger of disregarding the letter and the rite
is always possible with mystics, and it is in this disregard that
exaggeration, error and spiritual pride inevitably lie. The risk
taken is obvious: the substitution of one's own natural feelings
for the Presence of God is a terrible abyss to fall into. And
now in our century the revival of the mystic spirit will either
harm or newly inspire traditional Christianity, which, without
it, must necessarily degenerate into mere formalism, a religion
of credulity and ceremonial routine. But fear of that risk is
not only more injurious to religion that any error which may
result from a failure to keep on the knife edge, it is a denial
of life and the Holy Spirit Himself.

Mysticism is more, far more, than any experience of supreme
joy in nature. Its goal and way to that goal is not self or
nature, but God, and this explains why true mystics invariably
resort to analogies and symbols from natural things. Many

have taken refuge in trying to tell others of their experiences by
an explanation of Scriptures. Some have been inspired by the
Canticle of Canticles to sing out their experience in poetry.
Others have turned to the analogical terms afforded by philosophical speculation. Yet all seem to have the same message
about that truth which is beyond words, that experiential
knowledge of God.

Because the forces of nature are sometimes baffling to the
human mind, there have always been men and women who
have mistaken them for the supernatural. But there is a great
difference between the irrational and the supra-rational. Anyone who preoccupies himself only with extraordinary pheno-
mena, those as yet unprobed natural forces like hypnosis,
suggestion and telepathy, is a long way from an understanding
of true mysticism. For these are at best mystical symptoms
rather than cause. As the author of our book claims: "The
man who attaches importance to so-called visions, who preoccupies himself with images, shows that his ground is not
altogether pure and simple."[24] The true mystics are those
who ascend to union with God and leave behind them that
aspect of mysticism which intrigues the people of this world.
They have nothing to do with any form of self-seeking trans-
cendentalism, for in anything less than union with God the
chief agent, singly or collectively, is inevitably found to be
man.

Christian mystics concern themselves very much with mystery,
and this probably is the reason why so many people hold them
in low esteem. But the mysteries with which they concern
themselves are neither many nor fantastic. They are simply God
and the soul—and the Incarnation. They concern themselves
with this third mystery because through it God is made known
to the soul. In other words, Christian mysticism—and Rhineland mysticism is very Christian—views the following of Christ
as the soul's Way to the eternal Godhead. A few well-known
words from St. John and St. Paul sum up the whole subject.

Indeed certain mystics have, in moments of enthusiasm, said
more than this, and their statements are usually considered

exaggerated. Now exaggeration is not synonymous with untruth, but it sometimes evinces a dogmatism which is founded, not on tested and abiding wisdom, but on the individual passing emotions. Though the Church must guard herself against exaggerations, she can never eliminate mysticism. Since it is her very life she dares not even attempt to do so. For it is another name for love, spiritual growth, the rights of the human soul, for the privilege of immediate access to Christ. It is another name for the presence of the Holy Spirit in the heart of the pursuer of truth.

The mystic is always of his own age and environment. And it is quite evident that the basic beliefs of the author of this guide to Rhineland mysticism were precisely those of any other Catholic of his time. The spiritual element of his teaching is very predominant, but it never excludes the use of conventional language about the fall of man, the sufferings of human nature, the Redemption, and the precepts and counsels of Holy Christianity. In these teachings one will find the same spiritual substance which he has already found in St. Augustine, St. Bernard, the author of the *Imitation* and St. John of the Cross. He will also find, in this book particularly, a safeguard against exalting any strange intuition which he may think he has been granted into a cause of self-glorification. Moreover, he will not be tempted to imagine that he can become something merely by an act of acknowledging himself nothing. An act of faith alone is good and it has much to do with mystery. But it is not the mystic spirit. No, the spiritual life implies ceaseless perseverance in spiritual works.

Mysticism, then, is a way of apprehending spiritual truth and doing something about it. It implies a cultivation of a mode of thought which is really insusceptible of precise definition. It is neither purely intellectual nor purely intuitive, but a way that employs all the faculties of the human soul together. Reliance is placed on a spiritual awareness which somehow transcends the ordinary powers of understanding. The human soul perceives the ultimate reality of things, or the divine essence beneath the substance, and enjoys a real communion with the non-dual source of all being. Mysticism is a simple act of complete abandonment to God in the eternal now-moment.

This immediate knowledge of God and of things divine is derived neither from argument nor from observation. It ultimately involves the elimination of argument, concepts and images, or at least the transcendence of them. It is the result of a conscious spiritual experience, and hence grants, for the individual who holds it, a conclusive degree of certainty. One cannot acquire this knowledge in the way that one can acquire an understanding of the law of cause and effect or of the quantum theory. But one can prepare oneself for the reception of the divine influence which makes this experiential knowledge of God possible. And that is why the method of preparation is called mystical theology.

When mystics, especially those of the Rhineland school, sometimes apply the term *Nothing* to God, they neither admit to agnosticism nor insinuate that He does not exist. God exists, but in the sense in which no created thing can be said to exist, for His existence is *a se*, whole and complete. Since there is no name that human intelligence can think of adequate to define God, rather than lower God to a conditional status, they prefer not to name Him affirmatively. God is neither this nor that; He is not any *thing* comprehensible or limited. But this is not to say that human reason cannot know something about Him; because of its limitation it cannot know Him wholly, immediately. Since a concept cannot transcend itself it must be transcended by a kind of awareness which integrates all the faculties of the soul into one act. Whether the act is one of love or of knowledge was a question much debated among the fourteenth-century friars.

To study the Rhineland school of mystical theology is to study a most instructive part not only of Christian but of universal religious experience. It would be impossible for one to read their writings, any more than those of the later English, Spanish or French mystics, without realizing that their way of detachment and their profound speculations plumb the universal depths of theology and metaphysics. They are distinctly Christian, but they are also connected with those traditional doctrines which have prompted the truly great of every race which has left behind it more than elaborate grave-yards. In the Sufi, the Greek, the Buddhist and Hindu, one will discover the same craving after the eternal Spirit, the same attempt to put into words that experience of union between the soul and the Absolute.

If the student has not already made this discovery two courses will be open to him when he does. He can put aside all such thought as worthless, assuming that anything which Christianity has in common with Greek or Eastern traditions must be an intrusion and sophistication. Or he can regard these thoughts which spontaneously spring up among men separated from each other by race and time, to be the normal aspiration of the human spirit towards some real object. If he chooses the second course he can gain a sympathetic understanding of the aspirations, true or mistaken, of those who in darkness, and not in vain, sought a glimmer of light. And as he sees these Catholic teachings fulfilling those aspirations, he can renew his gratitude for them.

5

To the modern mind the writings of the fourteenth-century mystics frequently display a hard and didactic style. There is a certain arbitrary tone about them which makes even their concern for discretion and the *via media* seem a little hollow. Even Tauler, the most moderate of the school, appears quite exacting at times, a little too inclined to view spiritual matters in terms of black and white. Persistently concerned with the " best ", they were a little impatient with the " good " and the " better ". Gentleness was certainly not their chief virtue, for to them gentleness meant softness, and softness meant weakness. Theirs was not the age of devout humanism, but of cold Theism —the West had to wait another three and a half centuries for a St. François de Sales.

If the Rhineland mystics gave perfection a severe and almost superhuman description, their charting out of the way to perfection was just as barren. In composing a sermon or spiritual treatise they would select, by way of philosophical analogy, an attribute of God, such as simplicity, detachment, purity, freedom, and positivize it into a human virtue which men must perfect if they wanted to become godlike. Different ways to perfection were, of course, acknowledged, for they believed that all ways chosen, whether of detachment, of purity, of simplicity, implied the same exacting commitment. As Eckhart says:

> If a man is going to be like God, so far as any creature can be like God, it will be through spiritual poverty or detachment. For this leads to purity and from purity to simplicity and from simplicity to immovability. It is in these that the likeness between man and God is found. And this likeness is in grace, for it is grace which draws a man away from earthly things and cleans him from all things mortal. I would have you know that to be empty of created things is to be full of God, and to be full of created things is to be empty of God.[25]

Any way which could not be systematized into an all-out stripping of self was regarded with a suspicion which we in our day might call unwarranted. Now to understand this mode of thinking—a mode of thinking which did after all produce many holy people and preserve the Church of the "North Country" from a collapse into neo-barbarism—is perhaps the unique key to an understanding of Rhineland spirituality.

Surely the indispensable counsel of the Rhineland school was this detachment. Devotion, hope or the affective virtues did not preoccupy them in the sense that renunciation or spiritual poverty did. Rather than stress attachment to God, they stressed detachment from all that was not God. They wanted to lead man back to the state of his prime origin, a rather naked state and a desolate journey. Suso begins *The Book of Truth* with this theme, likewise the author of the *Theologia Germanica*, and Tauler says: " In the physical universe the movement of the celestial spheres is most noble and perfect, because it continually returns again to the prime origin and beginning from which it began. Hence, the way of man which is most noble and perfect is when it returns again toward its origin and source."[26] And Eckhart: "The spiritually poor man who has abandoned to God all things as he possessed them when he existed not is blessed. None can do this but a wholly detached heart."[27]

This chiselling away of self and all that clings to self is the underlying theme of all their writings and this is why *The Book of the Poor in Spirit* is so representative of the school. Just as Suso's *The Book of Truth* is centred around one theme— the pursuit of detachment—so in this work the author sets forth the theory and practice of self-renunciation, a teaching which advocates external detachment as the natural fruit of internal detachment. There is nothing new in this doctrine. Saints of every age have assumed the excellence of external poverty as releasing the Christian from many cares and temptations; moreover they have insisted, as the Dominican Père Régamey reminds us in his *La Pauvreté*, that those who have only interior poverty run the risk of having none at all. If there is anything new or different about our author it is that he never for a moment relaxes his hold on the reader.

The whole treatise might be considered as a further develop- ment of Eckhart's sermon on Spiritual Poverty,[28] in which he says that "outward poverty is good and much to be commended in him who practises it voluntarily for the sake of our Lord Jesus Christ whose lot it was on earth". In this commentary on the first Beatitude, Eckhart explains how spiritual poverty has three features. The first is poverty of self-will: "thus shall a man be poor of self-will, as little willing and desiring as he willed and desired when he did not as yet exist". The second feature refers to the understanding: "Being poor in spirit means being poor of all particular *knowledge*, even as one who knows nothing (particular), neither of God nor of creatures nor of himself." "Thirdly, a poor man has nothing . . . and this is the most intimate poverty. One must be empty of things and of self-willed activities if one would be a fitting place for God to work in." Eckhart then enlarges this teaching to the perfection of spiritual poverty which is accomplished in

eternity, "where God finds no place in man outside Himself
in which work . . . Then God is His own patient and He is
His own work room, since God is in Himself the working."
In one of his tractates on Poverty, Eckhart points out its five
degrees:

> The first, devilish poverty, applies to those who do not have
> what they really want, outward or inward. That is their hell. The
> second, golden poverty, applies to those who, surrounded by goods
> and properties, pass empty out of them. If all that they owned
> was destroyed, the effect on them would be to leave them quite
> unmoved. . . . The third, voluntary poverty, applies to those who,
> renouncing all goods and honours, body and soul, empty them-
> selves of everything with good grace. . . . The fourth, spiritual
> poverty, belongs to those who have abandoned, not merely goods
> and honours, but also friends and relations; furthermore, they are
> above external works. The eternal Word performs all their work.
> . . . The fifth, divine poverty (in heaven), applies to those in
> whom God can find no place to work. Theirs is emptiness with-
> out and within, for they are free from all contingent form. In
> them all men are one man and that man is Christ.[29]

The Book of the Poor in Spirit bases its theme on this
sermon and also on the third and fourth degrees of poverty
as outlined in the tractate. Echoing these teachings our author
says: "Man is not perfect only when he lacks everything in
the inner spiritual man; he should at the same time become
detached, as far as possible, in the outward man."[30] Though
he tends to positivize this doctrine in the typical fourteenth-
century German manner, he nevertheless always insists that
a man must retain his necessities, that he must renounce external
things "only in so far as it is possible". Thus he wisely steers
clear of the dubious teachings of those, like the Fraticelli, who
taught that, to any high attainment in the Christian life, a
literal renunciation of all goods was absolutely essential.

"One should consider the needs of the body in such a way
that one always remains on the *via media* between excess and
too little."[31] "If a man directs bodily things with discretion
and gives the body the needs that pertain to it and which it
utilizes in God's service and in accordance with the teachings

of our Lord Jesus Christ, he is against neither truth nor perfection."[32] Our author goes on to say that if one is in need
of help, then he must certainly accept it. "If he refuses it,
he has less merit than if he accepted it." But "if you receive
more than you need, give it to others,"[33] for "virtue has an
order, and if one gives away this necessity he would act counter
to order, and that which he obtains for his needs it as right
as if he gave it to a poor man".[34] Furthermore, "he who has
proper order and discretion, who always takes the right proportion in all his words and actions, will always find God".[35]

Poverty of the body in no sense guarantees blessedness.
"If Christ said: 'Blessed are the poor in body' a sinner might
also be blessed and all wealthy people condemned."[36] Our
author repeats over and over again that to choose outward
poverty alone is not enough, that when it does not spring from
inward poverty it may easily increase the dangers of Pharisaism.
A man is poor only when "his spirit becomes a pure instrument of God".[37] It is this alone which assures perfection as
"the inwardly poor life is only a condition which makes it
possible for one to attend to God".[38] Why? Because "true
spiritual poverty is also true humility"; because "inwardness
and spiritual poverty stand on the same level".[39]

Perfection is approached by becoming "freed from the *love*
of temporal things",[40] and the more one is freed from the love
of them the more he will dispose of those which he does not
essentially require. "Man is a man not only through the soul,
but through the body as well,"[41] which implies, according to
this author, that if the interior imitation of Christ does not
result in an exterior imitation—"in so far as it is possible
and pertains to him"[42]—the harmonious relation between soul
and body becomes broken. The real measure, then, is not
merely the degree to which one does not possess excess goods,
but "it is detachment from all accidentals", and "they are on
the way to perfection because they judge no one".[43]

Yes, the author has much to say about Pharisaism, about
those who "appear outwardly as very holy men but who inwardly do not follow the truth whole-heartedly".[44] He also

has much to say about "rich people", about "those who intentionally acquire and take pleasure in excess possessions".[45] For he never forgets what Christ said about the rich man, the kingdom of heaven and the eye of the needle. But one dare not judge others for the simple reason that others are, through Christ, one's own responsibility and a failure to recognize this responsibility " inevitably brings upon one a higher judgement". Turned around, this also means that spiritual poverty includes the acceptance of the judgement which others make of one, for " only by patiently suffering the judgement of others is God's judgement removed ".[46]

What is true of material obstacles is even more true of spiritual obstacles. Influenced by scholasticism as he is, the author readily acknowledges that " he who spurns reason does her a great harm ".[47]   Human reason *can* perceive truth, "but it can never fully embrace or hold it since truth outruns reason ".[48]   Reason affords us an indirect knowledge of God, but in order to know God directly reason has to be transcended. Sooner or later created images block the soul's return to her prime origin.[49]   And, as our author says: " Since man must finally know God without images he must be stripped of them."[50]   Hence to become poor in spirit also involves a poverty in the mere human and particular way of knowing. Ultimately it calls for the *via negativa*—" the stripping-off-reason "—so that " reason may be free from working and that only God may be the master workman".[51]   Tauler says: " Be certain that when the soul is liberated from all images and media, God can then unite her with Himself immediately."[52]   In other words, true poverty of spirit leads to mystic union.

This is not pseudo-Gnosticism, nor is it bold mystical speculation. It is the fourteenth-century way of saying what St. Dionysius meant when he wrote: " That the soul may lose herself in that which can be neither seen nor touched, let her give herself entirely to this sovereign Object without belonging either to herself or to others; let her unite herself to the Unknown by the most noble part of herself, and because of her renouncement of knowledge, finally draw from this absolute

ignorance a knowledge which the understanding knows not
how to attain."[53]

This is also the scholastic doctrine of the *intellectus agens*
and pure contemplation. To be "lost in darkness" is to
contemplate in darkness. For St. Thomas taught that, if a
contemplation without images occurs, and if the active intellect has, according to the nature of light, the special function
to enlighten the phantasmata and to make what is intelligible
in them perceptible to the mind, then in this case, during the
contemplation, the active intellect remains quiet and the
essential imageless knowledge is imparted to the spirit without
any co-operation on its part.[54] This is also, of course, the
doctrine held by St. John of the Cross. Our author, however,
deprecates visions more than the Schoolmen, though they
would have agreed with him when he says that since Christ
these are not so necessary; for Catholic doctrine has never
taught that divine faith must be attached to them, always
associating a human faith with them, as Pope Benedict XIV
stated.[55] When, however, our author speaks of God's action
in the soul as an "essential work raised above all grace and
reason, a work in the light of glory ",[56] he is speaking of *lumen
gloriae* in a way rarely used by the Schoolmen. And when
he refers to the *synderesis* as the highest power of the soul he
endeavours, like many mystics, to combine the doctrines of
St. Bonaventure and St. Thomas. Whereas the former regarded
the *synderesis* as belonging to the affective part of the soul,
the latter called it a *virtus*, which transcends reason, but
belongs to the intellectual part. Some mystics, our author
among them, prefer to hold the belief of the early Fathers
that in this highest part of the soul love and knowledge dissolve
themselves into one integral act. (See Addendum B, p. 287.)

Now to point this out he says that there is also a poverty
of loving that the truly poor in spirit experience. St.
Thomas said: *Quidquid recipitur, recipitur juxta facultatem
recipientis*,[57] which forms the principle of our author's teaching
that "That which is to receive light must be formed accordingly."[58] And in order to receive the light granted to them,

seekers must frequently renounce long-cherished aims, deny themselves many opportunities of doing good, and even, it may seem, the very powers for using goods. Not only is the opinion of the world to be sacrificed, but the good affection of many who are most dear to them.

It is here that the human soul shrinks and begins to hold back from such denial. Doubts arise to add to the bitterness of the journey. Can it be right to forgo so much that is good in itself? Can the voice of God—the same God who loves all created good—utter such a counsel? Is it not perhaps a self-willed notion of their own? Hardly. Though conscience is not always able to reveal the path of holiness, it cannot be in error when it tells them of selfishness. And what is this hard attachment to their own desires but the same determined resistance to God's will which makes the hardened sinner?

But when the author disparages "external works" as he sometimes does, he is saying nothing against the performance of duties, even the smallest, of ordinary life. What he does protest against is the reliance on unnecessary or self-appointed works and on extraordinary religious exercises, such as excess fasting, night-vigils and rigid disciplines. Even when the seeker must forgo the creature and adhere to God alone, it is no selfish shutting up of the heart within the narrow sphere of its own experiences, for we learn that one must "perform external virtue until one is free of accidents".[59] It is then and only then that one "attains to the essence of virtue", in which even those "acts of a *particular* love of God" are dissolved.

When he says that a truly poor spirit accepts nothing from creatures but all from God, he implies what so many saints profess—that there are only two realities, God and the self, and every human relationship is a speaking of God through that neighbour. There is no passive mysticism here: "Even if one were in the highest state of contemplation that can exist in time and he did not come to help his brother, he would err."[60] Furthermore: "To be against God and the truth by a neglect of virtue is laziness."[61]   No, poverty of spirit is not a trust in Divine Providence that leads to inaction.

Then we are told that: "He who desires to follow Christ must do so by good works according to His example."[62] "One must exercise himself in the virtues of his vocation;" also that: "The poor man should do all that relates to him under the law of the Church."[63]   But in placing human duties on their true level he measures their value, not by the nature of the act but by the obedience and love involved in its performance. In other words, "It is the degree of divine love in the soul that shall measure all one's words and works and life."[64]   As St. Thomas says: "Virtue is praised because of the will, not because of the ability."[65]

"There is a *mean*," says our author, "between little and much, and he who always hits the mean in his love-acts has them well-ordered and according to divine love."[66]   And "Necessity is the object of gifts and their mean." Hence, for a rich man to give to a rich man is off the mark, so is it off the mark for a man to fast in such a way that his nature is harmed by it. Nature has its order; so has grace, "and nothing is done in God unless it is in accordance with order".[67]

It is not, then, "exterior works of charity" in themselves that hinder spiritual progress. Because spiritual poverty involves a poverty in the particular way of knowing and loving and which shows itself outwardly in a poverty of externals, it implies first and foremost a poverty of self-will. The obstacle is only and always the *self*: it is the performing of these works "according to one's own opinion"; it is "refusing to listen to the better opinion of others"; it is being "pleased at thinking that one has made a great penetration"; it is "preferring to be preoccupied with God inwardly when He is asking one to serve Him outwardly"—"I say that this man still retains self-will."[68]   In other words, it is the sense of "personal ownership in spiritual things that obstructs one in his perfection". And just as he cautions against the exaggerations of the Fraticelli and the Catharists, he warns against these errors of the Free Spirits, against this notion of ownership in spiritual things which fosters a "misdirected freedom," "disdain of reason," "a pleasure in forming distinctions so satisfying that one gives no heed to virtue and good works," "a spurning of all the laws of Holy Christianity".[69]

To say that grace is lacking is no answer. "It frequently happens that a man believes that he is abandoned by God as well as by creatures and that he is without grace."[70] But if the self will not get out, grace cannot get in. It is not God's fault. "God damns no one. Rather man damns himself."[71] Nor is human nature to blame. "Nature is noble and does what is right. . . . God loves human nature so dearly that He created all things for its service and even suffered death in human nature."[72] No, "death to self" is the only answer He will give us, and "as is the dying, so is the growth in grace, and blessed are they who have chosen God in a dying life, for their wealth in grace is exceedingly great".[73]

This resolute author continually holds before us the utmost heights of perfection, and though he is very understanding, even patient, about our slow approach and how we must progress "one step at a time", he never lowers his standard of perfection in favour of what might grant us a moment of satisfaction. As long as man is in time he must move on. Time holds no resting-place. And though man may attain to a state in time where creatures find nothing more in him to kill, there is still a higher degree of perfection at which he must always aim. "But man never attains to this other state in time, for God always finds something in him to kill."[74]

Poverty of spirit, then, is detachment, well-directed freedom, purity, and continuous self-denial. It is also the acceptance of suffering, the physical sufferings which reveal to us that all things are but loss, and principally those dark sufferings in the mind, in the will and in the spirit itself. Then there is a suffering in God which is the utmost in loneliness. Now this sense of isolation from God was later to preoccupy Luther, but there is an important difference. With Luther the feeling of alienation was permanent; with our author the dark night of the soul was a passing phase between moments of intense joy. "When God is the working and man the suffering being, then all is made quiet within him."[75] Divine love and divine joy take over. "The greatest joy that exists in time is found in this."[76] It is the joy of union with God "brought about by the simple, pure ground, out of which simple, divine love springs. It is godlike, and it reveals the truth which is God."[77]

"Love makes other's sufferings its own, not one, but all."[78] But even the sufferings of others, of all mankind, are entrusted to God, for the truly poor in spirit calls nothing his own. He and all that he has are God's. He has "emptied himself even of the desire to accomplish great external works or to have any property". He desires to act and live only in the sense that God pleases to act and live in him. And "that is why the highest perfection of a spiritual poor life rests in being so wholly attentive to God that one does not notice the actions and defects of others."[79] Yet these poor spirits "remain unknown, because there is nothing singular about them";[80] "to give them a proper name would be to give them the name of *love*, for they are nothing but love."[81]

At the centre of Rhineland mysticism is the doctrine of the *visio essentiae Dei*, the blessed contemplation or knowledge of God. "Knowledge seeks that which is stripped, namely, the naked truth, and it is never satisfied until it enters in complete nakedness and sees God and knows Him without medium. When it comes into this Nothing, all natural marks disappear and the soul becomes unoccupied and rests in pure peace. It is then that the spirit arrives at the source from which she flowed."[82] Our author has taken this doctrine from the Schoolmen, and upon it has established the belief that a blessed unitive knowledge is, if only for a moment, attainable in this world by a perfect poor spirit, and that it should be sought by every means. Suso also speaks of this foretaste of heaven when he says:

D

Blessedness in the sense of participated union is very possible, though it may seem impossible to many, since neither reason nor mind can attain it. A certain theological treatise[83] states that there is a kind of men, chosen and well-tested, who are so thoroughly purified and godlike in spirit that virtue bursts forth in them, as in God, for they are transformed in the unity of their first exemplar. They arrive, in some measure, to a full forgetfulness of this changing and temporal life. They are transformed into God's image and are one with Him.[84]

The Rhineland mystics say that a direct knowledge of the Godhead is possible because "there is a speaking of God in the core of the soul where no creature can enter nor speak, for only God lives there, and only He speaks".[85] Again our author takes this from an old scholastic doctrine which states that only God can work in the essence of the soul.[86] God is ever transcendent. "Indeed, God has no need of His creatures," says Eckhart, "but everything created has need of Him."[87] And in order that the transcendent may appear immanent as a second subject, all particular thinking about God, all self-willed activity must cease. Aid is given in this effort by the ever-present light of grace which raises nature far above itself, for "with each stripping, each death, there is a new love".[88] The way to God is through love, and God replies to its highest development through His presence. To know and love God is to know and love Christ. And this is a self-stripping, following of Christ's spiritual poverty, in other words, His Passion, whereby the divine enters into the human subject which then "becomes God with God", for "he knows God by means of God, and loves God by means of God".[89]

This Plotinian emanationalism is only verbal. The Rhineland mystics believed that, since God is eternal, and since His actions are not bound by the limitations of time as human activity is, then God's activity by way of creation or procession is one and indivisible. The begetting of the Son by the Father and procession of the Holy Spirit from the Father and Son are continuous. The generation of the Son takes place in the soul since God is in the soul through grace when she has become poor in all that is contrary to God. Now if a man has left himself and all things, then " God necessarily fills him " because there are no more obstacles present. The fact that God "must give Himself up" not only relates to what the Schoolmen called the *necessitas coactionis*, but also to the *necessitas infallibilitatis*. In other words, God's design would be defeated if He did not give Himself to a soul prepared to receive Him, since He is also responsible for the preparation. Hence the greatest experience of these mystics is "to know and love God by means of God". Tauler also says: "No one can attain to God or know God except by means of the un-created Light, and that is God Himself."[90]

A few men in every age have passed on to others their accounts of this divine knowledge. From those of Plato and Aristotle and the East, the mystic spirit of the Greeks, as a stream distinct from that of the New Testament, was passed on to Plotinus. Thus through his fellow Neo-platonists, and through Philo, it became an intricate element in the writings of St. Augustine and the Pseudo-Dionysius, and hence in Christian theology. This is not the place to trace the filiation of the doctrine from the fourth to the fourteenth century. One need only say that the Rhineland mystics had access to at least four Latin translations of the Pseudo-Areopagite's writings. Many of the Scholastics, including St. Thomas, had already commented on St. Dionysius, most of them using the version of Scotus Erigena. When one considers that passages like the following, along with many others, were heartily studied by our author, it is easier to appreciate the part his prede-cessors played in his thinking.

Distinct from the soul is that Light by which she is so en-lightened that she may behold all things, whether in herself or in Him, truly understanding them; for that Light is God Himself. But when the soul tries to look at that Light, even though she is rational and intellectual and created in His image, she throbs through weakness and cannot. . . . However, when she is then transported and withdrawn from the bodily senses, she is placed in the very presence of that Vision: not in local space, but in a way all her own, she beholds That . . .[91]

—St. Augustine

Exercise thyself ceaselessly in mystical contemplation. Leave on one side the senses and the operations of the understanding, all that which is material and intellectual, all things which are, all things which are not, and with a supernatural flight, go and unite thyself as closely as possible with that which is above all essence and all idea. For it is only by means of this sincere, spontaneous, and entire surrender of thyself and all things, that thou shalt be able to precipitate thyself, free and unfettered, into the mysterious radiance of the Divine Dark.[92]

—St. Dionysius

Learn to stand above the images of the material world, for God finds surpassing delight in a mind which is thus purified. . . . Thus one is, as it were, transformed into God; he cannot think, understand, love nor remember anything that is not God; He does not see other creatures nor himself except only in God; he loves nothing except God alone, he does not even remember others or himself except in God.[93]

—St. Albertus Magnus

When the good and faithful servant enters into the joy of the Lord, he is inebriated by the riches of the house of God. . . . He forgets himself, he is no longer conscious of his self-hood; he disappears and loses himself in God and becomes one spirit with Him, as a drop of water which is drowned in a great quantity of wine. For even as such a drop disappears, taking the colour and taste of wine, so it is with those who are in full possession of blessedness. All human desires are taken from them in an indescribable manner, they are rapt from themselves, and are immersed in the divine Will. If it were otherwise, if there remained in the man some human thing that was not absorbed, those words of Scripture which say that God must be all in all would be false. His being remains, but in another form, in another glory, and in another power. And all this is the result of an entire and complete renunciation of all things inwardly and outwardly.[94]

—Heinrich Suso

When our Lord went into Egypt, all the idols of the land fell. However good or holy anything may appear, if it obstructs the real and direct divine generation in you, it is an idol. Our Lord tells us that He has come carrying a sword cutting away all things that adhere to men, even mother, brother, sister. For all things, outward or inward, that are joined closely to you without God are your foe, forming a multitude of obstacles which cover and hide the divine Word.[95]

—Johann Tauler

All these teachings are summarized by our author and he takes us through the same arid no-man's land of mystical theology. Eckhart is the metaphysician, Tauler the preacher, Suso the poet and psychoanalyst; the author of *The Book of the Poor in Spirit* is the instructor, the Don who attempts to set down the perfectionist aims of his colleagues. He does not try to classify religious experiences as St. Teresa does three centuries later. Nor does he advocate a technique of mysticism. Steeped in the early Fathers as he is, he has no doubt that if one aims at the highest degree of spiritual poverty, which is a God-likeness, that if one aims at the Godhead by following Christ's Passion and poor life, the technique will take care of itself. (See Addendum D, p. 288.)

Because of its profound depth it is possible to criticize certain aspects of this book without detracting from its perennial value. Written as an attempt to counter a tendency towards excessive spiritual laxity, we dare not judge it in the same light as, for instance, St. François de Sales' *Treatise on the Love of God*, which was written in the early seventeenth-century France to counter a tendency towards excessive spiritual rigorism. No doubt our author, not unlike his enthusiastic confrères, is a little too anxious for quick results, is not content to let the good wheat and the tares grow in the same field until the harvest, is insufficiently cognizant of the various temperaments to be considered in his recommendation of contemplation and mysticism as a duty for all Christians. Is it not a little dangerous to advocate one principle for all, even though that principle is truly Christian? For in doing this, is not one apt to minimize the worth of other principles equally true and Christian? But the paramount truths which he does so courageously expound and constantly reiterate are verities of which not only the children of St. John the Baptist but also the children of St. John the Evangelist need daily reminding. St. François himself admits this and " was fond of quoting that holy man [our author] who wrote a book on mystical theology ".[96]

This " holy man " is quite generous in granting to the spiritually minded pagan a sufficient knowledge of truth. Like his colleagues, he holds that in the inner ground some of the Greeks apprehended God's essence. And so he wisely counsels: " Let no man try to find the difference between pagans and Christians unless he has the divine light."[97] Furthermore, a prince may even rise to a high degree of spiritual poverty if there is nothing that he is not prepared to abandon to God's will. The " evangelical counsels " are greatly emphasized, but we also learn that a householder, working to maintain his family because God so ordains it, is by no means deprived of those graces which lead to sanctity. What this author does not sanction is the least taint of a rationalization. But we must not forget that his age, unlike our own, was not the age of the layman or of the emancipated woman. To become a religious, to enter a school of charity where one might attend to spiritual realities more effectively than the multiplicity of secular life afforded, was the popular, if not the only thing to do for the concerned believer of the fourteenth century. It was for these vowed religious that this treatise was obviously written.

Is this book, then, meant only for monks and nuns? The author would no doubt answer this by asking if the Beatitudes are meant only for religious. By no means. The highest degree of spiritual poverty is here set forth for all who are willing to aim at it, and the householder who fulfils these conditions of inward and outward detachment, " in so far as he is able and necessity permits ", and " according to his vocation ", may be assured of being on the highest path. Since it is agonizingly hard to remain detached from things as long as they are possessed, our author, along with Christ, counsels the man who is free from lawful commitments to get rid of his possessions.

> *Pulchra quae videntur,*
> *Pulchriora quae intelliguntur,*
> *Longe pulcherrima quae ignorantur.*

"Beautiful are the things that are seen, more beautiful are the things that are understood, but by far the most beautiful are the things not understood." True to Christian tradition, the Rhineland mystics maintained a hierarchic view of the sacraments—this world was an outward *sign* of the Godhead, of the presence of God who sows His likeness in man. It was a unitary perception which gathered every fact, thing or discovery into its range. In no way limited to the elements of bread, wine, oil and water—as some non-Catholics frequently surmise and some Catholics unfortunately forget—all this signification was centred in Christ, the unique sacred sign, in that His human and divine natures were one; in receiving His body one received God. Furthermore, they indigenously believed that the faithful were themselves the very preservation of this " sign ", experientially realizing themselves as *members* of the Mystical Body. Rarely dreaming of an outwardly triumphant Church, rarely judging it in terms of advance or retreat, they instead taught a contemplation of Christ's Passion, fully convinced that, like Christ, the Church must suffer till the end of time. It is this same suffering, they said, which is necessarily involved in the quest for that which is " by far the most beautiful ".

No doubt the conception of " nature " held by the fourteenth-century mystics is for us a narrow one. Surely it should include, apart from those natural gifts which constitute personal character, such social virtues as benevolence, love for the family and community, a concern to make the kingdom of God on earth as much a reality as is humanly possible, to master the earth and make it the home of a well-ordered society. But the social elevation of mankind here and now was completely outside their strict and systematic mode of thinking and we find it in none of their writings.

No, their way is dark. These are men on whom the "nothingness" of all created things has flashed, not as a sentimental metaphor, but as a cold, logical fact. They have realized, if only for a moment, that all they have seen and known is empty; they have looked over the abyss of boundless doubt, shuddered as they saw the beauty of the heavens, hills, trees, even the faces loved, perhaps passionately; even the earth beneath their feet, their own flesh and bones—all this they have seen spin, melt and disappear until nothing of the entire universe remains but the lonely, ugly, grasping self—and God.

Yet, this is a problem which our author does not attempt to solve for any man, for it is one which everyone must solve for himself when he comes face to face with God alone. But for those who are willing he does pass on instruction about a way which others, like himself, found to be true. Though usually published in two parts, the book tends to divide itself into the four secondary treatises, as here presented. The first is a systematic treatment of the nature of spiritual poverty; before going into detail about the way he wants to make sure that his readers understand the goal and all that the journey towards that goal implies. He then considers God's work in the soul and how man should co-operate with Him. In the last two divisions he lays out the steps, but steps which are so constructed that the goal always remains in sight. Difficult as those steps may be and distant as that goal always remains, joys, more of grace than of nature, are assured to the person who perseveres. He does not attempt to make the way attractive, but in that utter darkness he is certain that there shines an eternal light which belongs neither to that darkness, nor to the outer world, neither to time nor to space nor to anything that the human mind can comprehend, and that its source is the abiding One, whose love is all-embracing. It is a simple way of honest self-knowledge and self-stripping, in which every step is a following in the footsteps of the Incarnate Son, whose Passion was this same self-knowledge and self-stripping—a way which ultimately penetrates the very centre of the Godhead. It is the simple way of the poor in spirit.

6

Who, then, can the author of this book be? What we can gather about Tauler's life has been greatly coloured by an old Latin biography which was often bound together with his sermons, and was therefore looked upon as genuine. One of the features of this *Life of Tauler*[98] is its telling of how a famous Master of Theology was converted by a saintly layman who, after hearing him preach, had accused him of hypocrisy. The layman became the Master's spiritual guide and directed him to perfection. After the Master's death he appeared to the layman and revealed how he had been taken to heaven by the angels, where he was granted the beatific vision; he assured the layman that he too would come to a blessed end. By degrees this legend grew, and by the middle of the fifteenth century the Master of the story became associated with the name of Tauler.[99]

Within the last hundred years scholars have discovered the suspicious circumstances surrounding this "biography" and how it will not stand up under critical examination. They have discovered that Tauler and the Master of Theology in the legend could not be the same person. They claim further that Rulman Merswin was the probable author of the narrative and that this Master and layman are as much an invention on his part as his Friend of the Oberland. Since the *Life* had been proved untrue, it meant that all the treatises attributed to Tauler were deprived of their claim to genuineness. Hence the *Divine Institutions, The Exercises on the Life and Passion of our Lord Jesus Christ, The Marrow of the Soul, The Prophecies of the Enlightened Dr. Johann Tauler*, and *The Book of the Poor in Spirit* were put aside for further examination and only the *Sermons* retained.

The original task of compiling Tauler's work was done in the middle of the sixteenth century by St. Peter Canisius and Surius the Carthusian. They gathered together sermons, treatises and other works which, strictly speaking, contained the same thoughts and phraseology as Tauler's. In 1543

Canisius quoted several extracts from *The Book of the Poor in Spirit* in his *Holy Instructions of Tauler*, and in 1548 Surius translated the entire treatise into Latin along with the other attributed works. His publication became so popular throughout Europe that French, Italian, Spanish and Dutch translations of all the treatises which bore Tauler's name were circulated.[100] The first complete modern edition of *The Book of the Poor in Spirit* was published in 1621 by Sudermann at Frankfurt. This rendering was a "faithful word-for-word reprint" of one of the earliest manuscripts. Since then many editions and translations have been published.[101]

Both Professors C. A. W. Schmidt and W. Preger,[102] two of the scholars who began to investigate the authenticity of *The Book of the Poor in Spirit*, upheld the tradition which regarded Tauler as its author. They even considered it as his most important book. In the 1870s the Dominican H. S. Denifle, one of the leaders of the German school of destructive criticism, broke with this tradition.[103] He argued that Sudermann published the 1621 edition without any real proof that Tauler was its author. Denifle compared this book with the authentic sermons of Tauler and concluded that an essential difference exists between the two. He argued that certain passages in the book which dealt with the doctrine of spiritual poverty, external works, the receiving of the Eucharist, do not fully coincide with the spirit of the *Sermons*.

So far as concealing one's identity is concerned, our author certainly practised what he preached in Part III, Chapter iv, Section 1. Commenting on these words, Denifle says that "this anonymous Friend of God, by hiding himself from all creatures so that neither good nor evil may be spoken of him, has perhaps deprived us of the hope of ever knowing his name".[104] Denifle did not attempt to say precisely who wrote the book, but rather than attribute its authorship to Tauler or even to a direct disciple of Tauler, he suggested that it may have been composed by an anonymous Franciscan, but a sincere Friend of God who undoubtedly wrote the book shortly after 1346. He believed that the theme of spiritual poverty was more Franciscan than

Dominican. Professor A. Ritschl, another critic, followed Denifle most of the way, but tried to develop the hypothesis that the book is a heterogeneous composition consisting of different treatises and written by different authors.[105]

Just as Suso in his *Little Book of Eternal Wisdom* has frequently been accused of being carried away by the bodily sufferings of Christ, our author has been criticized for paying unnecessary attention to the bodily poverty of Christ. Indeed, there are passages in both books which tend to confuse the average reader. But is it possible that these criticisms spring from a failure to understand the mystical doctrine of these fourteenth-century Dominicans? When *The Book of the Poor in Spirit* advocates that all men are called to spiritual poverty, and that outward detachment is obviously the corollary of inward detachment, Denifle and his followers interpret it in such an absolutist way as to regard this as one of the points of departure from the general theme of Tauler's preaching. The twentieth-century scholars, who do not go as far as Denifle, agree that in one sense this may be true, but they say that it is true only if one makes a point of exaggerating differences and overlooking other passages in the book which clarify and moderate this teaching.[106] And this, they say, holds for other points which Denifle observes as departures from the teachings of the Dominican friars.

We are reminded that many of the lectures, conferences and sermons of the Rhineland friars were compiled from detailed notes taken down by their hearers, which accounts for the little differences in style and for the various readings to be found in the early editions. Further, it is worth noting that a man may have an altogether different approach in a lecture on the spiritual life from that in a sermon on the Birth of our Lady. It should also be remembered—Denifle's impression to the contrary—that the author for ever keeps ultimate perfection in view, frequently observing that as long as man lives in this world, absolute spiritual poverty, like absolute perfection, cannot be obtained any more than the final beatific vision can be fully obtained in this life.

It is no doubt most important to realize that the Dominicans of the thirteenth and fourteenth centuries held rather definite views on the doctrine of poverty. According to the plan of St. Dominic, the friars were to go about in twos, to possess nothing, but to live on alms. Before St. Dominic died he adopted the ideal that the individual religious should not be an owner, and that the Order should be dependent on what the providence of God sent it. Nor had this plan been altogether altered or shattered by the fourteenth-century Rhineland Dominicans;[107] out of it a profound doctrine of spiritual poverty emerged, occupying a central place in their teachings. As a virtue and work of perfection poverty was a means to the contemplative life; hence it shared in the relationship between contemplation and apostleship: if it was not primarily an act of pure love of God, it was considered useless. External poverty and abandonment never became absolute; rather they were the natural and unquestionable continuation of internal poverty and abandonment—so different from the doctrine developed by many Franciscans. Since, for these Dominican mystics, the highest perfection of the spirit implied a likeness with God, then all things, when seen through the eye of the spirit, became nothing—that is, nothing worth *possessing* except in so far as necessity required. Spirit and body were not to be separated into contradicting realities. As our author says: "The outer life is imperfect without the inner, and likewise, the inner life without the outer. They both belong together in the building up of perfection, and neither is sufficient without the other."[108]

Hence, it would seem that Denifle not only misinterpreted the views of poverty held by our author, but he also failed to grasp the meaning of that subtle, yet essential approach which dominated the teachings of these great mystics. In a sermon for All Saints' Day, Tauler's comments on the First Beatitude further illustrate the views held by our author:

The fourth and highest kind of poverty is that of a man who wants to be poor both outwardly and inwardly, after the example of our Lord Jesus Christ, who out of true love follows His poverty, neither bothered by it nor hiding it, either outwardly or inwardly. Only such a man has a true, pure, immediate and continuous communion with his Source and Beginning, so that there cannot be a sudden falling away without the heart being aware of it and quickly returning. This is the highest poverty of spirit, for its most noble form is a turning to God, pure, free, unhindered, now and for ever, like the poor saints.[109]

In another sermon he says:

The following of Christ in poverty, outwardly as well as inwardly, is the highest way. But no man can attain to this in his own strength, for he must forgo all temporal advancements and outwardly deny himself all temporal goods. Nature does not willingly act in this way, for it is difficult. Yet, the more arduous it is to nature, the more pleasing it is to God. . . . And if this exterior poverty is to work for their real good, it must, of course, spring from within. Therefore, exterior poverty is most beneficial when it becomes a help to interior poverty.[110]

Further support for the approach to spiritual poverty found in *The Book of the Poor in Spirit* may be gathered from other preachers, not to mention some of the foremost Catholic commentators on Holy Scripture.[111] Compare the following passages from these most prominent Dominicans:

Regarding the "Seven Rules of Virtues", Nicholas von Strassburg says: The third rule is that the spiritual man should most sparingly use the things of this world, as far as his necessity demands, in food, clothing and shelter, and such things. Our Lord Jeus Christ, who would not have so much from the world as even where to lay His head, teaches us this rule. Indeed, the more sparingly one uses the goods and pleasures of this world, the more quickly he ascends to the height of the heavenly kingdom. . . .

He who even for a short way (to the kingdom of heaven) burdens himself with much grain soon tires and suffers great trouble before reaching the end. Thou, O Lord, desireth that Thy people be prepared for the journey and not burdened with earthly things. Should they have something to carry, let them share this with their shipmates who have not. Thus their burden is smaller and they travel faster. For Thou has taught us this with Thy perfect poverty.[112]

Meister Eckhart also says: The poor in spirit go out of themselves and all creatures. They are nothing, they have nothing, they do nothing, and, save by grace, these poor are not but God with God. . . . The deeper the mind penetrates, the more the incomprehensible splendour of the Godhead is reflected in her poverty. For as far as she has gained awareness of divinity with her inner man, so far has she followed the voluntary poverty of her example Jesus Christ in her outer man. The poor spirit uses all things and creatures only as she needs them, always without attachment, and if she does not have them, she can do as well without them and with the same detachment.[113]

Even St. Thomas says: External works conduce to the increase of the accidental reward; but the increase of merit with regard to the essential reward consists chiefly in charity, whereof essential renunciation borne for Christ's sake is a sign. Yet a much more expressive sign thereof is shown when a man, renouncing whatsoever pertains to this outward life, delights to occupy himself entirely with divine contemplation.[114]

By a scissors-and-paste method one could, of course, argue in favour of both sides of the question, yet ample reasons can be shown to point out that this unknown author of our book was not at variance with the Dominican school. One should also remember that the natural tendency of destructive criticism is to point out differences rather than similarities, to exaggerate these and even forget that many of the paradoxes found in spiritual writings (and there are many in *The Book of the Poor in Spirit*) are inevitable simply because they are about the life of the spirit. The parallels to Eckhart, Tauler and Suso which appear in *The Book of the Poor in Spirit* are very numerous; Denifle himself admits this. The birth of God in the soul, the word spoken by God in the soul, the soul's withdrawal from the obstacles to true contemplation, the soul's death in God, the mystical devotion to the Passion of Christ are, among others, stressed by the author and these points are not unlike the teachings of his colleagues.

Other points recall some of the teachings of David von Augsburg—there is even an attempt to combine ultimately the teachings of St. Bonaventure and St. Thomas. Certain passages resemble Ruysbroeck, Mechtild von Magdeburg and Nicholas von Strassburg. On two or three occasions the author confuses his terms, fails to distinguish one concept from another, over-emphasizes a particular point of doctrine to the neglect of others, so that one wishes he were a better theologian. Yet in spite of these little faults which at face value appear as inconsistencies, he has constructed an entire treatise which points out, particularly for men and women under religious vows, the nature of spiritual poverty as it was so profoundly emphasized by the Rhineland mystics, and the means of attaining to that true poverty of spirit which is to be found perfectly exemplified in the poor life of Christ. As Professor F. Vernet says: "Their mysticism is very austere, very prayerful, very loving; it is the *familiaritas stupenda nimis*, by which the most beloved names reserved for father, mother, brother, friend and spouse are lavished upon Christ; the pseudo-Tauler *The Book of the Poor in Spirit*, by the very title under which it became popular in the sixteenth century, *The Following of the Poor Life of Christ*, well summarizes this theme."[115]

The term "poverty" has a sacramental significance for Catholics which is not accepted by members of other faiths, and this was especially true in the Middle Ages when it had mainly a spiritual rather than a material meaning.[116] For the Rhineland mystics that spiritual meaning implied an inflexible act of self-renunciation for the sake of Christ's love; to become poor in spirit was to become a Friend of God, wanting in God only; it was to become nothing in the world's opinion. Indeed, one may find them too cold, too systematic, too uncompromising, too full of paradox—and all these characteristics are found in our book. But it would be difficult to deny their perennial significance or that they are needed in our time. Nor can one say that they did not spring from a deep concern for true spirituality or that they did not encourage one of the outstanding revivals in the development of Christianity.

Those, then, who regard *The Book of the Poor in Spirit* as a guide to Rhineland mysticism have much to back their opinion, for it contains the profoundest truths and enthusiastic faith of that school—also its little faults and sometimes boring rigidity. The modern critic must, of course, agree with Denifle and disregard Johann Tauler as the author. No doubt he is obliged to do so. But he will also agree with Denifle in maintaining that the book has a very special value and that many of its chapters are equal to anything to be found in the writings of the Christian mystics. Denifle says further in the Introduction to his own published edition of the book:

> Let it not be inferred from our representations that all the teachings in this work are exaggerated. Such a conclusion would be unjustified. The chapters on the Passion of Christ especially belong to the finest things that the mystics have written on the subject. And when the author advances the sound normal doctrines of the other mystics, he develops them in an original manner and his presentation is always supported by a high moral conviction.[117]

Such, then, is the state of the question as to who was the author of this book. On the one side, for over four centuries it was unanimously honoured and regarded as coming from Tauler's own hand. Schmidt, who was certainly not adverse to admitting that not all the works formerly attributed to Tauler were authentic—he was in doubt about the *Life of Tauler*, some of the *Sermons* and the *Meditations on the Passion*—nevertheless believed that Tauler was the author, that it contained his spirit, doctrine and style. On the other side we have Denifle's view.

A contemporary opinion should perhaps side with Denifle and say that Tauler did not personally write the book. It should not, however, argue that it is necessarily not Dominican in spirit and doctrine, rather that the author was far more influenced by Tauler than Denifle will admit. It would be far nearer the truth to regard this treatise not only as having been written by a mid-fourteenth-century Dominican but, as Professor A. Chiquot says: "even by a close disciple or perhaps some friend of Tauler".[118]

The original text of *The Book of the Poor in Spirit* is in Middle High German, quaint and hard, but charged with great simplicity. Though some of this simplicity is naturally lost in the softer and more sophisticated New High German editions, the essential quality of the original has been retained. My translation is not made directly from a manuscript; I am no scholar of Middle High German. I have referred to *Johann Tauler's Nachfolgung des Armen Lebens Christi*, Frankfurt am Main, 1833, and the 1855 Regensberg edition. The former entirely coincides with the 1621 publication which is a faithful reprint of one of the earliest fifteenth-century manuscripts. And in examining the 1670 Frankfurt edition I noticed that it also follows, without altering a single word, the 1443 copy (No. 263.2°) which I have investigated together with another manuscript (No. 4415) in the Staatsbibliothek, Munich. All these I have compared with the edition of Fr. H. S. Denifle, O.P.— *Das Buch von geistlicher Armuth*, Munich, 1877, which he made after a study of the best manuscripts, especially the early 1429 MS. in Leipzig, and hence have relied greatly on his work.

I have also referred to the Latin translation of the book made by Surius in 1548, a modern French edition, *Imitation de la Vie pauvre de N. S. Jésus Christ*, Paris, 1914, and the only other English translation, the *Following of Christ*, by J. R. Morell (Burns and Oates, London, 1886). This last translation was, to my mind, unfortunately rendered literally into antiquated English; nor did the translator help the modern reader by properly dividing the book into the obvious chapters and sections which it contains. This I have done by following to a large extent the divisions made in Denifle's edition, and the suggestions made by Professor Ritschl.

A literal translation of the book would tend to falsify the spirit of the original and even make many passages unintelligible if not ridiculous. But I have had no thought of "popularizing" the author's words. He was an early *Friend of God*, an orthodox mystic who held all the beliefs of his age and of the Church without any trace of reserve. Sometimes he expounds his theme like a homilist, at other times like a lecturer. Sometimes his use of passages from Scripture may appear strange, even arbitrary to the twentieth-century reader. But it is a method which is justified, both in the fact that it

E

is in accordance with the tradition of the mystical school to which he belonged, and also in the experiences of appreciative persons who have always found spiritual guidance in its use.

It has not been possible to trace all his quotations of various writers. In the custom of his time, he frequently refers to them simply by saying "a teacher says"—teacher or Meister in this case usually implies a prominent Master of Theology, Doctor of the Church, or early Father. Regarding several terms, the thing I have tried to keep in mind is finding a word which supplies the necessary warmth of modern speech in contrast to the hardness of the German of the fourteenth century, without detracting from its strength. I have also tried to remember that the author is voicing, in the language of the Rhineland school and the "classroom" of St. Thomas Aquinas, the message of a great mystical tradition which goes back to St. Augustine and St. Dionysius.

I wish to acknowledge my indebtedness and thanks to the Librarians at the Handschrift Abteilung, Staatsbibliotek, Munich, and at Bonn Universität; to Dom Urbanus Bomm, O.S.B., Bibliotekar, Maria Laach Abtei; to Dr. J. Krump, O.P., Bibliotekar, Dominkaner Kloster, Walberberg, Cologne; to friends who have read this work in manuscript, especially R. and B. Freeman, Dom. F.J.B.P. and Fr. H.S.S.

C. F. KELLEY

DOWNSIDE ABBEY
5 - VI - 1954

PART I

On the Nature of True Spiritual Poverty

CHAPTER I

TRUE SPIRITUAL POVERTY IS DETACHMENT

****

SPIRITUAL poverty is a God-likeness. What is God? God is a being detached from all creatures. He is a free power, a pure act. In the same way spiritual poverty is a state of being detached from all creatures. And what is detachment? That which clings to nothing. Spiritual poverty clings to nothing and nothing to it.

1

WE MUST KNOW AND LOVE GOD

Now one might say: since all things are contained by something, all things must cling to something. What, then, does a poor spirit cling to or hold to? He clings to nothing beneath him, but only to Him who is elevated above all things. As St. Augustine says: "God is the best of all things."[1] Spiritual poverty seeks God; it clings to Him and to nothing else. And that poverty should cling only to the very highest, and quit, in so far as it can, the lowest, is indeed its foremost quality.

Many say that the highest poverty and the most intimate detachment is when a man becomes as if he had no separate existence of his own. Then he understands nothing, he wills nothing; then he is God with God. If this were possible, it might indeed be true. However, since man has a natural being, so must he also have a *doing*. For his blessedness rests in his knowledge and love of God, as St. John says: "This is eternal life: to know Thee the Father, and Jesus Christ whom Thou hast sent."[2]

But how shall a man know and love God and at the same time remain poor in knowing and in loving? He must know God by means of God, and love God by means of God.[3] Otherwise he can neither know nor love Him so as to become blessed. And he must become poor in human discernment. What is this discernment? It is in images and forms which one draws in through the senses; otherwise one cannot know through nature. And if he would become blessed and stand in true spiritual poverty, he must become poor in this.

2

DETACHMENT FROM ALL THAT IS CREATURELY

What use, then, is it for one to have in himself a reasonable discernment in images and forms, if it will not bless him? Further, if he must become wanting in the power to reason, shall he then become poor? I answer that reason is useful as long as man has not yet attained true spiritual poverty; as long as he is weighed down with multiplicity, so must he make use of this power of discernment. Thus is it useful and must not be discarded. But when a man comes to the point where he is made simple and stripped of multiplicity, and hence attains genuine poverty, he then must forsake all discernment through images and transfer himself with One into One, without any unlikeness.

If a man remained on the level of discernment, he would make many mistakes and would not be really poor. Also this power of reason is useful since in this way only can man be taught. Thirdly, since man is in time, he must be active in time in accordance with the outer man. Hence, in order that man may not altogether remain in time and that the outer man may be properly subordinated to the inner, a reasonable discernment is needed. Again, this power is useful because man cannot remain long without many manifold weaknesses, and he must resist these by reasoning if he would remain pure and poor. In this way spiritual poverty is a God-likeness; it is a pure, simple state of being detached from all creatures.

Must man, then, be poor even in virtue and grace, since grace is a creature and virtue creaturely? Grace is simply a light which God draws from Himself, and He pours it into the soul. In this way the soul moves from the bodily on to the spiritual, from time to eternity, and from the manifold to the simple. When the soul is lifted above the bodily, above time and manifold things, she becomes a naked spirit. She lives in eternity and unites herself to the only One. Then grace is so changed into God that God no longer draws the soul after the manner of a creature, but He leads her with Himself in a god-like manner. He leads her from Himself to Himself, as St. Augustine says: "O Lord, give me another Thyself, that I may go from Thee to Thee." When this point is attained, the soul is poor in grace.

Again, must a man be poor in virtue? In operation, virtues are creaturely; in intention, they are godly. God does not accept virtue according to the doing or operation, but according to the intention; man should act from a pure intention—God. See, then, that virtue is no longer creaturely but godly, for all things work in accordance with their end. Hence, God should be your end—nothing else, and then virtue will consist well in poverty.

Man should be poor in virtue in such a way that he has so thoroughly worked out all virtues that the mere image of virtue is lost and he no longer has virtue as an accident but in essence —not in a manifold direction, but in unity. When this point is attained, virtue is no longer creaturely but godly. For as God comprehends all things in Himself, so a truly poor spirit also comprehends all virtue in a simple love, and he performs all the virtues in love; these virtues are essential and they consist well in poverty. Indeed, a man can never become truly poor in spirit unless all the virtues become part of his being.

Is, then, poverty of spirit to be understood, as some say, to mean that when a man has what he needs bodily, he still inwardly holds this possession unwillingly? Does such a man have virtue essentially, like a poor spirit, who is wanting in all things both outwardly and inwardly?

Man begins to enter into what is essential when he is free of all chance or accident. For if he is free of all accidents, it is a sign that divine love has raised him above temporal things in such a way that he stands naked and free, empty of all things outwardly and inwardly. In this state he does not have the power of performing various virtues with materials; he can only let himself be in all virtue, with his will simply abandoned to God.

But a man who is not yet free of all outward accidents and from whom God has not taken away all external things, and who is not stripped of worldly possessions, can hardly be like this. He can have accidental virtue but not essential. Now what is accident? It is that which now is and then is not; and hence it now works virtue, but only as it presents itself to one. Now a truly poor spirit always performs virtue, and as his very being is indestructible so also his virtue cannot be destroyed. This is why it is called essential, since it is similar to being.

Some have said that the man who has one virtue has all virtues.[4] And that is true. For all the good that a man can do outwardly or inwardly belongs to a virtue which should be perfect. If he directs all things towards this virtue he then gains the essence of virtue, and with this essence he draws to himself all other virtues and makes them essential. If, then, a man has not placed all things in virtue, the essence of virtue escapes him. Nor can he have all virtue essentially since he himself is not like its essence.

It follows, then, that the perfection of man not only implies the emptiness of the internal man, but also of the external. For a man is a man not only through the soul, but through the body as well. Man is not perfect only when he lacks everything in the inner spiritual man; he should at the same time become detached, as far as possible, in the outer man. In other words, when a poor man directs all things into virtue, outwardly and inwardly, he then, and then only, is perfect, for perfection is founded on virtue.

3

MAN SHALL RECEIVE ALL FROM GOD

Suppose a man has detached himself from all creatures, yet creatures turn to him with favour; would not this hinder spiritual poverty? To this I say that if a man is in himself free of all things, whatever happens to him without his co-operation is a gift from God, and this is the best thing for a man regardless of what it is, whether something joyful or painful, sweet or bitter. For when a man turns himself away from all things and clings to God, God must necessarily go out to him with all that is good, be it bodily or spiritual. And he should take it all from God, and not from creatures.

But what shall a man do if too much or too little falls to him? If too much falls to him, he must not stand on the level of accidents, but see to it that he may always remain a detached man. Should someone give him a hundred pieces of gold, let him be sure that he does not become richer. God and not temporal things is his wealth. Should he then accept all that is given to him? If he accepts it, he makes himself heavy with it and no longer free. But if he refuses it, he has less merit than if he accepted it.

Let us suppose, however, that a man who wishes to give to you is also poor—or, perhaps, that he is so abundant in charity that he retains nothing but gives all away, or that he wishes to give it out of natural love. Then do not accept it, rather let him be burdened with it while you remain free and empty. But if the giver is rich in goods yet poor in love, and he gives through God and you are really in need of help, then accept it. And if you receive more than you need, give it to others. If this comes to you as a burden, it is not really one, but a work of God.

Should too little fall your way, then seek to free yourself from your necessity. If someone gives to you, accept; if no one gives to you, suffer it patiently. For to want is sometimes as profitable as possession. In wanting a man knows himself better than in having, since, in the absence of temporal things, man is better prepared for the reception of eternal things. In the weakness of bodily power man sometimes gains much in a spiritual strength which exceeds all bodily powers, as St. Paul says: " Strength is made perfect in weakness."[5]

Now let us suppose that a poor spirit addresses himself to worldly people with acquired riches. Can he find in them complete love and truth? I would say " No," and I will explain this with a little discourse:

First, " Like adheres to like "[6]—a teaching of Aristotle. In other words, where there is dissimilarity there is no love. Secondly, these worldly people do not have the real ground from which love and truth spring forth. Thirdly, the charity they render to the poor is done usually from fear of hell and love of heaven, and this is not real charity or truth, since it is themselves whom they love in it. If they could get to heaven without poor people they would have little care for them. Fourthly, if they ever give witness to the truth and love for the poor, it is not wholesale but fragmentary; and it is not perfect, since they do not learn to love all that belongs to perfection, but only a little and even that with difficulty. Fifthly, a poor spirit is detached from all creatures and these worldly people are still attached to creatures; they cannot show with love that they care for the poor spirit out of love, and so he remains unloved by them. Sixthly, true love is a complete going out of yourself and a separation from all things; if these people have not gone forth from themselves and all things, they cannot have true love. Seventhly, true love is spiritual, since it springs from the Holy Spirit—whereas these people are bodily-minded and so cannot show true spiritual love. For this reason a truly poor spirit when he is in want does not depend much on people with acquired riches. Eighthly, a poor spirit is unknown by all these rich people and is therefore not rewarded by them, for the ignored being is also the unloved being, as St. Augustine says: " The things that we see, we love them well, but the things that we do not know or recognize, we love not."[7]

CHAPTER II

TRUE SPIRITUAL POVERTY IS FREEDOM

****

GOD is a free power. Poverty of spirit is also a free power, not bound by anyone, for freedom is its nobility. The soul, while she is weighed down with temporal and feeble things, is not free but is burdened. What makes a burden? Coarseness, blindness, weakness in virtue. And temporal things are coarse, blind, and they cause the soul to be weak in virtue. Hence, if the soul wishes to be noble and free, she must empty herself of temporal things. Now spiritual poverty is noble and free, since it is empty of all things.

1

WHAT IS FREEDOM?

Freedom is a perfect purity and detachment which seeks the Eternal. Freedom is a withdrawn and separated being, similar to God or wholly attached to God. Now spiritual poverty is also an isolated condition, apart from creatures, and in this sense it is free. A free soul sets aside all feeble and created things and penetrates into the uncreated good— God. And this she attains by violence, as Christ says: "The kingdom of heaven suffereth violence, and the violent bear it away."[1] To the soul, God is the kingdom of heaven; hence, when she withdraws from all things and adheres only to God, she attains God by violence. For God cannot withhold Himself; He must give Himself to her, since it is His nature to

59

communicate Himself to the soul that is ready to receive Him.

Now all things are equal to a free soul—pain or pleasure, slander or praise, poverty or wealth, weal or woe, friend or foe. A free soul never permits herself to be drawn away by anything that might keep her apart from God or mediate between herself and God, as St. Paul says: "Who shall separate us from the love of Christ?"[2] All things then tend to aid her towards God; she presses on through all obstacles towards her origin. A free soul grasps and wins virtue; and not only virtue but even the essence of virtue. Nothing holds her except virtue, the most intimate and purest virtue. Yet this is hardly a bond, rather it is a kind of freedom. Then, when the soul can endure only what is best, and can entirely discard evil, she is wholly free. For freedom does not consist in sins. But slavery does, as St. John says: "Whosoever committeth sin is the slave of sin."[3]

Real freedom is so noble that no one gives it except God the Father. It is a power which flows directly from God the Father into the soul and it grants all possibility to the soul, as St. Paul says: "I can do all things in Him who strengtheneth me."[4]

The soul, when she turns in upon herself, becomes aware of what she was, what she is, and what she is not. She perceives what she was in feebleness, and this she apprehends with bitterness—and bitterness, dissatisfaction, remorse and displeasure make her pure. Out of this purity a clear light springs forth which reveals the truth to her. The Holy Spirit causes the light to burn, brightly and intensely, and urges the soul to pass through it towards the truth which has been made clear to her; and in no way does it allow her to return to her old feebleness, but leads her freely into all truth, without the need for more insight.

When the soul comes in this way into the truth, is preoccupied with the truth, and when its freedom has tasted the truth, this truth becomes so sweet and satisfying to her that she forsakes all things and adheres to it. She then surrenders the freedom of her will and makes herself poor. In the departure of her will, God receives her, covers her with His will, frees her and grants her full power with Him, as St. Paul says: "He who is joined to the Lord is one spirit."[5]   Her own will is ennobled and elevated in this spiritual poverty—not degraded, but liberated as though she had not really been emptied of her will. The Philosopher of Nature (Aristotle) says: "Everything that is most intimate with the first cause is the most noble."[6]

In other words, when the soul has united her will with the divine Will, she becomes truly noble and free; if she is otherwise she is not free.   And in the union of her spirit with the divine Spirit, the soul is freely able to do all things; for "Where the Spirit of the Lord is, there is liberty,"[7] as St. Paul says. Spiritual poverty then, is a God-likeness, for with God it can do all things.

2

IS OBEDIENCE OPPOSED TO FREEDOM?

Now if a man goes out of his own will and abandons himself in obedience to another man, does he not lose his freedom? My answer is that there are four ways in which a man may abandon himself to another.   First, in so far as he is ignorant and is taught, he abandons himself to another.   Again, in so far as he is not dead to all sins and in order that he may more quickly die to all contradiction in truth, he also abandons himself to another.   Thirdly, he abandons himself out of true humility, not even looking to see if he comprehends the truth; he is merely dead to sins, always regarding himself to be nothing else than a sinner.   In this way he gives himself up to another and does not rely on himself.   Fourthly, he abandons himself to the commandments of Holy Church; he does willingly what he is obliged to do.

But in the case of a truly perfect, poor man, who has become empty of himself and all things, there is, as I will explain, a difference.   For instance, he does not have to abandon himself through ignorance, for a spiritually poor man is a pure man.

Now where purity exists, light also exists; and where there is light, it shines and it reveals what is hidden.

A spiritually poor man has a pure light in himself by which he recognizes all truth, and he does not need to go out of himself to seek it elsewhere. Were he to go out of himself in this way he would quickly find intermediate and manifold obstacles. Instead he goes deeper into himself where he finds all that he needs. When he thus abandons himself and external things, God must give Himself to him in all truth; and when he has God, he requires nothing else.

Furthermore, it is not necessary for him to go out of himself for the sake of dying, for he is dead to all sins. And he who is dead to them has no need of further dying. But, in time, can a man attain to this state—that is, to where he has no further need of dying? Man may certainly attain a state in time where creatures find in him nothing more to kill, for he has gone out of himself and all creatures. St. Paul was in this state when he said: "I count all things but as dung."[8] Indeed, the deaths of a spiritually poor man are so secret and subtle that few creatures can recognize them. But man never attains this other state in time, for God always finds something in him to kill. Hence, the man who has abandoned self does not need to abandon himself to creatures, rather he should at all times abandon himself to God.

Now a perfectly poor and pure man does not need to abandon himself to another through humility, since he has within himself the very roots of humility. Nor is it necessary for him to show his humility to creatures, for God well understands his heart, as Christ says: "Learn of Me, because I am meek and humble of heart."[9] Be humble in your heart, that is sufficient!

Someone may say that it is not sufficient for a man to have virtue in him, but he should show it to others in order that they may be helped. To this I say: If you are truly gone out of yourself and thoroughly detached, others, if they wish it, will be helped, more through your detachment than through your actions. Another may say: Let us suppose that a man understands in himself all truth and has overcome all sin; still it is not good that he should keep this all to himself, better would it be for him to give it to others. My reply is that he should not keep it to himself, but leave it to God; for no creature can give this truth and detachment. God alone can give them.

The spiritually poor man should also have confidence in all men and he should always set them before himself. But his first confidence should be in God, and he should place Him before everything else.

A truly poor spirit is not obliged to take externally all that is legally prescribed in Holy Christianity. Those who do this do it because they are not in themselves wholly and perfectly empty. That which Holy Christianity performs in an external manner the spiritually poor man performs inwardly and essentially. The manifold enters in manner and form, but being is without manner and form. The perfectly poor spirit is so simplified in his being that he cannot abide in the manifold, as St. Paul says: "The law is not made for the just man."[10] For the law is only there to make people abandon sin and gain virtue. The perfectly poor spirit has overcome sin and attained virtue.

But how shall a spiritually poor man regard himself under the law? In simplicity he should certainly do all that he can and all that relates to him, and the rest he should leave. He should not, however, look down upon it nor regard it as inferior, but good; for all that Holy Christianity has prescribed is good. Hence, freedom always reigns in the poor spirit, yet he is ever obedient and ever submissive.

CHAPTER III

EXTERNAL WORKS OF CHARITY

✳✳✳✳✳✳✳✳✳✳✳✳✳✳✳✳✳✳✳✳✳✳✳✳✳✳

HOW is it with those spiritually poor men who live in monasteries, when a man abandons himself to another and is obedient to him? Is this not against freedom? On this I shall speak, because a man who is poor in spirit can abandon himself through external works of charity in three ways.

1

WHY ONE MUST PERFORM EXTERNAL WORKS OF CHARITY

First, one may abandon himself out of bodily necessity, such as to seek food, through God, for his own needs or for the needs of his brother. If he acquires what is needed for himself, he should abandon himself to God, attend to his heart and grant God freedom to work in him. The strength he has received from food he should let God use, and he should not allow himself to be led astray. For if he lets himself fail in God's work, he will not be entirely free. It pertains to the nature of gifts that they should be utilized in God. He who uses them in any other way, either in worthless works or in idleness, does not make a wise use of his gifts nor act according to the true principles of a spiritually poor life.

Should, then, a poor spirit always attend to his heart and not trouble himself about external things, such as weaving and other such work? And if he should trouble himself about outer work, is this against spiritual poverty and freedom? No, a truly poor spirit owes no one anything—only God. And if he wishes to do God's work, he should always hold himself empty in order that God may find him ready. If this pertains to external works, he should leave them; nor should he consider obedience to man, but please God and not man. And if the body can no longer endure what it utilizes internally, let him perform the nearest external work of charity.

Secondly, a poor spirit may abandon himself for the sake of virtue in himself and in his brother. In himself this may occur in the following ways: If his nature is weak or bored so that it cannot attend to the heart and turn inwardly to God; hence, he will do well to perform some work of charity. Again, if he has not yet acquired the external virtues, he should practise them until he has attained the essence of virtue. Further, he should practise works of charity to aid his brother in order that he might give him a good example; what he does he should do out of pure love, and this does not detract from freedom, but increases it.

It should here be added that a poor spirit *ought* to abandon himself and perform acts of charity to his brother. For instance, when he is lacking in virtue and has no one to aid him, he should abandon himself and go to help his brother. Even if he were in the highest state of contemplation that can exist in time and he did not go to help his brother, he would be in error. Also, let him remember that he is the disciple of our Lord who performed outward works of charity towards his followers, and he ought to imitate His example. And he must do this work if he hopes to gain eternal life, as Christ says: "Come to Me all you that labour and are burdened: and I will refresh you."[1] This, of course, implies the acts of mercy that God expects from every man.

It is in this way that a man can abandon himself and ought to give himself over to works of charity. This does not hinder a man nor does it detract from his freedom; rather it helps in a real way and even increases freedom. A man is not pure and free simply because he is pure in virtue. He must exercise himself in all the virtues that belong to his vocation; then is

F

he pure and free; then, without sin, he can turn in upon himself and attend to his heart.

Thirdly, a poor spirit should abandon himself to an external work of charity when he is advised by God to do so, and he should not resist God. He should please his Creator and renounce himself in all that God requires of him.

2

TRUE AND FALSE MOTIVES FOR EXTERNAL WORKS

How, then, is a man to understand if the motive to an external work is from the evil spirit, or from nature, or from God? For the internal works that God performs in the soul are better than external works, and yet both must exist. Though much might be said on this point, I shall pass over it at present and merely consider this difference briefly.

Let us first see how the evil spirit is to be recognized in the way in which he promotes acts of charity. Now if a man is attracted from his inner recollection to address himself to people of acquired riches, and if he abandons himself to them and endeavours to please them without any necessity of virtue, and if he wastes his time unwisely with them and lives with them in comfort, in eating and drinking, and if he imagines that his nature requires this comfort so that he may become stronger and may better serve God, and if he seizes more than he needs and becomes weighed down, distracted and preoccupied with manifold concerns so that he cannot return to his heart as though he had remained at home—these motives and tendencies are from the evil spirit and from his bodily nature. For bodily pleasure also finds its satisfaction in these things. St. Paul says: "The kingdom of God is not meat and drink, but justice and peace and joy in the Holy Ghost."[2]

Another motive proceeds from the evil spirit when a man endeavours to please these rich people and give them what should be given to poor people. For example, to entertain them and to live in equality with them; for in this action such

a man seeks praise and honour, and that people should entertain him in return. Hence, he overlooks virtue and merits no
reward for his behaviour, but much sorrow instead. Christ
says: "When thou makest a feast, call the poor, the maimed,
the lame and the blind. And thou shalt be blessed."[3]

Also, if a man is by himself and God performs works in
him, and if he thinks himself too weak to bear these works, and
hence turns himself outwardly into time, to unnecessary works,
this is a temptation of the evil spirit and of nature.

It may be added that the motive is also inspired by the evil
spirit when a man directs himself to external works over and
above all measure of necessity. For example, in excessive
fastings, night-vigils, and other severe exercises, by which a
man becomes unbalanced and his senses become in some
degree perverted so that he becomes half foolish, and by which
he alters so much from himself that he can never again turn
to his own heart, and he becomes so seriously ill that as a
result he must abandon many good works which God would
have performed through him. Of this St. Paul spoke when
he said: "I beseech you, therefore . . . that you present your
bodies a living sacrifice, holy, pleasing unto God, your reasonable service."[4]

To recognize whether the external work of charity is prompted
by nature, consider this: It is a work of nature when one is
turned to self or considers self in a work of charity. For nature
always loves and promotes self. If a man indulges in bodily
pleasures and displays love for them, it is also readily seen to
be from nature, for even sinners practise those things.

Likewise, if worldly people display faith in each other, it
is also from nature, for by nature like clings to like. Hence,
if a poor spirit consorts with these people, it is a sign that he
has a certain likeness with them, and has not yet put aside
all things. If he had spurned all things he would not keep
close relations with worldly people, since virtue consists in
doing this only in so far as it is directed by necessity.

And how is a man to recognize whether an external act of
charity is prompted by God? Let us first consider the need of

the person whom he serves—if that person requires his help. In this sense he ought to come to the help of friend or foe, good or bad. For in a case of necessity no one is excluded, as Christ says: "Pray also for them that persecute that you may be the children of your Father, who maketh His sun to rise upon the good and bad."⁵ If it is a case of necessity and if it is performed in humility, it is then a divine work of charity.

Besides, a man should remember the distinction of persons in his works of charity. He should be more inclined towards a holy man who utilizes all things in God, than towards a man in whom he does not recognize much good. For in a holy man all things are fruitful and praiseworthy of God, and all things in him are referred to their original source.

Though it is true that God always acts in a holy man, to strengthen him so that he may be able to carry on God's work, nevertheless you should still come to his assistance rather than to that of another through whom God's will is not so perfectly fulfilled. All things are more the property of a holy man than of him who possesses many things; and for this reason, if a man wishes to make amends for his sins, he should give what he has to a holy man. A holy man can obtain much more grace for him for whom he prays; and God lends His ear to him sooner than to another.

A man ought, moreover, to remember the right order of time and of himself in his external works of charity. As to time, in the morning a man should give special attention to his heart and not worry much about external works, unless a great necessity arises. For things come more easily to a man in the morning, and at that hour he can more effectively turn to God than at any other hour. Later, in the afternoon, a man may very profitably exercise himself in acts of charity. But again, in the evening, he should take care of the state of his heart. Thus we see that he should keep order in the regulation of his time.

He should also observe order in the management of himself. If he feels himself attracted towards God, and if God leads him from external things to Himself, he should attend to God and allow Him to work in him. At these moments he may be quite empty of all external works, unless, of course, there is a case of great necessity. Afterwards, when God no longer works so intimately in him and this working is withdrawn from him, he should turn himself to external work in necessary acts of charity. When he works in this way it is a divine act of charity.

A man may also recognize a divine work of charity when he is always inspired by a wholesome devotion to the work, and when he performs it for nothing save the glory of God and the needs of his neighbours; or when he does not seek any natural pleasure in it. A spiritually poor man should perform such works of charity, and he should readily leave all other works, whether encouraged by the evil spirit or by nature. From all this it is seen that spiritual poverty is a free power.

CHAPTER IV

MISDIRECTED FREEDOM

✳✳✳✳✳✳✳✳✳✳✳✳✳✳✳✳✳✳✳✳✳✳✳✳

O NE will naturally wish to ask more about freedom and now especially about misdirected freedom. In other words, how is a man to discern whether his freedom is directed by God or not?

1

THE DIFFERENCE BETWEEN WELL-DIRECTED
AND MISDIRECTED FREEDOM

Godlike freedom springs from true humility, and it ends in humility, patience—in fact in all the virtues, and in God Himself. When a godlike poor spirit, who is free, is assailed either by man or by the evil spirit, he becomes more humble and patient, drawing closer to God, abandoning everything to Him. He remains silent, endures and gives thanks to God.

But freedom of an inferior kind springs from pride and ends in pride, anger, presumption and other vices. When imperfectly free men are assailed, they become angry and seek immediate revenge; they fall into pride, hatred, self-righteousness and slander against their adversaries, and, rather than control themselves, they break out into revenge by means of vices. It often happens that they wish to do this out of a sense of justice; hence they believe they are honouring God by their opposition. This is false justice, for it springs not from humility but from pride, as St. Gregory has said: "False justice hath hardness, but true justice hath compassion." [1]

In this sense misdirected men are to be recognized by their unvirtuous assaults; just and free men by their humble silence, long-suffering and abandonment to God. Their silence is not from fear. On the contrary, they are silent because they realize that their speech does not bear fruit. Should, however, God wish them to say something, they do so without fear. Indeed, they are able to endure much for the sake of truth, whereas unjust men are always disturbed by the urgent need to eliminate the suffering and so help themselves as much as possible.

It frequently happens that a just and free man is thought to be misdirected. For instance, when something good is proposed to him, and realizing that it is not the best for him, he turns to this best—such behaviour is frequently judged to be bad. On the other hand, a disorderly free man is also often thought to be well directed. For instance, when he ought to practise a certain virtue which is one of necessity, and he does not do so, preferring to remain particularly preoccupied with himself. This is frequently considered as good, yet it is not. For we should perform virtuous acts when the need arises, and remain preoccupied with ourselves if that is also expedient and wise.

2

BODILY MISDIRECTED FREEDOM

Now there are two kinds of misdirected freedom. One is bodily and the other is spiritual. Bodily freedom comes from temporal goods, from honours and friends and power. He who has considerable property, honours, friends and power, always desires to be the best; he desires to be noble and free. This freedom is not well-directed, for it does not spring from God. It is indeed rare that a man preoccupied with property and honours, or with friends or power, is at the same time dissatisfied with a freedom that is not rightly directed. But he who wishes to be perfectly free must have detached himself from property and honours and friends and power, and must have persevered to the true ground of humility. For true freedom springs from this ground and from no other; true freedom is a foundation for all virtue and an abandonment of all vice.

It is often said that no one is capable of all virtue, even though he has abandoned the cause of vice. Now temporal goods, worldly friends, honour and power are a cause of vice and sins; hence it must follow that he who desires true freedom must detach himself from these. Seneca refers to this when he says: "He who wishes to be free in his mind must be poor and like a poor man."[2]

Spiritually poor men are accused of being free in a misdirected fashion, but it is the worldly rich who are so, those who hold on to property in temporal goods, who try to assert themselves with clever pretences, who desire the same height of perfection as a completely poor spirit, and who think they can gain the best within by not bothering about external detachment. Should this happen, it is good. But the Gospel speaks otherwise. It says: "Sell all whatever thou hast . . ."[3] Those who keep their possessions and yet desire perfection realize only an inferior kind of freedom.

Misdirected freedom has still another trait. It sins without remorse or fear, it assumes virtue to itself without acquiring it, and it imagines itself in perfection without having abandoned itself and all things.

3

SPIRITUAL MISDIRECTED FREEDOM

The other kind of misdirected freedom is spiritual. It springs from the spirit and is sometimes possessed by spiritual people. It arises in three ways:

First, when a man turns away from a sinful life and severely mortifies his body, and exercises himself in a life of penitence, and performs virtues only outwardly, and does not attend to his heart, and fails to see God within himself, thus remaining always an external man—this man remains unknown to himself. True knowledge springs not from without but from within. Since, however, he is external, the truth is unknown to him, and from blindness he falls into an ignorance of himself. If he performs a great number of exercises, he thinks himself perfect, and from this a questionable freedom springs up in him, counselling him to submit to no one, for he considers himself perfect because of the manifold nature of his exercises.

Such a man is, perhaps, a good man, but he cannot remain without some infirmities, since he is ignorant of an inner light. Hence, he falls into misdirected freedom, into looking down on others and judging them. It is a sad thing to live with such a person, for as long as he stands alone in his external works, he never attains true humility. Indeed, he may evince outwardly a humble attitude, but fundamentally he is not humble. The ground of true humility is born from within, not from without.

What, then, is the use of external observance, penance and so forth, since these things do not themselves place a man in perfection and even sometimes foster misdirected freedom to arise in a man? I answer that external observances are very good and useful if they are performed in moderation and in a regulated manner, and provided, over and above them, a man attends to himself within and gives himself to God. The outer life is imperfect without the inner, and likewise, the inner life without the outer. They both belong together in the building up of perfection, and neither is sufficient without the other.

In the same way, misdirected freedom may arise if a man has exercised himself in external good works, and he then abandons the manifold and turns in upon himself intellectually and remains there. For in this turning into himself there usually springs up a natural light in him, and this reveals the distinction of natural truth. This distinction sometimes produces a great pleasure, and this pleasure urges him on to know still more truth, so that he grows intellectually. But reason and the intellect are from nature. Hence, he remains in this natural light and he understands what he will through discernment to the point where he imagines he possesses all truth and distinctions. He then falls back with pleasure on himself and imagines that he is superior to others and that he is free to the extent that he should submit to no one, for he thinks that no one comprehends the truth which he now holds. He begins to judge others and pride arises in him, and the pleasure he takes in forming distinctions is so satisfying to him that he gives no heed to virtue and good works.

From this springs misdirected freedom, and he spurns all the laws of Holy Christianity. In so far as he abides by this natural light to discern all things, it happens that he wishes to know faith wholly according to a figurative fashion, and this he cannot do. And in so far as he thus remains ignorant of faith, and yet would happily know it, the evil spirit enters and presents a false light to him as a true one. He surrenders himself to it, accepts it as the truth, and through it falls. His fall is in a certain degree similar to Lucifer's fall, for he is spiritual, and he can hardly ever rise again, and since he does not regard his actions as sinful, he remains unrepentant. No man can come to this man's assistance—only God.

Yet these men are often called *free spirits*. However, it is an evil freedom, and it is never the freedom about which we have previously spoken and which relates to a pure, poor spirit. It springs from the evil one, whereas the other freedom springs from God. Indeed, it is necessary to be cautious when in contact with these men.

Thirdly, misdirected freedom is sometimes fostered by visions, as when a man is so enraptured that he sees something that was previously hidden from him, and this does not take place without means, as St. Paul says,[4] and hence a man begins to fancy that he is in a very lofty state. From this we see that a freedom that is often without proper direction arises in him, for it does not spring from true humility.

Furthermore, the evil spirit can fool this man, for he may grant him a false image which makes him think that he is favoured; for, as St. Paul says, the evil angel may take upon himself the likeness of a good angel.[5] No, we should not believe in all spirits, for man is easily fooled. And these men much resent your attempts to correct them.

CHAPTER V

TRUE SPIRITUAL POVERTY
IS A PURE ACTION

****

GOD is a pure action. Spiritual poverty is also a pure action since each thing acts according to its form. Now spiritual poverty is a pure and simple form and hence it also has a pure and simple action.

But what does *pure* really mean? Well, a thing is pure which is one and separated from all else. Spiritual poverty is one and separated from all difference and hence it is pure; and that which is pure also acts purely. And what does *action* mean? Action is simply the making of something out of nothing, or the making of one thing into another, or the making of a thing better than it was before, or the making of something into nothing. Now spiritual poverty has these characteristics.

1

HOW SPIRITUAL POVERTY ACTS

Spiritual poverty makes something out of nothing. For instance, when a person abandons all that is not God or god-like and clings only to God, God must necessarily give Himself and all things back to such a person. He now obtains what he did not previously have, such as the good works that others perform and even those that Christ and all the saints and holy men performed or still perform or will perform—all these belong to a pure man as though he had done them himself.

When a truly poor spirit goes out of himself and out of all

things that are not God and turns to God with love, he gains a fellowship with God and all things that are godlike. What he is then unable to accomplish by action he accomplishes through love. Through love he makes his own what another does through action, for "Love appropriates others' virtues",[1] as St. Gregory says.

This man's action is so far-reaching that he performs all actions in a moment. Inwardly and in detachment he performs all external and internal works that are good, not accidentally but essentially. Since the essence of a thing is much nobler than its accident, his virtues are much nobler than those of another who performs virtue accidentally.

Next, spiritual poverty makes one thing into another. When a man is weighed down with time and creatures he also acts in time and with creatures, and he cannot be free from them. But when he turns himself away from time, away from creatures and towards God and eternity, he obviously acts with God and in relation to eternity. Out of time he makes eternity, and, out of the creature, God. Spiritual poverty seeks precisely this, and for this reason it is a pure action.

Spiritual poverty converts a good action into a better and more perfect action. When a man walks in God's way his journey is always towards something better and more intimate, as St. Gregory says: "The going in the way of God is always a forward march."[2] A man who is poor in spirit always walks in the truth, and always increases while he is in time; hence spiritual poverty is a pure action because the poor spirit continually makes things better and better.

Again, spiritual poverty has the characteristic of even annihilating one thing and making another in its place. Man has inherited from Adam's fall a nature full of sinful inclinations, and to annihilate these he must cultivate virtues; man must build a virtue in the place of each sin.[3] In this way he may overcome vice with virtue. He who desires to annihilate vice must cultivate virtue, and in no other way can vice be overcome. Since spiritual poverty continually annihilates vice, strives for and obtains virtue, it is a pure action.

Truly, we must daily exercise ourselves in virtues if we would become free of vices. When a man is idle regarding the cultivation of virtue, vice gains the upper hand. But if a poor spirit continually performs virtuous acts, vice has no control over him. If he always aims at God's glory, everything becomes virtue to him. Of this St. Paul speaks when he says: "All things are clean to the clean."[4]

2

SPIRITUAL POVERTY PERFORMS ALL THINGS IN GOD

How can there be action in spiritual poverty, since it is a mere state of being? In other words, it is simple and immovable, whereas action is movable and takes place in movement. How, then, can spiritual poverty and action go together?

My answer is that spiritual poverty is a God-likeness. Now God is in Himself immovable, yet He moves all things. Spiritual poverty is also immovable, yet with God it moves all things, for it is fused in God and united to Him. Now that which is one has but one action. God and spiritual poverty are one and therefore it performs all things with God while remaining pure and simple and immovable with God.[5]

Furthermore, man is compounded of time and eternity. But when man is lifted with the highest faculties out of time into eternity, he becomes immovable in accordance with these highest powers. For eternity is immovable and that which is in eternity is also immovable. If man is with his highest part in eternity, he is immovable, yet he moves the lowest faculties in accordance with time. (See Addendum C, p. 288.)

Spiritual poverty, in other words, is to be considered in relation to the highest faculties, and these are immovable. Hence, it also is immovable—it acts with the highest powers in the lowest, not the lowest in the highest. For example, the angel moves heaven and the things that are in heaven, yet he remains unmoved. It is the same here—and in this way spiritual poverty is a pure action, though immovable.

CHAPTER VI

THE WORK OF NATURE

✹✹✹✹✹✹✹✹✹✹✹✹✹✹✹✹✹✹✹✹✹✹✹✹✹

IN man there are three kinds of work—a natural work, a work of grace, and a divine work. One should make the first pure, the second acts in a pure way, the third is pure. Now the natural work in man is of three modes: bodily, sensual and intellectual.

1

THE BODILY WORK

The first natural work is bodily, such as eating, drinking and sleeping, and all this man should purify so that he may not stray from God. And this may be accomplished in the following way. Above all, one should observe measure and moderation. And moderation simply implies neither too much nor too little. In other words, a man should consider the needs of the body in such a way that he always remains on the *via media* between excess and too little. In this measure the work remains pure and well directed in God, but without this proper balance it is neither pure nor well directed. If a poor spirit directs all his actions according to God, they are pure.

Another property that belongs to a bodily work for it to remain pure is that one should take his necessity from truth and from the Holy Spirit. He should not try to aid himself with untruthfulness. What is this untruthful assistance? Well, it is when a man asks for gifts that he does not need, or addresses himself to others and exaggerates his necessities. This is an untruthful way of seeking help, and if a man desires his work to be pure he should stop it. He should take his need from the Holy Spirit. In other words, he should not be prompted by his own will because people do not give him anything from natural charity, or for his services or for his speeches. After all, only the Holy Spirit is the Giver of the gifts that are bestowed on him, and in this way the work remains pure.

It also belongs to a pure bodily work that what a man eats or drinks should be consumed in the Holy Spirit. For the heart of man ought to burn with the love of the Holy Spirit, and the strength which man has taken from his meal the Holy Spirit draws to Himself and burns it in the fire of charity, making it completely spiritual. Thus, instead of a bodily force, man becomes a spiritual force which surpasses all bodily powers.

Men like this are truly spiritual, and their eating is dearer to God than the fasting of others, and those who so eat actually consume God Himself. And God consumes in them what they eat and drink. Let us compare this with the sun. Its hot rays draw the dampness on the earth's surface to itself and make the earth dry. In the same way, when the divine sun shines in a pure heart, it draws to itself all that is in the heart and at the same time makes it light and dry, which, thus escaping from man, exceeds all power, yes, far more than if he had worked in a mine.

To give strength to these men is to give strength to the work of God, in which God is well pleased, and in which He purifies all things in time. If God did not continue to perform this work on earth, all that is in time would disappear. Indeed, this is a particularly pure work which, nevertheless, belongs quite essentially to a man who is poor in spirit.

2

THE SENSUAL WORK

The second natural work is sensual, such as seeing, hearing

and the other three senses, which man should also control so that he may remain pure. He should always hold them under the restraint of modesty and grant them only what is necessary. For if the senses stretch out beyond reasonable necessity, man becomes distracted and can scarcely remain as pure as when his senses were gathered into one. True purity is in unity and not in the manifold. When a man is distracted he wishes to see and hear many things which cannot abide with purity.

Man should also control the senses because the faculties hang on one another. When one works, the others are hindered and obstructed. For instance, if while he is wastefully seeing and hearing outwardly, his inner sight and hearing are led astray; it is a hindrance. Man should only take what he needs from his senses and nothing more, in which case he remains pure and he can always use them to the glory of God rather than for the lust of the body. Since God will request an account of our five senses we should direct them in a useful way.

3

THE INTELLECTUAL WORK

The third natural work is intellectual, such as to know, to love, to remember, and this, too, should be directed in accordance with need. And how? Well, man has from nature the power of knowing, and this forms a distinction between him and other animals. But he should direct this natural knowing to God and to godlike things, and hold himself back from things which he does not need. If he directed it towards something other than God or godlike things, God would remain unknown to him and he would go astray.

Had Lucifer directed his understanding to God when he turned it to himself he would not have fallen. But as he turned it to himself he necessarily had to fall, for by mere force of nature he could not subsist. It is quite similar if a man turns his reason and understanding on himself and on things other than God, for he must fall, even were he of as noble a nature as Lucifer. Yes, he must fall; he cannot stand, for no one can stand by nature alone.

But if he directs his natural understanding in the light of faith to God and to godlike things, and if he lives accordingly, then God changes his natural understanding into a divine understanding and establishes him in it so that he may not fall. This is the case with angels, who live with God and whom God strengthens in such a way that they can no longer fall. For at the very moment that they turn their understanding from themselves to God, God produces His divine nature in them and this draws them immediately out of themselves and confirms them.[1]

The same thing happens with man. At the very moment that a man turns his knowledge from himself towards God he also becomes strengthened by Him. This happened to the Apostles on the day of Pentecost. For he who truly knows God can never take pleasure in mortal sins. Had Lucifer truly known God he might never have fallen. Hence, it is in this way that a man no longer acquires a natural understanding, but instead a godlike understanding. And what he then knows is never from a natural light but from a divine light.

Let us again take a comparison from the sun: As soon as it rises it changes all other lights into its light so that there is no other light. Its light is above all other lights and hence, all lesser lights must vanish and the sun shines alone with its light. It is the same in a pure soul. When the divine sun rises in it all other lights change into the divine light, so that no other light remains but the divine light. God is a light above all lights. When He shines with His light it is necessary that all other lights should cease, whether they are of nature or of grace.

Now it does not follow that the natural light is destroyed. Though it still burns and is not as a thing that does not exist, it is, however, changed into a divine light and glorified, just as when the moon's light is changed into the sun's light and is magnified. As St. Augustine says: " God is never a destroyer of nature, but He ordains it and makes it perfect."[2]

G

4

THE NEGATION AND AFFIRMATION OF NATURAL KNOWLEDGE

Some negate natural knowledge and others affirm it. Yet it must be both negated and affirmed. It is to be negated, for, though man's mind may penetrate all knowledge and distinction, and though man may have a real distinction of all truth in himself, still he must forgo all distinction and carry himself towards his centre with unity and into unity. And he should remain in this unity and contemplate it with a simple and single urge. Then all natural knowledge should leave, for it consists in images and forms, and man can never really know God through images. Since he must finally know Him without them, the spirit must be stripped of all images; for a teacher [Eckhart] says: "He who wishes to know God must be stripped of all creaturely art."[3]

Knowledge seeks that which is stripped, namely, the naked truth, and it is never satisfied until it enters in complete nakedness and sees God and knows Him without medium. When it comes into Nothing all natural marks disappear and the soul becomes unoccupied and rests in pure peace. It is then that the spirit arrives at the source from which it flowed. In this way natural knowledge is negated, and in this way it is necessary that one should become empty of his natural knowledge if he desires true spiritual poverty. His knowledge is so magnified with divine charity in this nakedness and poverty of spirit that nothing remains of the knowledge that belongs to him only naturally.

Man, then, knows all truth when he knows what is good or harmful to him. He can no longer be deceived by a false light since he is removed from all falsehood, and falsehood can no longer find a place in him. For this reason Christ says: "When He, the Spirit of truth, is come, He will teach you all truth."[4]

But natural knowledge should also be affirmed. For instance, when a man is in doubt and he is still exposed to error in distinguishing the truth, he must then seek distinctions in himself and out of himself. Man can never live in accordance with the truth unless he has first known it. Hence, if knowledge is wanting to a man, life is also wanting, for a true life springs from a pure knowledge. When a man needs distinctions and does not seek them, he lives like the beasts and not like a human being.

Man naturally desires to learn much. Because he comprehends the truth and seeks that which fails in him, he is human. In this sense natural knowledge is not to be negated but affirmed. For it leads a man, if he is willing, into the knowledge of grace, and this knowledge of grace leads him to divine knowledge. It is in this way that a man attains to perfection.

What is the difference between natural knowledge and the knowledge of grace? Well, consider this: Natural knowledge seeks distinction in created things, whether spiritual or bodily, and man naturally desires to know all created things, and the distinction that he perceives in them is granted to him by his natural knowledge. The desire to know produces in him a great pleasure, and this pleasure drives him on to know more and more. If a man remains on the level of natural knowledge so that he does not arrive at the knowledge of grace or at divine knowledge, he turns his knowledge towards himself and regards it as his property, and never attains to a true and proper self-denial. Mere nature bends back on itself and seeks her own pleasure.

One may wish to ask: How does one recognize a man whose knowledge is merely natural? Among other things, he is to be recognized by three conditions. First, by his desiring to be always the most distinguished in speech and honours; he desires to dominate the conversation, for he believes that no one can do it as well as himself. Secondly, he always desires to have the privilege of a question and regards his own words as the truest; and if others attempt to dispute his remarks, he becomes angry and grasps at any support for his opinion and will not listen to the opinion of anyone else. Thirdly, he believes that all that people credit him with is right and proper, for he considers himself worthy of all things, and he thinks a person is lacking reason and sense who finds anything more worthy of praise in somebody other than himself.

Natural knowledge, then, is indeed harmful if it remains in the self and does not attain to a true denial of self. But if a man who is by nature discreet attains to a genuine self-denial, his natural understanding does not injure but greatly aids him; he comes more easily to divine truth than one who is by nature coarse and stupid.

What the stupid man seizes with great labour, the intelligent man acquires without much labour. For if a well-directed nature has a good will, it is a great help towards God. But if it has a perverse will and keeps to itself, it falls much sooner than a stupid nature. This happened to Lucifer who was one of the noblest by nature, but because he kept to himself he was the first to fall. Yet this still happens, and for this reason spiritual poverty should be regarded as very noble and useful provided a man is humbly established in it alone and in the denial of himself and all things.

CHAPTER VII

THE WORK OF GRACE

****

WE must now speak of the knowledge which is of grace. This, of course, implies that the man in this state is given the power of distinguishing the Holy Scriptures so that he understands them in truth, and that, when hearing and reading them, he understands them in the most profitable way. This knowledge is of grace and not natural, for one cannot come to a true understanding of Holy Scriptures by mere natural knowledge.

1

UNDERSTANDING HOLY SCRIPTURE

The Holy Scriptures are from the Holy Spirit and he who desires to comprehend them correctly must be enlightened with the grace of the Holy Spirit. It might be objected that many understand the Holy Scriptures who have not much grace nor live a holy life. That is true, but they understand them only according to the senses and not properly according to their true groundwork. He who desires to understand them on their true ground must form his life to divine grace. Thus it is that Holy Scripture is understood in the light of grace and not in the light of nature.

True spiritual poverty is full of grace and so Holy Scripture is understood by a truly poor spirit. Of this Christ says: "The poor have the Gospel preached to them,"[1] for only they comprehend it correctly. This may also be observed in the Apostles who preached the Gospel and converted the people; they did not do this by cleverness of natural knowledge. Rather they did it in the power of spiritual poverty, for by it they sur mounted all things and in it they comprehended all things. Surely grace is a flowing-out from God into the soul, but only into the soul that is empty and poor of all things that are not of God. And since Holy Scripture is to be understood by grace alone, and since only a man who is poor in spirit is receptive to the grace of God, then only a spiritually poor man correctly comprehends Holy Scripture.

This is not to say that a spiritually poor man comprehends Holy Scripture in all the ways in which it can be understood, but he does comprehend it in its essence and he comprehends the naked truth about which Holy Scripture has been written. Since he understands the essence of truth it is not necessary for him to consider truth according to accidents nor that he should understand all figures of speech which are in Holy Scripture. As Christ says to His disciples: "To you it is given to know the mysteries of the kingdom of heaven: but to them it is not given. . . . Therefore do I speak to them in parables."[2] He who comprehends the naked truth does not need a parable. Hence, because a poor spirit is empty of all things that are not like the truth, he then comprehends the naked truth and he has enough with that alone.

2

DISTINGUISHING VIRTUE FROM VICE

In man the knowledge by grace is also the distinction of virtue from vice. It is hardly possible to abandon vice and introduce virtue without understanding them. Therefore it is from grace that man is able to understand virtue and vice properly. Philosophers of nature have written about virtues, but they do not always penetrate to the real foundation of virtue. They wrote about how much pleasanter and sweeter virtues are in their nature, since virtues are without a doubt and naturally a greater source of pleasure than vice. In this way they sought their pleasure in virtue and nothing else. But they never really penetrated virtue since it consists in the denial of all natural delight, and they never possessed virtue completely because they sought themselves in it.

Now he who desires to have virtue in a hearty stripping of himself must acquire it from grace and not from nature, for virtue is quite at home in grace. But when a man has himself in view in virtue, it is not true; it is only a natural virtue—not of grace, for sinners also have it. They cannot possess virtue except in true self-denial. When, then, a poor spirit stands in complete denial of natural pleasure, he understands virtue in its groundwork. The philosophers of nature could not come to natural truth with vices so they left vices through the power of natural knowledge.

No man can attain to natural truth who is too heavily burdened with the coarseness of sins. It was through nature, and not grace that these philosophers left vice. Virtue by grace is only for the sake of God; it is not from natural knowledge, and so they did not arrive at the true knowledge of virtue. This knowledge is of grace.

A man's awareness of his faults is also of grace. As St. Gregory said: "It is a great perfection that a man should know his imperfection, for sin blinds a man so that he may not understand his faults." When a man feels displeasure in sins, a light springs up in him, revealing to him his defects so that he knows what a sin is, and thus he forgoes his sins and turns to virtue. And this knowledge is of grace.

When a poor spirit feels a thorough disgust at all sins, he then has a divine light revealing to him all sins—and not only sins, but even the causes of sins, and not only gross sins, but also spiritual and secretive sins which occur in the reason and in the will. A man who understands all sins must have much light, and this knowledge can only be had by a simple and poor spirit who stands firm in the denial of himself. Only he can really understand sin, whether spiritual or bodily. For this reason perfection rests in spiritual poverty, since only in this is all truth, all good, all evil properly understood.

No one can be deceived in true spiritual poverty, for deception is in a manner of adhering to and taking possession of a spiritual or temporal good, or even what seems to be a good. It is in this point that we may possibly be deceived, but in true detachment, self-denial and humility, no one can really be deceived. When, then, a poor spirit has abandoned himself to God and has truly denied himself, and when he does not take truth according to appearance or display or splendour, but in its essence which is without all this or that and un-disguisedly God or godlike—in this state he cannot be deceived, either in himself or in others.

A Master says: "He alone cannot be deceived in whom the heavenly Father begets His eternal Word." And this happens only in the man who has thoroughly abandoned himself to God, who is thoroughly self-denying, who has thoroughly gone out of himself and who has considered the being of things according to their essence and not their appearance. No deception can be hidden in this. All is manifest so that the man knows what is evil; and in this state he forgoes the evil and chooses the good.

3

UNDERSTANDING THE DANGER AND DEGREES OF SIN

It is of grace when a man realizes the danger inherent in sin. No one can really speak of the amount of harm that lies in it; it robs man of all good, not only natural good but spiritual as well. Sin pulls nature down from its nobility and debases it to the ignoble which all creatures hate. No, even the devil hates it, though he can never be free of it, and that is hell.

Some people say that it is human to sin. It is not human but devilish, for sins make a devil out of a man. Those who live conscious of it in mortal sin are hardly men but devils and are even more wicked than devils. For if the devil could return he would not abide in sin; but these men, though they may return, continue with the same evil and are therefore worse than devils.

Now an inclination to sin is certainly human, since man acquired this from Adam's fall. But his actual sinning is committed because of an evil will; it is not from nature, but really against nature. Nature is destroyed by it and degraded from its nobility. He who wishes to acquire a proper nature must do it through virtue, not through vice. Nature desires good, not evil, and whenever evil takes place it is a suffering to nature. Since nature is created for good and not for evil, it despises all evil.

No, a man's love of sin is not from nature but from devilishness and it is even worse than the devil. For the devil hates sin naturally and yet the fact of his loving it unnaturally makes him a devil. Sin does the same; it makes all who love it into devils. Many people woefully blame nature, but they do not know what nature is. Nature is noble and does what is right. Men should blame evil, not nature; for God loves human nature so dearly that He created all things for its service and even suffered death in human nature, and by His death in human nature a man is elevated above all the angels.

Natural men are often spoken of as if they were harmful, but I say that a completely natural man is a pure man, for everything is to be taken according to its best. Now nature is good, and what is good is also pure and without any sinful accidents. Hence, when a man stands in his true natural nobility, he is without any sinful accident, and that which is without sinful accident is pure.

Finally, a completely natural man is a pure man. That which makes nature impure is a defective accident of nature, and not the essence of nature. Just as accidental virtue regulates nature and leads to its true source and essence, so vice destroys nature and removes it from its source so that it never arrives at its true essence. Indeed, it is far more according to nature to work virtue than vice, for virtue firmly establishes nature and sustains it, whereas vice disestablishes it.

All of this may be recognized in the pagan who, prompted by nature, forgoes vice and performs virtue. He knows from nature that vice keeps man from happiness, as Seneca said: "Even if it were true that the gods did not know my sins and did not avenge them on me, I would still leave sin and its ugliness." But where natural men are to be questioned is where they keep selfishly to themselves and hold themselves in their own property and ease. These are harmful men since they change their human nature into devilish nature. Lucifer, when he stood in the natural nobility in which God had created him, was a pure noble creature. But when he kept to self and held himself as a property with his natural nobility, he fell and became a devil.

It is the same with man. If he arrives at the summit of his nature and stands free of all accidents, his nature is quite noble. But if he remains in himself and holds himself as a property, he falls and becomes a devil instead of a man. For this reason sin is wicked.

If they who lived in sin only knew in what good they were lacking, yes, even natural good, they would suffer the greatest pain to be inflicted upon them before they would commit a mortal sin. Sin is so bad that it robs man of all good. They who live in worldly riches and in sin imagine all is well with them, but they do not know what suffering it really is. The devil prompts them to sins and especially to those of unchastity, but when one is unchaste, the devil flies and prefers not to see it. Though he is at the root of all iniquity, yet he naturally hates this sin for its very uncleanness.

It is truly a great sign to know the injury of sin. And no one can know it except they who have been in sins and have departed from them and turned to grace. It would be a torment of hell for them to fall into sins again. They have more joy in one day than all sinners have ever experienced. Their labour is more pleasant than the repose of a sinner, who really can have no repose. Sinners always labour and never rest, and yet their labour is fruitless.

But truly good men always rest; not that they sit in idleness, but their labour is repose. As Solomon says: "They have rest in all things."[3] The sinner has disquiet in all things; let him eat or drink or sleep or wake, it is all painful; let him do what he will—never will his heart be joyful. He may certainly display an outward joy and others may think he is cheerful. But true joy is not there. For the ground of joy, out of which true joy springs, is broken. He may sometimes indulge himself, but dogs also do the same.

It is of grace when a man knows each defect according to its degree. One is called a fault, another a debt, another a sin. And one kind of sin is called a venial sin, another a mortal sin, one a cardinal sin, another a sin against God the Father and God the Son and God the Holy Spirit.

A fault is when a man knows what is good for him and yet adheres negligently to what is less good. For instance, when a man has a useless thought, or speaks a useless word, or performs a useless action, though he knows there is a better one and he fails to attend to it. This is a fault.

Now it is a debt if one dwells with pleasure on a thing that is bad, as when an evil thought occurs to a man and he lingers on it rather too long and with pleasure. This pleasure creates guilt and he must suffer pain for it. Also, if he speaks voluptuously improper words and performs improper actions, this is guilt.

It is a sin if one consciously does a thing that is wrong, such as telling a lie, which yet does not hurt anyone; this is venial sin; or speaking loose words and indulging in loose gestures so that others are made angry by them.

It is a mortal sin if one, with an evil and determined will, does that which is forbidden. For example, he who deliberately breaks the Ten Commandments in which the seven deadly sins are forbidden. Thus in the first commandment, "Thou shalt believe in the Lord thy God," which condemns unbelief, and unbelief is a mortal sin. Then, "Thou shalt love the Lord thy God . . . and thy neighbour . . ."—in this envy and hatred are condemned. "Thou shalt observe the holy days"—in this indolence is condemned. "Thou shalt not covet any man's wife," in which unchastity is condemned. "Thou shalt not covet any man's property," in which greed and avarice are condemned. "Thou shalt not worship idols," where gluttony is condemned. "Thou shalt not kill any man,"[4] where anger is condemned. Furthermore, maliciously to break the commands which Holy Church has established is a mortal sin.

It is a cardinal sin if one does what is unnatural and inhuman —such as to kill, rob and burn father and mother, and other sins that are contrary to nature.

A man sins against God, and first in God the Father, when he is tempted and in the resistance is so rigid that he sins through disorder. This sin is in the Father. Also one sins against the Son when one sins unwittingly. And one sins against the Holy Spirit in many ways: First, if a man sins against God's mercy; if having sinned, a man despairs in God's compassion; if a man altogether resists the counsel of the Holy Spirit and destroys it in himself; if a man attributes to himself the good that he has from God, whether spiritual or bodily, and thinks that he has it from his own worthiness and fails to thank God for his goodness; if when the Holy Spirit desires to do his work and a man turns away from him, refuses to make room for him, burdens his heart about other things that are contrary to God and drives out the Holy Spirit. All of this is called sinning against the Holy Spirit and is not lightly forgiven.

It is, then, a great grace when a man knows each sin in its degree, for then he can more easily guard against sin and keep himself pure. Since a spiritually poor man is full of grace, he has the light of grace which reveals to him all faults so that he can properly guard against all defects and preserve his purity. Therefore, as we see again, spiritual poverty is a pure action, for no impurity can hide itself in it.

CHAPTER VIII

THE FOUR SPIRITS THAT
SPEAK IN MAN

****

WHEN man knows the distinction of spirits it is indeed
a great grace. Now there are four kinds of spirit
that speak in man—the evil spirit, the natural spirit,
the angelic spirit and the divine spirit—and he who wants to
know them must have considerable light.

1

THE EVIL SPIRIT

There is an evil spirit that speaks in man and this speaking
is in one direction to sin and in another direction to virtue.
A third direction is to perfection. The evil spirit advises sins.
In other words, if a man finds himself inclined to bodily
pleasure, he presents the sin to his mind with great sweetness
so that the man thinks that great pleasure lies in this sin.
The body is inclined to luxury, and if the spirit inclines to the
body and the body to luxury, man comes to his fall and slips
into mortal sin.

Should the spirit turn from the body and the body remain
in its inclination while the spirit does not concede to any deadly
sin, then the evil spirit advises man in favour of great venial
sins, and so he falls into them daily. If it happens that the
spirit of man turns from the body and the body desires to
follow the spirit and not sin, either mortally or venially, then
the evil spirit attacks man in his belief. It is in this way that
a man has a spiritual conflict.

If, in this condition, a man strongly resists and calls upon God to help him to conquer the evil spirit, and if he should win out, this evil spirit makes himself look like a good angel and thus advises the man towards virtue. But this virtue is above the power of nature and the Evil One does this in order to destroy nature and in order that a man should become feeble and so lose his sense of direction. For the virtue which the Evil One advises is irregular and without measure, and the end of the virtue is evil, for it does not teach the mean but reaches beyond it to seize the end.[1] For instance, fasting and night-vigils beyond measure, and other such severe exercises, which result in a man becoming ill.

All this is neither useful to God nor to oneself nor anyone and it usually results in a man having to cease midway in the exercise of many good works. This is what the Evil One often proposes in his advice in order that by it a man may altogether perish.

But when a man enters into himself and views each virtue in its proper measure and performs virtue according to it, he begins to move towards perfection. When he moves thus from virtue to virtue he is purified from all faults since virtues are purifying. Light appears in purity and this light enlightens man in distinguishing manifold truths, and in this distinction the Evil One hurries to deceive him.

When man understands much truth he arrives finally at a truth that he cannot well understand. He would gladly understand it but he is unable to do so. Then the evil spirit enters and presents a false image to him, one which is against faith. If it happens that the man accepts this image for a truth, as often is the case, he is deceived and makes a spiritual fall, which is injurious in a way that he does not realize at the time. If man is to be warned against this it must come from God without any mediation.

Now if man has been warned by God so that he realizes that the image is false, he then turns away and perceives what is best and clings to it. Hence, when he stands in perfection so that he accepts all to be good that God wills to have from him, then the Evil One comes again and fosters pride in him and makes him think that all others err and go astray, and that only he dwells in the truth and that only he comprehends it. Should he resist this, conquer the Evil One and realize what he truly is in himself—that he is capable of nothing good without God—then he gives the honour to God and makes himself truly poor.

Man comes to the ground of humility by spiritual poverty. The evil spirit cannot injure him there, for he cannot enter upon this ground. Spiritual poverty is a strong fastness which no one can capture. Indeed, men often attack it and seek to storm it, but it is not to be taken. It is the same with true humility; in it man cannot be conquered. The evil spirit attacks the humble man in many ways, but he cannot harm him.

Should man stand on any other ground than true humility and detachment and spiritual poverty, then the evil spirit can certainly harm him and can tear down the house, for the foundations are not deep enough. True humility has deep foundations on which all that is built upon them stands firm. Without humility every building must fall. He then who desires to overcome the evil spirit should place himself on the ground of humility where no one can injure him.

Now true spiritual poverty is also true humility and so no harm can be done to a poor spirit. He may certainly be helped, but he cannot be hurt. For all things take him nearer to God— yes, even the evil spirit himself is of no use and cannot obstruct him, for, as St. Paul says, he tempted him grievously,[2] and the temptation placed him in a genuine humility, and, as he says: "Power is made perfect in infirmity."[3]

2

THE NATURAL SPIRIT

Another spirit that speaks in man is natural, and its speech is in images and forms by which man seeks the distinction of created things. If man's spirit comprehends all created things and if he is free of accidental faults, he is in nature's nobility. But if he keeps to himself and is satisfied with his nobility, he cannot remain in this, the highest state of his nature. He falls into an ignoble state and clothes himself with mortality and many defects, for no nature can subsist long without accidents, whether these be from sin or grace.

When the natural spirit has reached the highest summit of its nature and turns itself to God and contemplates His nobility, then the natural nobility of this man is clothed with a godlike nobility and it becomes immortal. Light and life and truth flow into him, and God then continually produces these in him.

When the spirit of Adam stood on the highest summit of his nature he understood all created things, and that was his delight. It is the same with the spirit of man when it is stripped of faulty accidents—man understands much natural truth and this truth produces pleasure in him. Now pleasure is of nature, though man often imagines it is of grace, and for this reason nature is frequently taken for grace. Just as divine light and life and truth flow into the spirit which is raised above itself and all things in God, so also flow natural light and natural truth into the natural spirit that stands on its mere nature.

What is the difference between natural truth and divine truth? Natural truth consists in man knowing the distinction of manifold things in such a way that the understanding creates images of each and every thing, and that it understands each thing from its image. Now if these representations are evil they are from the evil spirit; if neither evil nor good, they are from nature; if they are good they are from the angels. But by this is meant that these images are evil only if they are turned to sins or to the cause of sin. If they do not acquire eternal happiness for man and if they are turned to the mere work of knowing things in general, they are neither good nor bad. Man is not saved by this knowledge, but only by knowing God who is eternal life. This knowledge, then, is not to be called good since it does not gain eternal life for man. Nor is it evil since sin is not committed with it. But these images of the understanding are good when they direct man to virtue, for through them eternal life is gained.

We see, then, that natural knowledge consists in the distinction of manifold things that are neither good nor evil. Divine truth, however, is a pure distinction of eternal things which man realizes in himself without images. That is, he realizes them by an internal consciousness and feeling showing him what God and creatures are, time and eternity, sin and virtue, manifold and simple, useful and harmful, evil and good. But can this be known without images? Yes, for those men who are touched by God within know all without natural images, for the truth reveals itself to them in a pure consciousness without representations.

The man who has left creatures and turned himself to God, finds in himself, without intervening images, the very sweetness of God and the bitterness of creatures. It is not necessary to say anything to him in images or in manifold forms, for the divine image and the simple form reveal to him all things. This knowledge is a unity and not in the manifold. Hence it is called divine, for it is similar to God. As God comprehends all things in Himself without created images, so likewise a godlike man comprehends all things in God by a pure indwelling in God. For he who realizes God realizes all things in God.

This realization is nothing more than an understanding of God's work and its fruit. Through this work and fruit man measures and examines all other works and fruits that are not from God. God's work is pleasant and its fruit is bitter. Take a man who eats a sweet apple and also a sour one: after doing so he knows the sweet from the sour. It is the same when man tastes God; he then knows that all other things are bitter and he measures their worth accordingly. As Christ says: "By their fruits you shall know them."[4] And this is the difference between natural and divine truth.

When a spiritually poor man is free of all fallible accident he has no impediment in his natural perception because the natural spirit takes its object in images and forms that are created. All that obstructs a man in understanding, whether

H

natural or divine, is a fallible accident, and when a man is free
of this he has a pure understanding of all truth, whether natural
or divine, and from this position he can extract the best in each.

It might, of course, be objected that there are many pure,
poor men who still do not realize or discover such truth. I
say, however, that where there is a pure, poor spirit, all truth
is revealed in the inner part of his soul. And if he does not
understand the truth in images and forms, he nevertheless does
understand it in its essence. And if he does not discover the
truth in natural powers he does discover it in being.

3

THE ANGELIC SPIRIT

The speaking of the angelic spirit to man is about that virtue
which leads man to God. The highest angel draws his image
from God and, as this is increased in him, he turns it over to
an interceding angel. This one again turns it over to the lowest
angel, who at length gives it to the soul which thus gains the
power of distinguishing how she has to seize and hold the truth
and how she must practise each virtue in proper order, discretion
and necessity. This clear distinction which man obtains is
granted by the angel who also lets him see vice so that he may
guard against it. When a man knows vice he also knows virtue
just as one can recognize the colour white through black. Should
man deny vice he would draw closer to virtue, but should he
leave virtue, vice would return to him, for the man who turns
away from virtue inevitably arrives at vice.

You may say that if a man feels remorse for his sins and
God forgives him so that he is free of sin, he still does not
possess all virtues. I would say, however, that a true repentance includes both the forgiveness of sin and the acquisition of
virtue. If virtue is actually lacking to a man he at least has it
in the will and if sin is not to find a place in him he must carry
out his will in works as far as possible. Through the strong
will that man has to gain virtue and sin no more, God forgives

him for his sins. But he must conquer every sin with a virtue, for by them the causes of sin are uprooted.

If a man is lacking in virtues and good works then the roots and impulses to sin must continue to grow, and if he is attacked he easily falls. As the tree that lacks deep roots easily falls if the wind blows violently against it, so man must strike deep roots of virtue in his heart if he wishes to stand firm and not fall. Virtue guards a man from sin; if he is lacking in virtue he has no support and sin soon establishes itself in him.

But if a man has a true repentance, does God forgive him so that he immediately has no more sin in him? Yes, this is accomplished by a true repentance. There are, however, many who guard themselves against sin but who still lack virtue. Yet I add that a true, earnest *avoidance* of sin is a true possession of virtue.

If some guard themselves against sin yet lack virtue, they only guard against it outwardly in their actions, and they frequently do so only because of the disgrace involved since they fear dishonour in the eyes of the world. They do not do it for the honour of God and they do not inwardly avoid sin. If they avoid mortal sins in their will and actions it is from fear of hell, and they do not avoid venial sins for they frequently indulge in these. Hence sin is not properly avoided. If these men, while guarding against sins, moral or venial, do not at the same time possess love, it is because they unconsciously commit many sins. In this sense unawareness is itself a sin.

Indeed, a man who wishes to guard against sin must possess all virtue and hence the angel advises man towards virtue so that he may be empty of vice. The more a man realizes virtue in himself the freer he is from vice, and he who cannot find any virtue in himself should know that he is full of vice.

It might be stressed that a child is pure and free of sin, yet it does not have all virtue. Yes, but a child possesses purity in the lowest degree which is a mere necessary first condition for heaven. The child also has virtue only in the lowest degree. Since it possesses purity only in an unmerited way, so also does it possess virtue in an unmerited way and its virtues are imperfect, for both qualities may come to nothing. It is clear, then, that genuine purity is a vessel full of virtues and to the extent that a man fails in virtue he also fails in purity. Hence the absence of all sins is the possession of all virtues.

In this way the angel counsels the soul to virtue and advises her to fly from vice. His speech is also in images and forms, but his images are useful and good. They direct man along the path of truth and without these images no one can practise true virtue. If a man needs these images he should not avoid them, for it he were to reject them he would lack the order of virtuous practice and he would hardly be able to execute a good work in proper order and discretion.

Now these images come from grace and do not hinder a man from what is best but aid him towards it. As a man who sees clearly leads a blind man so that he will not fall into a ditch, so these images lead man so that he will not fall into sin. And he who most has angelic ideas and images in himself can best keep in proper order both outwardly and inwardly. Some indeed avoid images without knowing what they avoid, and God frequently grants to them the grace to deny them in themselves. But we ought to receive gladly those that aid us towards divine truth.

4

THE DIFFERENCE BETWEEN THE EVIL, NATURAL AND
ANGELIC SPIRITS

Now there is a great difference between natural, angelic and devilish images. Natural images lead a man to the preservation of nature. They direct all things to man's nature and all men have these images. Every man is by nature more directed to himself than to others, and that which man loves in nature, he loves for his own sake and for the delight it gives his nature. Were it not agreeable he would not love it. The angelic image directs man away from himself and all things to God. It refers all to God and few have such an image, except a spiritually poor man. Most men are more considerate of themselves than of others, whether in spiritual or bodily things, since every man seeks his own.

Here one naturally asks if perhaps a spiritually poor man has too many natural images in himself. I say that a truly poor spirit is empty of all natural images, for he is placed in a true denial of himself and all things. Hence the images that are in him proceed from the angel and not from nature, since he refers nothing to himself but all things to God.

A spiritually poor man also has more knowledge than another, but he directs his knowledge to virtue and hence it is useful rather than harmful. They who for the most part possess natural images in themselves are also mostly considerate of themselves and cling too much to temporal things, since temporal things are to them a sustenance of their nature. And those who are most concerned about keeping temporal things are also the most immersed in nature and they have mostly natural images in themselves. They are too natural, since they cling too much to bodily things and by them hope to gain the best. They desire temporal and eternal things at the same time, which, however, is impossible, for two things that are unequal cannot subsist in the same being. They certainly wish to be poor in spirit but at the same time rich in the body. They want to eat the pure grain before removing the husk. They want to have God and the creature at the same time.

Such men are natural and have the greatest number of natural images in themselves. These are not spiritual images, but bodily images, yet for that reason they are more defective than if they were spiritual. A genuine poor spirit forgoes temporal things, outwardly and inwardly. Hence his images are not natural but angelic. And since the man with this image is led to God's holiest will, his image is also similar to that of the angel; that is, it is not natural but angelic.

But how does it happen that natural images are frequently similar to angelic images, for one often accepts the natural to be an angelic image? Well, the likeness is in the forms. In a spiritual way they both have a similar form. In their aim, however, they are very dissimilar. Natural images are aimed at nature and they have nature since Adam's fall. But the image of the angel is turned away from nature towards God, and we have this image from Christ.

Prior to Christ everyone was concerned with his own self-hood and everyone wished only to possess and no one wanted to be poor in spirit. But when Christ came, He brought with Him the angelic image which we had lost in the fall of Adam. It is in this true spiritual poverty, both outwardly and inwardly, that that angelic image rests, for Christ has brought it with Him.

No one, then, is free from the natural image which we have inherited from Adam except a truly poor man who is detached both outwardly and inwardly from all temporal things and who follows the image of Christ by a spiritually poor life. He has the image of the angel since he lives in true self-denial, and hence he is like the angels and not like Adam. He who lives with external accidents is like Adam, but he who enters with self-complacency into himself is like Lucifer; for he sinned spiritually whereas Adam sinned only bodily, and so his fall was greater than Adam's fall.

Likewise the fall of the person who refers all things only to his selfhood is greater than the one who clings outwardly to accidents. But those who are empty, outwardly and inwardly, are like Christ according to the angelic image which Christ has brought to us from heaven. When nature is criticized it is because of its similarity to Adam and Lucifer, but when it is praised, it is because of its similarity to the angelic. Hence, nature is itself very noble and such a nature is readily adopted by a perfect, poor spirit. This is the difference between natural and angelic images: Natural images are directed to the pleasure of nature whereas angelic images lead one from the pleasure of nature to virtue and God.

Now the devilish images have a likeness to the natural and the angelic. If man directs the image to his own nature and seeks pleasure in it, then the devil enters and presents a sensual object to man which promises increased pleasure. Should man follow this and seek the pleasure, the natural is then turned into a devilish image. But should he turn away and remain in a state of surrendering all the pleasure of nature, his image then becomes angelic. The evil spirit then forms himself in the mode of this image and advises man to surrender all natural lust. But his advice surpasses all the powers of nature and he does it in order that these may amount to nothing and destroy themselves. It is in this way that an image of the devil has a likeness to the natural and angelic images.

When a poor spirit has denied himself all bodily lust and pleasure and holds all things in their right order, neither natural nor devilish images have a place in him. They may certainly present themselves to him, but he does not linger with them. Instead he holds on only to those of the angel which lead him through virtue to God.

Perhaps one might say that a man really poor in spirit is lifted into God above all creatures, whether they be angelic or whatever creatures they may be. If, then, a man is lifted above them and is also lifted above their images, how can he live by the images of the angels or another creature? My reply is that the raising of a poor spirit is to be taken according to the highest faculties of the soul and according to the likeness of God which is impressed upon the soul. In this way the poor spirit is lifted above all creatures and their images regardless of what they may be.

According to the lowest faculties or powers man must have images to the end that he may direct things according to their measure. These images must be angelic so that he may be able to accomplish all things in their right order. When it is said that man must be freed of all images, this is to be understood according to the highest powers of the spirit. But this cannot be in the lowest powers, for these must have either good or bad images as long as man is in time. If a man desires to practise his work in images according to the likeness of the angelic, that is, in complete abandonment, the work is then perfect and directed as the best.

If, however, man performs his work so that he is perfectly free in all his actions, he must also be free from this image, whether it be angelic or natural. And he must permit God alone to act without images. God does not act or work in images, but in essence, and for this reason the spiritually poor man must increasingly be free from images.

5

THE DIVINE SPIRIT

The speech of the divine spirit which speaks in man is nothing else than a revelation of divine truth. By it man is lifted out of sensuality, above *all* images and forms, so that he attains to the divine essence. The spirit now realizes her nobility and her nobility is now in company with the godlike. By this entrance the spirit is united with the divine spirit, as St. Paul says: " He who is joined to God becomes one spirit with God."[5]

This joining is simply the spirit going out of herself, out of time, and entering into a pure *nothingness*. That which *is* and which forms her being is the divine likeness which dwells in man and which man can never destroy. God takes this likeness and unites it with Himself and in this way the spirit of man becomes one spirit with God according to the divine likeness.

Man's spirit is also one spirit with God when he acts and brings forth all in essence that God performs. But what does God work and produce? He has produced all things out of love, and because He produced them, they are good. Hence the spirit should also perform all things from pure love, and that which she produces is also good and is the work of God. All things are good in the divine Love, as St. Augustine says: " Love, and do what you will."[6]

CHAPTER IX

THE FRIENDS OF GOD

✱✱✱✱✱✱✱✱✱✱✱✱✱✱✱✱✱✱✱✱✱✱✱✱

THE spirit of God speaks in man so that man may again speak all things through the divine spirit in God. But the spirit speaks in God when in all her works she proposes God's glory and when, regardless of what challenges her, she always remains pure and never clings to any accident. Thus she always finds herself in a state ready to accept God and listen to Him whenever He wishes to speak to her. She returns all to God through this hearing which is such a joy for her that she puts everything aside in order to listen to His words. This hearing is also called "returning all things to God", and thus the spirit speaks again in God. Man, then, becomes one spirit with God when he returns all to God as God has given all to him. By this return he makes himself a friend of God.

1

A FRIEND IS AN "ALTER EGO"

Where there is friendship there is union, for "a friend is another myself,"[1] as Aristotle says. The spirit is united with God when she has gained God as a friend. Christ said to His disciples: "Now I call you no longer servants, but friends."[2] He used this word *now* when they had abandoned all to follow Him. No longer were they servants, but real friends. He, therefore, who wants to be a real friend of God must abandon all and follow God. He who is attached to things and who does not follow God is not a friend, but a servant. And he who is not a friend is also not one spirit with God, for it is friendship and not servitude that establishes union.

2

WHAT FRIENDSHIP WITH GOD IMPLIES

What does a friend imply? The first thing a friend implies is likeness, for " like admires like ". God is free of all temporal things, and he who desires to conform to Him should detach himself from all that is temporal. Where likeness reigns there is also friendship. Where friendship reigns is also union. God is the Giver of all gifts, and so man must return all to God. God loves virtue and hence man, too, should love virtue.

Friendship also implies the same willing and the same not-willing. As Aristotle said: "True friends have the same willing and not-willing."[3] He who wants to be a friend of God should will what He wills and despise what He despises. And what does God will? He wills that man should be holy. As St. Paul says: "God's will is our sanctification."[4] Man should also will this. And what is holiness? To be holy is to be clean of all that is earthly; therefore he who desires to be holy should strip himself of all earthly things. This is God's will and if man wants to be a real friend of God he should also will this.

There are some who say: If I only knew what God's will is, I would do it. But they hardly speak sincerely, for they surely know it well enough, though they may not do it. Christ has frequently pronounced for us God's will and he who follows His teaching fulfils God's dearest will.

We know that Christ has taught us that we should abandon self and all things and follow Him. And in so far as we do this we follow His will, and as often as we neglect it we speak dishonestly when we say that we live according to His will. He who desires to fulfil God's will should abide by His teaching. His teaching, however, is simply that we should give all to the poor if we would enter into a perfect life, as God's will consists in nothing other than this.

But do I know that God wills precisely this of me? Yes, God wills it. But first look and consider if you are willing to have it! God will give you all the gifts, but what will you accept from Him? If some of His gifts are spurned, it is only your fault.

But you may say: Since God has ordained all things, He has perhaps placed me in a condition which obliges me to marry and have children for whom I must secure temporal goods so that they may not suffer want. Yes, God has ordained all things for the best, and if it is otherwise it is no longer God's order. But man frequently orders things for himself and then considers it still to be God's decree.

You may perhaps go on to say: Let us grant that I regard it as the will and decree of God that I should arrive at perfection, but I am not fit for it, nor can I find myself well in a perfectly poor, spiritual life, and this perfection is not meant for me and I am not able to act in what does not apply to me, in the same way that a sick man is not able to engage in combat with a strong man. Ah, but the best belongs to every man, and God will grant it to you no matter in what condition you may be—if you will accept it.

If we are not worthy we should try to become worthy. If we want to stand on the highest level of life we should humble ourselves and practise lowliness in highness. If we do not find it easy to do this we should nevertheless seek all the possible ways that lead to it. If we are too weak and sick, we should call on God to help us, unite our weakness with His strength, and what we cannot do He will fulfil in us. It is God's will that we should thus regard His teachings. And if you want to be a friend of God and one spirit with God, this, too, should be your will. If a poor spirit accepts this teaching of our Lord and lives accordingly, he will then fulfil God's dearest will. In this way he will become a true friend of God and one spirit with Him.

A man who wants to be a friend of God should also despise what his Friend despises. What does God despise? Sin, and if we want to be His friends we should shun it. But it might here be said that God is love, and since His love is not accidental but essential, no accident can enter into God. But to despise is an accident; how then can one say that God despises sin?

Let us try to understand this in the following way: God is a pure being, unified in Himself with essential love, and no accident is possible with Him. God has also created man after His likeness, as St. Augustine said: "Lord, Thou has made us after Thy likeness, and my heart is in unrest till it rests in Thee."[5] If man is burdened with faulty accidents, he cannot attain to God. Man's turning away from God is what stirs His wrath, though it is not the same in Him as it is in man. It is merely a displeasure that the likeness which He has impressed upon the soul and created after His own is now turned away from Him and not formed as He wished. It is the disorder that man creates against God's order that causes His displeasure, not a wrath from accident, not a hatred, but an expression of divine justice which is not contrary to His love.

Real hatred is only in man—never in God, and God does not will it. The man, then, who wants to be a friend of God should also not will what God does not will. This is erroneous accident of which man should become empty if he desires to be a friend of God and one spirit with God. Man becomes precisely this if and when he is free from all feeble accidents.

Another thing about friendship is that gifts procure a friend. As a teacher says: "Giving makes a man well-pleasing to God," and Christ says: "Give alms, and behold all things are clean unto you."[6] Purity is a likeness to God, and where God finds His like, there must He also love. In this way, giving makes man a friend of God.

3

THE NOBLEST GIFT OF A FRIEND OF GOD

What gifts will God have from a man that will make him

His friend? The noblest gift that he can give is himself. And when he gives himself he gives all, for man is himself in all things and for this reason it is not necessary for him to give anything but himself. As David said: " I blame thee not because of thy offerings, for I eat no flesh; if I am hungry I say it not to thee. Give God the praise and the desire; this offering God wishes to have from thee."[7] The same thing is implied in the words of Solomon, who said: " My son, give me thy heart."[8]

If the greatest offering consists in man's giving himself, what is its value, since some people say that one should give other things for God's sake? Man is created for time and eternity. But time and eternity are contraries.[9] He, then, who desires to win eternity must forgo time and all temporal things. Hence it is necessary that the person who retains many temporal goods should give them to others for God's sake, so that he may not become immersed in them. Otherwise, he would depart from the eternal. It is only by abandoning temporal things that there is entrance into the eternal. One should also be empty of these because many accidents cling to them.

Indeed, he who really wants to be free from all faulty accidents must be freed from the love of temporal things. The person who is overburdened with them can never gain true peace of heart. Since time itself is always in a state of change, a man cannot gain peace if he is always influenced by time and temporal things. Man should also be detached from these because they obstruct him in the knowledge of truth and the fire of divine love is then extinguished. As St. Augustine said: "These things we should freely value as a poison which kills not only the reason of man but also his soul, if he practises them and gives himself up to them." Another teacher says: "To kindle fire in water is just as impossible as the heart of man is to be enkindled with divine love in bodily delights."

The giving away of temporal things is also useful in the sense that Christ meant when he said: " Give alms, and behold all things are clean unto you."[10] One may have made himself impure in many ways by the use of temporal things. If he desires to purify himself from them, this must be through detachment.

Through detachment from temporal things the wounds which man has inflicted on himself are healed. As a teacher says: " I know nothing more useful to heal the wounds of the sinner than that he should give alms out of love." It is also a teaching that a man should help his neighbour in his necessity, as Christ says: " All things whatsoever you would that men do to you, do you also to them."[11]

One should also abandon temporal things if divine love requests it. As St. John says: " He that hath temporal things and seeth his brother in need, and closeth his heart against him, how can the charity of God abide in him? "[12] Where divine love is, it expresses itself outwardly, as St. Gregory said: "Where great love is, it works great works, and if it does not work these, it is no divine love at all."[13]

A heart that is full of love and a purse full of gold can hardly subsist with one another, for love is a fire by which all that is temporal is consumed. Where real love reigns, there can only be a free heart. He who is weighed down with temporal things gives evidence that the fire of divine love does not burn well in his heart. It is the nature of fire that it destroys all that its flames grasp. Likewise the divine fire destroys all things. It was this fire that burned in St. Paul when he said: " I count all things as dung."[14]

One may well ask: Is it not possible that the fire of divine love should burn in man and destroy all temporal things only inwardly, while the outward man might retain them? Well, if a man keeps himself pure, guards his heart, practises holy contemplation, especially the contemplation of the Passion of our Lord—for this makes a man pure—then in his purity rises a light which burns, and this inner burning shows itself outwardly. If it is great it consumes all things, outwardly and inwardly. But if it is weak, then man despises these things in his heart while he outwardly holds on to his possessions.

In order to gain heaven it is necessary to become free of all things spiritually. Now those who do this are certainly good men, yet it is also true that those who do this perfectly are those in whom the fire of love has consumed all things inwardly and outwardly. These alone stand on the level of perfection, of whom the Gospel speaks: "Blessed are the poor in spirit, for theirs is the kingdom of heaven."[15]

Some may object to my referring to the fire of love by giving it strength and weakness, and say that it is neither great nor small, since it cannot be divided. And that which has no parts also does not have these qualities, but is a simple being in itself. True, divine fire of love is neither great nor small, hot nor cold, in itself. But it is in its operation, for it effects in every man according to his ability to accept and according to his longing for God. If this earnestness and longing are great, the flame is also great; but if small, then the flame is equally small.

If man has a will free from temporal things, the divine fire enters and consumes them, outwardly and inwardly. As St. Paul says: "God is a consuming fire."[16] This fire arises in the man who wills to renounce all. And with the man who will not do this, not all, of course, is consumed. If a man's soul is empty through love, his body must also be empty and poor in so far as he can strip from it all that is not necessary. And even this he should keep in a way most spurned by the world, namely in a truly spiritual life, according to the teaching of Christ. For the soul governs the body, not the body the soul.

He from whom demands are made should be obedient. A lord commands his servants and his servants do what he commands; if they do not he discharges them. Likewise the body is the servant of the soul and what the soul commands, the body ought to do. If the soul is detached from temporal things, she requests a similar detachment from the body. When a lord becomes involved in a dispute, his servant should stand by him and aid him in his trouble. The soul, too, while she is in the body must protect herself against her enemies and the body should assist her, for without the body she could not conquer. For this reason she gives to the body the same weapons that she has. If she is detached from temporal things, the same applies to the body. And if the body wishes to have a reward, it must work with her and help her conquer all things that are not God.

Soul and body are one person, and what the soul receives from God she passes on to the body. And the same sweetness that the soul experiences with God the body also experiences with the soul. If the body wants to feel this blessedness, it should co-operate with her. Hence, when the spirit is stripped in a most perfect way, the body should also strip itself in so far as it is reasonable.

4

THE UNION OF BODY AND SOUL

St. Paul says: "The flesh lusteth against the spirit, and the spirit against the flesh."[17] And it may be said that where there are unlike desires, there are unlike results. How then can one say that the flesh must be subjected to the spirit?

Man is created for time and for eternity—for time in his body, for eternity according to his spirit. Everything strives according to its origin. Since the body is made on earth and for time, it leans towards earthly and temporal things, and seeks its pleasure in them. But the spirit has issued from God and is created for eternity; hence it leans towards God and eternity. The contrary tendency of both causes this opposing desire. However, soul and body are one and things which are united have mutual trust. Hence the soul is devoted to the body and the body to the soul.

When the soul, however, out of blindness of its knowledge, selects a false good for a true good, she turns to sensuality and the senses turn to this good which can be seized by them. But this springs from ignorance. To be sure, the soul finds no rest in it. She longs for something else but cannot seize it, since the body obstructs her and since her knowledge is blind. The soul then follows and takes the likeness of the body—that is, mortality, for the body is mortal. She becomes spiritually dead;

she ought to live, but she dies, as St. John says: "Thou hast the name of being alive. And thou art dead."[18]

But when the soul arrives at the knowledge of the truth, recognizes the real distinction of all things, learns that all bodily things are passing and feeble, and beholds in the light of faith that she herself is eternal, she then, fearing mortality, turns from the body to God, from the temporal to the eternal. In this craving for God the soul lifts the sensual desires up to herself and unites them with herself so that the senses can desire nothing save what the soul wills. The body must now follow the soul and be subjected to it. The body follows wherever the soul leads. What God has given her she passes on to the body and this is a greater satisfaction to the body than all that is merely bodily, and this satisfaction makes the body so strong that it endures all for God's sake.

When the soul has abandoned bodily things, she requests the same of the body, which, because of its very nature, causes suffering. It is this suffering that is a striving against the spirit. Nevertheless, the body now follows the spirit, and as the soul follows the body when she leans towards it, so the body follows the spirit when the spirit turns to God. Just as it was contrary to the spirit to lean to the body, though she did this in blindness, so it is also a suffering to the body which yields to the spirit.

When man's body is united with his spirit and the spirit with God, no further conflict arises—only a pure peace, a one-pointed will; just as with two spouses, of whom each wills what the other also wills. This is God's holiest will, and this they both accomplish and each does all it can so that His will may be fulfilled. This union results in utter abandonment, so that each stands in resignation—the body abandons itself to the spirit and the spirit clings to God alone. If the body does not forgo temporal things in so far as it is possible, a true union of body and spirit can never be established, nor of the spirit with God. There could never be a true peace but only a continual combat. He, then, who desires to be a friend of God so that he may be one spirit with God, should forgo

I

all out of love and unite his love with God alone. It is in this way that giving makes true friendship and union.

5

WHAT CHRIST MEANS WHEN HE SAYS: "BLESSED ARE THE POOR IN SPIRIT"

If one cannot be truly perfect without being poor in body, what does Christ mean, then, when He says: "Blessed are the poor in spirit"? For He also says: "Sell what thou hast and give to the poor."[19] My reply is that if two things are united in one you should always look at the best. Since soul and body are one, and the soul is the nobler, happiness should be chosen on account of the soul and not the body. The soul is receptive of true happiness whereas the body is not, and hence Christ says: "Blessed are the poor in spirit." If He said: "Blessed are the poor in body," a sinner might also be blessed and all wealthy people condemned.

Blessedness rests in spiritual poverty, and no sinner possesses this. He may certainly have poverty of body, but he cannot be blessed through this poverty. The person who retains his resources in a proper way can guard himself so well that he may be blessed. His happiness is not perhaps as high as the holiness of those who do not cling to even these outward things, for to a rich young man Christ also said: "If thou wilt be perfect, go sell what thou hast and give to the poor. And come follow Me."

What does He mean when He says: "Give to the poor"? And what does St. Peter mean by: "We have left all things"?[20] Can a person leave his things unsold and yet be perfect? Let us try to understand it this way. If a man has great possessions and sells them, he should pass the money on to the poor who need it. It is a great virtue that he should come to the aid of his neighbours, for the poor cannot give him anything in return. Instead, God must repay the giver, and what God gives him is a perfect gift which also makes him perfect.

Furthermore, wealthy people do not require another man's possessions, and so it is not a virtue if he gives to them. For they can repay him and such giving does not lead to perfection. What a man gives to wealthy people, God will not return to him, and so Christ says: " Sell what thou hast and give to the poor." What you do not have you should forgo just as though you had acquired it. As St. Peter was poor and had nothing except what he gained by the work of his hands, he said: " We have left all." This he was obliged to forgo, since he could not sell it.

A person, then, who possesses many temporal things should not go away and leave them. He should sell them and give them away and follow God. And that which he does not have, yet might possibly gain, he should forgo for God's sake. And this is very consistent with perfection.

Moreover, the words " Blessed are the poor in spirit " should be understood in another way. Where there is genuine poverty of spirit there is also poverty of body. The highest always contains in itself the lower, and what the highest does the lower should also do. If the spirit, which is the higher, is really poor, then the body, which is the lower, should also become as poor as possible. For instance, as the servant must always do what his master requests, so also the body must do what the soul requests, and not the soul what the body desires. Hence, it was not necessary for Christ to say: " Blessed are the poor in spirit and the body," since poverty of spirit includes poverty of body.

Where there is true poverty in the spirit, there must also be true bodily poverty. Poverty of spirit agrees with perfection and perfection agrees with a spiritually poor life. He who chooses poverty of spirit in another sense than this, has it, no doubt, only in so far as he needs it for salvation. However, for the perfection of which Christ speaks one should have both poverty of spirit and of the body, for it can hardly exist otherwise.[21]

PART II

God's Work and Man's Co-operation

CHAPTER I

GOD *IS* HIS WORK

✳✳✳✳✳✳✳✳✳✳✳✳✳✳✳✳✳✳✳✳✳✳✳✳✳✳✳✳✳✳✳✳

WHAT is God's work? It is simply a revelation of God in the soul when God shows Himself to the soul. God acts, and He Himself *is* the work that He performs. God leads the soul away from all things so that she may be able to receive His work. And this preparedness and the action of God makes the soul one spirit with God. Indeed, the dearest and most desired thing that God wants from man is that he should, like a child, constantly be prepared for God to work in him without obstruction. And He therefore says: "My delights were to be with the children of men."[1]

1

THREE KINDS OF MEN

There is always a dissent between two different classes of men. One class surrender themselves internally to God but do not bother with external works. They reproachfully guard their heart and consider God's work and what He wants to do in them. This keeps them so preoccupied that they care very little for the opinion of others. It also happens that these men acquire interior contemplation and even bold divine graces. And this comes about through their turning in upon themselves and through their contemplation of the Passion of our Lord. Such contemplation not only protects them from sinful mishaps, but it also corrects them. God then pours His

119

grace into them so that they become aware of these mishaps within themselves.

Furthermore, if these men abandon themselves to God and do what He counsels them to do, they readily forgo all things and follow Him in a poor life. In this way they rise to a high level of perfection. If, however, they retain something in excess of their need, yet give away the remainder for God's sake and guard their heart, they are indeed good men, though not in the highest level of perfection.

Now the other class of men give away all outward things for God's sake, but they do it more from rumour, as they have no doubt heard that perfection consists in giving away everything that a man possesses and in following Christ in a life of poverty. This they do, but they retain and cling primarily to external poverty; they pay little attention to their heart; they do not attend to the inner contemplation of the Passion of our Lord nor to other devout practices that keep a man pure from sins and prepare him for divine graces. Yet they perform many external good works. They are certainly good men, but they lack light and know nothing of real friendship with God or of His work. God's work is only in the ground of the soul, and while He works within, these men are always turned outwardly. Hence they can hardly understand the truth which is God Himself in a pure heart. Nor do they come to the right degree of perfection which pertains to a man truly poor in spirit.

Well, these two classes of men dispute with one another, and each passes judgement on the other, considering how mistaken the other class is. And so it must be, for they both lack the most essential and perfect thing. But there is a third class of men who do become truly poor in spirit. They make an earnest turning in upon themselves, look to what God wills, try to please Him in all things, busy themselves diligently with contemplation of the Passion of our Lord, avoid all that obstructs them in this, and accept the real truth, which is God, and allow Him to work in them—all these men are on the road to perfection. What they cannot accomplish in works, they accomplish with their will, and God accepts the intention for the act as long as they do their best, and God does not require from them what they cannot do.

Yes, these men, I say, are on the road to perfection, for they dispute with no one, nor do they judge anyone. Instead they offer all things to God, since they have altogether abandoned themselves and never demand anything for themselves. And through this abandonment the spirit of God comes into them, draws them to Himself, uniting them to Him in such a way that they become one spirit with Him. Thus God works in man in order that he should be empty of all things.

God is now able to act without hindrance in this emptiness. And such an action in a pure soul is far nobler than all other works which God performs in time and in eternity. And for this reason: when God created all things He had no obstacles in His work. But the work that God performs in the soul may be obstructed through the freedom of man's will, and that is why it is the noblest work when men unite their will with the will of God and co-operate with Him.

2

CHRIST IS ONE WITH GOD

If man follows Christ as He has gone before us, his spirit also becomes one with God. For Christ is one with God and hence it is necessary that he who desires to be one spirit with God should first unite himself with Christ. And this union of man with Christ implies that he do all things as Christ did them when he was man, in so far as it is possible and he is able. Christ taught us in his action what we should do so that we may become one with Him. He says: "Father, I pray Thee . . . that they also may be one in Us . . . as we also are one."[2] Man is one with Christ when he has one action with Him.

One might, however, say: Since Christ is God and man, how can a mere human have an action in common with Him?

There are two kinds of action in Christ. The one is divine, such as, to walk on the sea, perform miracles and signs, to fast forty days. Such actions do not pertain to us, and we should not try to perform them. The other kind is human—to be detached, spurned, insulted, to suffer hunger and thirst, to endure pain. Also the virtues that Christ had—humility, patience and gentleness. These actions pertain to us, and we should adopt them and execute them, for by them we become one with Him. That which we lack in these virtues indicates how much we rely on ourselves and how far we are from Christ.

He who desires to be one with Christ and empty of himself, should do all that He did as man and in so far as it pertains to his condition. In an Old Church prayer we read: "Christ's working is our teaching."[3] Christ also did these things to teach us how to act, and what He taught is His will, which we should accomplish. And His will causes our will to become His will, and His will our will. Thus do we become one with Him, and this is only attained by good works which we perform in imitation of Him. St. Peter says: "Christ also suffered . . . that you should follow His steps."[4] And as He walked, so should we walk.

What is meant, then, by the expression that we come quite near to God in heaven? It means simply that we follow Him closely on earth. St. Bernard says: "Many would walk with Christ in heaven, but they are unwilling to suffer with Him on earth."[5] But these can hardly be one with God, for real union implies one action, and he who does not co-operate in it, is separated from Him, for He says: "Where I am, there shall My minister be."[6] This minister, or servant, is the man who performs the works which He has inaugurated. He who fails to do this cannot be His servant, nor shall he become one with Him.

No one comes to God except he who abandons all to follow Christ in the way in which He has preceded us. Christ is the eternal aim of all men, and he who comes closest to this aim is also closest to God. It certainly happens that some men come close to this aim by good works alone, yet they fail in utter abandonment. But the nearer they come to this aim, the nearer they also come to God, and the more earnestly they practise good works, the more they avoid sins. If they have many good works, they are that much closer. If they have few, then they are further from Him. But if they have none, they stick in sins and are wholly separated from Christ.

On the other hand, if they have all good works *and* all virtue, they are then one with Christ, and where Christ is, they are there with Him. He who desires to be one with Christ must have gone wholly out of himself. But he who neglects the virtues of abandonment and yet performs good works, certainly approaches this aim, but never reaches Christ.

Only he who wears Christ's robe and follows Him wholeheartedly reaches Him. For example: a master, who has many servants, permits those whom he likes most to stand nearest to him, to wear his cloak and to bear his arms. Also those who wear the cloak of Christ, exercise themselves in all virtues and bear His arms, are the men who endure the poor, despised life that He had on earth. They are the men who suffer patiently all that hurts them, all that happens to them. This is the best sign that they are dearest to God, and these are the ones who first attain to Christ. But they who fail to do this, who have not all virtues, even though they perform good works, may approach the aim, but they do not find Christ.

Now we approach our aim by two kinds of action—an inward action and an outward action. An inward action should have the following objects in view—knowledge of our failings, the Passion of our Lord, and God and His Godhead.

3

SELF-KNOWLEDGE

A man should first consider his failings, try to know himself within, and by this self-knowledge, free himself. If he does not turn into himself, if he neglects to consider his failings, he never gains a true insight and hence cannot free himself in order to become really pure.

He who attends only to external works, and clings to them, never arrives at proper self-knowledge and in fact frequently fails in them. Such men believe that they are performing a virtue when it may be a vice, and this results from a certain blindness wherein the evil spirit may deceive them. He who does not wish to be deceived, who desires to attain the aim of Christ without hindrance and by the light which God has kindled in him, should consider everything whether it is good or bad. Then by rejecting the bad and choosing the good he may approach his aim.

4

THE CONTEMPLATION OF CHRIST'S PASSION

A man should also consider the Passion of our Lord, and this he should impress upon his heart and by it discover how he may avoid all that is not God and how he may practise virtue so as to attain to God. As he contemplates the Passion of our Lord, God pours a power into him and by it He draws man to Himself. This is the great fruit produced by the Passion of our Lord. If man turns himself to this with an earnest desire, and if he remains there, God will reveal to him the fruit of His Passion, which is so wonderful that it flows all around him, and by this stream of grace he is drawn with power and energy to God.

Just as a mighty river with overpowering force carries everything along with it, so is it with the man who earnestly attends to the Passion. Into him flows the stream of divine graces which sweeps him forcibly away from himself towards that prime source from which he has issued.

Those, however, who do not practise such an inner contemplation of the Passion of our Lord, who only perform certain good works, certainly may approach God. But often they stand still or even go backwards. The force that is granted to men in the contemplation of the Passion is not a human but a divine force, and it is so great that they can hardly resist it. Hence, they always flow forward and, even if they lived till the Judgement Day, they would always hurry on, never ceasing, for it is not they who urge themselves on but God.

As God the Father begets His Son in Himself and in all things, so in this very birth He draws man to Himself through the Passion of His Son and all virtues. Since God's begettings are eternal, the initiation of man into the bodily and spiritual sufferings of His Son is an eternal process, and nothing can obstruct man in this work. Just as little as God can be obstructed in the birth of His Word, so little will He permit to be disturbed the man who gives himself with complete love to the Passion.

They who contemplate the Passion of our Lord most intensely are in a sense a second Christ. For love unites, and hence they cannot get lost as long as they cling to Christ. As God the Father did not let His Son go astray, so does He not let these men go astray. Instead He wills that they should always move onward towards their aim.

He, then, who wants to attain to this aim, which is Christ Himself, should whole-heartedly sink himself in the Passion and consider it with perseverance. In this contemplation he receives so great a power that in one hour it draws him further than he would have attained to for a very long time by any natural means. And he who fails to do this is idle, and even if he succeeds in attaining God, it is only by the utmost effort and by tremendous difficulty.

Christ says: "I am the gate through which a man must go to God. He who enters elsewhere is a thief and a murderer. The thief comes to steal and the murderer to kill."[7] As the thief takes that which does not belong to him, so do those who wish to gain heaven without the Passion. They wish to take what is another's. The kingdom of heaven is ours through the Passion of our Lord, and he who takes it in any other way takes it by an injust means and is a thief. He is also a murderer who wishes to enter otherwise than through the Passion of our Lord. Christ has been killed and murdered by us and through His death we have been saved from eternal death and given a new life. He who kills himself—that is, inflicts penance on his body—without considering the Passion, kills himself unrightly, and by it can hardly come into the kingdom of heaven. That is why he is called a murderer.

One can only get there through an inner death. He who wants to mortify his body properly and strip it of lusts, let him sink into the Passion in which all lusts disappear, for otherwise no man can properly die to himself. If a man is thus dead to all bodily lusts, a divine ecstasy arises in him surpassing all bodily lusts, and this joy drives man on towards his aim—Christ.

Some people greatly exert themselves in the knowledge of truth. But he who wants to acquire genuine truth, let him with all possible diligence attend to the Passion of Christ in which the fountain of all truth issues forth. Christ is the truth and he who wants the truth let him seek it in Him. He will certainly find it there, but elsewhere with great difficulty.

To be sure, he may discover the truth of the world in his natural knowledge, but even if he has this it will not necessarily help him to real happiness. If a man wants the truth which alone is blessed, he should seek it in the Passion. For there is the real fountain of divine truth and he who drinks from it drinks a living water. To this fountain Christ calls us with a loud voice, saying: "If any may thirst, let him come to Me and drink. He who drinks of it, out of his body shall flow streams of living water flowing into everlasting life."[8]

He, then, who desires to drink the real truth let him hold his mouth to the sacred wounds of our Lord, from which the truth flows. St. John rested on the breast of our Lord, and took in the wisdom and truth of God which was hidden from others. Those who earnestly sink themselves in the Passion of our Lord do the same. They sleep on His breast and take from it all wisdom and truth and the friendship of God that was hidden from others. Yes, a truth, an unutterable truth, as St. Paul says: ". . . which it is not granted to man to utter."[9]

When men receive such a truth they too ought not to speak of it, for the fountain of grace and truth flows through them and the stream is so great that they overflow with it. No man can know this—only God, for that which God performs in them is above all human comprehension. No one is required to direct or guide these men; they are directed and guided by God towards perfection. They arrive at the true and final aim—God. They travel by the right road, and they are there at home in their due dwelling-place—the kingdom of heaven, of which St. Paul says: "Our conversation is in heaven."[10]

Now what does St. Paul mean by this? Well, there are two aspects to heaven—the heaven that is above us, and the other heaven which is spiritual, or rather, which is the soul in which God lives. And where God lives, there is heaven. Hence, Christ says: ". . . The kingdom of God is within you."[11] If, then, the being and essence of our soul is heaven and God lives there, why do we not have this heaven here and now, and why do we not know God?

Two things obstruct us. One is faulty accidents. For instance, when a person is too greatly weighed down with these, they prevent him from reaching the essence of his soul. Hence he does not have heaven and cannot know God. The essence of the soul is simple, but if the soul is dissipated in manifold things, she cannot utilize her essence. St. Paul was freed of all faulty accidents, and so he entered into the essence of his soul, realized its nobility and immediately knew God. He could well say: "Our conversation is in heaven."

But why did he not possess the kingdom of heaven which he later had? This has to do with the second hindrance, which is the coarseness of the body, and is why he said: "I have a desire to be dissolved and to be with Christ,"[12] and also: "Unhappy man that I am, who shall deliver me from this body of this death?"[13] For this reason he could not have the kingdom of heaven which he now has. However, his dwelling-place was in heaven—the essence of his soul—and in it he knew God. Therefore he said: "I judged not myself to know anything among you but Jesus Christ and Him crucified."[14]

A man must be free, then, from all faulty accidents if his dwelling-place is to be in heaven. And it cannot be that he should be free from them except in the Passion. He should turn to it with diligence and then all faulty accidents will fall from him, and he will then enter into heaven, into the essence of his soul and see God within. There no defect can fasten hold on him, since it melts away in the wounds of our Lord. Just as snow when held before a fire melts and becomes water, so is it with sins which are held in the wounds of our Lord. They all melt away and disappear and man enters into the true centre of his soul where he realizes all truth without any blemish or untruth.

Pagans have also sought the naked and simple essence of the soul, but they could never completely arrive at it without Christ. Hence they could not fully know God, nor be truly happy, though they certainly wished to be happy. It is still the same with all men who seek the naked essence of the soul without the Passion. They never arrive at a complete comprehension of the truth which is God and by which they can be blessed and made happy. For our salvation and happiness rest in Christ in His Passion, and he who desires blessedness should enter into this Passion. As Christ says: " It was necessary for Christ to suffer to come into the kingdom of heaven."[15] We, too, must suffer with the Passion in the kingdom of the soul where we may see God immediately. In this way we arrive at our true aim through the Passion of our Lord.

5

THE CONTEMPLATION OF GOD IN HIS GODHEAD

Now the third object that a man should have in his inner work, in order to arrive at his aim, is the contemplation of God in His pure Godhead. If one has seen inwardly what he really is and puts aside all faulty accidents, and if the contemplation of the Passion of our Lord has directed him to virtue, he may then behold God in His true essence, simplicity and nature. Through this vision he goes into God, unites himself with Him, and God leads man with Himself into Himself so that he has a never-ceasing entrance into God. He is so completely encircled by God that he loses himself and knows nothing more save God alone. So he sinks and is drowned in the fathomless ocean of the Godhead.

He lives in God as the fish in the sea, and as the sea encircles the fish so is the soul encircled by God and is hastened towards her end where she shall live for ever. She aims at it and hits it, as it is written in the Canticles, when the Lord, speaking to His bride, says: "My friend, thou hast wounded Me with thine eyes."[16] The eye is the love of man penetrating into God, and with this love the soul compels God, so that He must do what she desires. And this is called "wounding" because she has potency over God and has mastered Him. She stretches her bow and shoots God in the heart and the bow that she stretches is her very own heart. She stretches this and shoots with a burning desire at God and hits the true mark. In this way she attains to the highest degree of perfection.

6

THE PRACTICE OF VIRTUE

The other action by which man draws closer to his aim, which is God, is outward. It consists of all the virtues which pertain to a perfect life. One must necessarily have these if he really wishes to arrive at the right aim. Because these virtues have been previously mentioned we shall pass over them here and only say that the man who really desires to be one spirit with God should be directed to this by the life, Passion and works of our Lord Jesus Christ. When a completely poor spirit is led through all this, he clings to God and becomes one spirit with God.

K

CHAPTER II

GOD'S INTIMATE SPEECH

✳✳✳✳✳✳✳✳✳✳✳✳✳✳✳✳✳✳✳✳✳✳✳✳✳

THE spirit of God speaks intimately in man without images and forms, or rather above images and forms. And this speech is Life, Light and Truth.

1

THE SPEECH OF LIFE

The speech of life is nothing more than a godlike power whereby man can accomplish all things. As St. Paul says: " I can do all things in Him that strengtheneth me."[1] But this force was simply the abandoning of all things that were contrary to God, and an acquiring of all virtues that led to God. If a man enters into this power, putting aside all that is not godlike, and seizing all the virtues that lead to God, it is by this living force which God pours into him that he overcomes all deadly things and comes to a real life.

God lives in this life; God is this life, and the soul lives in the life that is God. No longer is her life earthly but godlike. God plants the soul in His life, and all that is planted elsewhere fades away. That which the creature sows is perishable and because it rots and decays, it must be removed. Death and life cannot subsist together. That which God sows is life and when the soul turns to this life she lives.

One cannot very well say what life is in itself. Man certainly experiences something in himself, but he cannot describe it. It is beyond words and he cannot explain it in images and forms. And because he cannot speak of it he is silent and passive. Yet this is perhaps the best thing a man can do—be silent and endure that silence.

Silence and long-suffering are the most perfect acts that a man may have. For it is by this silence and patience that he lives, and, if he wants to speak, or if he wants to let others speak through him, it makes him mortal. If he really wants to live, he should always remain silent and suffer God alone to speak, for what God utters is life.

Christ says: "My sheep hear My voice, and I give them everlasting life."[2] The sheep of our Lord are men in which all creaturely things keep silence and who are in a pure passive state of receiving God. These hear the voice of God—the eternal Word which God the Father utters in the soul. The hearing of it grants eternal life. Our Lord says: "They follow after Me."[3] And this "following" is nothing else than that they live in the very life in which God Himself lives.

If, then, the greatest happiness of man consists in his keeping silence and listening only to the eternal Word, some will ask: Why should we then listen to preaching? Well, preaching is simply a leading to God, a capacity for realizing the eternal Word. If a man is remote from God, he can hardly hear the eternal Word, for, when one is far away from another, he cannot understand what the other says to him in secret. Hence much of this has to be said to man in images and forms so that he may arrive at a perception of it and recognize God's secret Word.

Through the outer word that men hear they come to the inner word which God utters in the centre of the soul. Christ says: "I have other sheep, these also must I lead up, that there may be one Shepherd and one fold."[4] Hence preaching is necessary to inform those who have not yet entered the fold what to do in order that they may hear the voice of the Shepherd. But the fold is simply the centre of the soul in which the eternal Father utters His Word. And if a person reaches the point where he recognizes the eternal Word in himself, he need not attend to anything else, but place himself in complete silence. This is his best condition, as St. Augustine said: "The man who hath learnt of our Lord Jesus Christ to be meek and humble of heart, for him it is better that he pray and think of God than that he read or listen to preaching."[5]

They, however, who have not attained to this should hear preaching and learn and follow what they hear or read. In this way they come to genuine truth, they come into life, which is God. Even if a man is so advanced that he hears the Word in himself, he is, nevertheless, not always prepared for it, since bodily nature cannot always endure it, and since a man must sometimes turn to his senses and be active. He should indeed direct this work of the senses to the best end. If preaching is useful to him, he can perform it. He should practise in himself that which he perceives to be the best.

Now this in no way hinders him from hearing the eternal Word, rather it furthers him towards what is best. If he has practised it, if he has strengthened the outer man and directed it according to the inner man, he should, nevertheless, continue to turn it upon himself, perceive and listen to the eternal Word, for by this hearing he may attain to eternal life.

All that hinders man in this listening should be cast aside with great determination. For then he will have the power of denying himself all that is not God and of continually hearing within himself the eternal Word which issues from the living ground in which God dwells. He drives these obstacles away as Jesus in the Temple drove out buyers and sellers and said: "My house shall be called a house of prayer, but you have made it a den of thieves."[6]

A pure heart is a temple of God in which God the Father is worshipped. The merchants whom Christ drove out are the worldly gadgetry that rusts in the heart and ruins it. Should the heart now retain these useless thoughts and linger over them, it is no longer a house of prayer but a den of thieves, for these evil thoughts drive God out of His dwelling-place and kill Him. And this happens when the heart is so turned away from God that he cannot enter it. This indeed thwarts God and hinders Him from entering His own house, and that is why he calls it a den of thieves.

The person who resists all thought that separates him from God, who makes room for God alone to live in him, receives this living, godlike power from the Father who pours it into him. And this inpouring is His *inspeaking* of a life full of joy and rapture. He who does not have this life, who does not have God Himself in a pure heart, is also wanting in joy. He is, in other words, more dead than alive, always going counter to the very nature of man. Sin kills nature, but nature abhors death, and because sin is contrary to nature, sinners can never experience real joy. Just as little as the dead can rejoice can sinners rejoice, for the ground from which true joy springs is dead.

But in those who live in true purity there is a fountain of joy and ecstasy. It sanctions no sadness, since the eternal Word, in which all the angels and saints enjoy ecstasy, speaks in them as in the saints in heaven. That their joy is not as perfect as those in heaven is only because they still have their body with them. Were they free from their body they would have the same ecstasy as those in heaven. Nevertheless, their joy is now unutterably great, and the more they are empty of earthly things, the greater their joy.

If, then, earthly things even obstruct devout men from their joys, how can they who are immersed in them possibly experience joy? They imagine they are in a good state, but this condition is quite contrary to the real one, for just as it is never quite well with a soul as long as it is in the body, so also there is woe to those who are greatly weighed down with earthly things. They, however, who most put aside earthly things have the real joy which issues forth from a living, pure ground, and the Holy Spirit is the source from which this joy flows. Hence, St. Paul says: "The fruit of the Holy Spirit is peace, joy and justice."[7]

The inspeaking of the Holy Spirit is life, from which all joy springs. He who most listens to this voice, has life to the fullest extent and where this is there is also the greatest degree of joy. If, then, spiritual poverty is a pure instrument of God, with which God can work without obstruction, and where He can place His eternal Word which gives life to all creatures, then a poor spirit is full of this life, since he has the fullness of the eternal Word in himself, from which all joy springs.

2

HOW THE SOUL SHOULD LISTEN

One might, of course, say that if a person is saved by hearing the Word of God, he is also saved if he hears the preacher who presents it to him, since Christ also says: "Blessed are they who hear the word of God and keep it."[8] But I believe that the speaking and hearing of the Word of God is two-fold. It is internally saving, and it also leads one to and prepares one for blessedness.

There is a speaking of God in the core of the soul where no creature can enter or speak, for only God lives there and only He speaks. God speaks there when the soul puts aside all that is created, when she silences her powers and gains a vision into the foundation of her pure essence.

In this pure and silent soul God the Father speaks and she hears His voice. And this hearing is simply an inner feeling of God in the centre of the soul, a feeling which overflows into all her powers and with such a joy that she would gladly forgo her action and allow God alone to act, only attending to His leadings. The more she withholds from action, the more God acts in her.

And he who has felt this action in himself is blessed, for God will not perform His work in any creature except in the soul in which He has chosen to remain for ever. No creature which cuts itself off from God merits it, hence God does not work in it. Had Lucifer felt this in himself he would never have fallen, for this action is so powerful that it draws the soul out of herself to God. God gathers and unites the soul to Himself so that she will and must live with Him for ever. This was missing in Lucifer and that is why he fell. The action is God's speaking. His action is His word, the Son of the Godhead, and this action takes place in the centre of the soul.

God's action is also in the powers or faculties of the soul. The word is spoken by the preacher and man hears it with his bodily ears. But this will not bless him unless he follows it in his life. This speaking occurs in images and forms, but that which comes through media does not bless the soul. It can only direct it to salvation and teach it how to put aside the media so as to arrive at the pure essence where the soul beholds God without any intermediary.

If the soul can distinguish by reason so that she is free from all faulty accident, then she should pass beyond all external words that are spoken through man. She should direct herself to the inmost centre of her being and there attend only to the eternal Word which God the Father utters. She should listen to no other speech even if it came from the angels.

Indeed, the word of the preacher is not his own but God's. Nevertheless, it is a means, and the mediate does not penetrate like the immediate Word of God. Should the soul empty herself of all intermediate things, strip herself of all images, she should also not linger with the media itself but recognize God in His pure being as her sole objective, and into this she should essentially enter. As long as one has the external and material about him and has not arrived at his inmost centre, so long must he listen to the external word. In this way he is taught how he should deny himself in order to arrive at truth, and thus is God's external word useful.

3

THE SPEECH OF LIGHT

The second thing that the spirit of God utters in the soul is light. Light is simply a radiance of the soul with which God clothes her, adorns her and makes her attractive to Him. In the Book of Canticles He says to His bride: "Very fair art thou, My friend, and no stain is in thee; come from Lebanon come, thou shalt be crowned."[9] This crown is the clear light with which God surrounds and glorifies the soul.

Christ also says: "Father, glorify Thy Son, that Thy Son may also glorify Thee;"[10] and from heaven there came a voice saying: "I have glorified Him, and will glorify Him again."[11] If the soul penetrates so far that she brings forth the eternal Word in her and brings herself forth in God, then she is a child of God. Not a natural child, like the Word in the God-head, but a child of grace. Then she can say: "Father, glorify Thy child with Thy clearness and with the same brightness will I glorify Thee; this is the unutterable praise that pours forth from me to Thee." Then a new voice, the eternal Word, will speak in her: "I have glorified thee, and will still more glorify thee."[12] This glorifying is the being surrounded by God. He surrounds the soul with the same clarity that He has and that He Himself is, and it is this which glorifies the soul.

In this clarity the soul grows to perfection. As long as she lives in the body she will continually increase in this godlike clarity, and she will grow in godlike clarity according to the degree of her purity. We may take a parallel from the sun. The purer the air, the brighter the sun shines. And the purer the soul, the more the divine sun shines in her and purifies her. If she is pure of faulty accidents, then the divine sun pierces directly into her. But if she is weighed down with venial sins, it shines in her only like a flame, indirectly and not so brilliantly. If, however, the soul is burdened with mortal sins, the light of the divine sun cannot pierce her.

St. John says: "The darkness did not comprehend the light."[13] The light of the sun is simply an encompassing of light, and wherever the light pierces there it enlightens, and that which is a recipient of light receives it. Air is clear, glass is pure, a flame is light, and so they are recipients of light and they also receive it. But that which is rough, impure and dense cannot receive it, such as earth, stone and wood. They are coarse, thick and impure, and hence the light of the sun cannot pierce them.

So it is with the soul. She is coarse and dense when she is burdened with earthly things. She is impure when she clings to sensual pleasures, darkened when she preoccupies herself with external or internal complexities. Since she is not receptive of light, the divine sun cannot pierce through her or enlighten her. That which is to receive light must be formed accordingly. Light is spiritual, empty of everything earthly. And if the soul desires to be enlightened by this divine light she could become a pure spirit, empty of everything earthly, and in this likeness she then receives light.

When the soul is a pure spirit and empty of everything earthly, she then becomes a light herself, since what is pure is also a light. But what further light is she to receive? If the soul is a pure spirit, empty of earthly things, it is a light, but one of her real nature. God has put a pure light in the soul, yet this light is the soul herself so long as she stands in the highest nobility of her nature, so long as she comprehends the distinction of all created things. And the light which she continues to receive is a supernatural light which God draws out of Himself and pours into the soul that is capable of receiving it.

To the degree that the natural light is pure, the soul receives the supernatural light which is a light of glory. Take a piece of glass. The purer it is, the more it is enlightened by the sun. Likewise with the soul—the purer it is, the more it is enlightened by the divine light. But if it is darkened and distant from God, she can hardly receive the light. The sun cannot penetrate a prison that is completely walled in. And the soul that is burdened with sins is like a dark prison in which the divine sun cannot shine.

The soul must also be close to the light if she is to receive it. A piece of glass may be quite pure, but if it is not brought to the sun, it cannot be enlightened. The soul should lift herself to the divine splendour if she is to receive the clarity of the light. And this closeness is nothing but an intense longing for God with perfect love in the light of faith. This makes the soul receptive to the divine light. If she is wanting in purity so that she cannot receive the divine light, yet has perfect faith and love for God, then she will become pure and receive the light.

On the other hand, if a man is quite free of all sins, yet lacks faith and love for God, he cannot receive the divine light. Men such as these are also found among the pagans who kept themselves pure and virtuous, yet were without the divine light. The fault was simply that they lacked faith and love, though they certainly had more natural light than other men.

Indeed, there are many who keep themselves pure and free of mortal sins, but who are unable to guard themselves against venial sins, and so the divine light fails them. The reason for this is simply that they do not approach it in the light of faith. The faith is Christ. But they only follow Him outwardly and, since they do not follow Him inwardly, they lack the divine light.

The light of God shines in the heart and he who wants this light should turn himself within, and by this turning he will perceive the light in himself. But he who only follows Christ externally fails to receive the real light, for Christ says: "Unless your justice abound more than that of the Scribes and Pharisees you shall not enter into the kingdom of heaven."[14]

The Pharisees are those who appear outwardly as very holy men in good works, but who inwardly despise the truth and do not follow it in whole-hearted righteousness. These can hardly enter into God's kingdom which is in the ground of the soul. He who wants to attain to it must practise all good works inwardly as well as outwardly. Such a man far surpasses the Pharisee in righteousness and comes to God's kingdom in the centre of the soul.

To be sure, the Pharisees of the old covenant conformed to the laws outwardly, but inwardly they were altogether sham. This certainly did not make them righteous. They appeared righteous, but they were not. If we would gain heaven we must go beyond this apparent righteousness. The righteousness we show externally must be whole-heartedly governed by

the internal.   It is this that enables us to receive the living
light, and it is why St. Paul says: "Appear what ye are, and
be what ye appear."[15]

He who desires to have the divine light in himself must
follow Christ outwardly and inwardly.   Outwardly by a pure
life and all the good works that relate to it; inwardly by a perfect
faith, by the consideration of Christ's good works and His
Passion.   A perfect love is then kindled in him, a love that
prepares him to receive the divine light by which he surpasses
all Pharisees in righteousness.

One should also surpass the Scribes in righteousness.   The
Scribes in the old covenant were those who instructed the people,
but what they taught others they failed to practise themselves.
Such men show themselves as inwardly righteous.   But this
inwardness is only natural, not godlike.   The natural light of
their reason assists them; they are able to distinguish all things,
and this makes them eloquent and they consider themselves
to be spiritual men.   They are hard to detect and only the
perfect man who is enlightened with the divine light can always
recognize them.

He, then, who wants to gain the divine light should surpass
them in righteousness, for their righteousness consists only in
lifeless words.   If they turn within they only meet natural
images since there is so much natural truth in them that they
fail to recognize the supernatural light.   Their outward emptiness and their inward attention make them reasonable in a
natural way, but what a man speaks should have life.

A man should weigh his faults, put them aside and diligently
contemplate the Passion of our Lord.   And if one now wants
to distinguish how he is to forgo his faults and increase in
virtues, he should not tarry over these distinctions.   Rather he
should go beyond the distinction of created images and penetrate the uncreated best—God.   In this way he may arrive at
the true divine light.

4

THE DIFFERENCE BETWEEN NATURAL AND DIVINE LIGHT

How can one know the distinction of the natural and the divine light? Well, consider the moon and the sun. The moon receives its light from the sun—in herself she is damp, and, as a teacher says, the moon germinates like water, and this is because of its dampness. And that which is damp is naturally cold; even when the sun shines on her, it still remains cold. This is why the light of the moon gives no warmth and why it renders many objects doubtful when seen in its light, and why it is deceptive.

The natural light of reason is like this in man. As the moon receives her light from the sun so also is the natural light cold. As the light of the moon fails to produce fruit, so also is the natural light in itself unfruitful, since it produces few fruits useful for eternal life. If the natural light could produce fruits which would aid man towards heaven, then many pagans who perhaps are in hell would be in heaven. For man cannot attain to heaven by his mere nature—grace must co-operate with it. Also that which is seen by natural light always remains doubtful. It is only a conjecture, an imperfect knowledge. The natural light remains dim because it consists only in images and forms and one cannot see real truth in this way.

This is why natural men believe a thing is absolutely so and not possibly otherwise. The natural light is very much like the moon-light and the light of the sun is like the divine light. For the light of the divine sun shines upon the soul immediately. It gives warmth to the soul and it grows in divine love, and, because she receives the divine light, she also receives the warmth of the light, and all inequality, unlikeness and every doubt of truth disappear. The sun produces fruit, it is the mother of all earthly life and all creatures experience its influence. If it were to vanish and if its light were withdrawn from the earth, all would die. The sun is the begetter and the sustainer of all creatures, and their generation is wonderful.

No one can perfectly comprehend this, no wise man has ever been wise enough to know all that the sun brings forth—the fish in the water, the beast on the earth, the bird in the air, the phœnix in the fire, and countless other unknown beings that are known to God alone.

Now it is the same with the divine sun. It is fructifying and the Father of all spiritual creatures. God has created the soul and the angels without mediary, but He has created the bodily creature through the mediation of the sun. Since the soul and the angels have been created immediately by God they have also received the immediate influence of the divine sun, the divine light. If the divine sun were to take away its light from the soul, she would die, not as earthly things die. No, the soul dies when she lacks the divine inflowing, since of herself she does not possess the life that blesses. This she must receive from God.

But it will be said that there are many good people who do not have a great inflowing from God, yet their souls are not dead. There are three kinds of people. Some live in mortal sins and these altogether lack God's inflowing. These are spiritually dead. But that they are still brought back to life is a greater miracle than the resurrection of the bodily dead, since the soul is far nobler than the body, it is that much greater that she live again. Concerning this, a teacher says: "It is a greater work to convert a sinner from his sins than to create heaven and earth."[16]

There are others who abstain from great mortal sins but who by no means abstain from venial sins, and these are neither dead nor alive. They do not completely lack the divine co-operation, but it is so weak that the external powers feel nothing. They think that they are lacking a divine inflowing; yet they are good men since they practise many good works.

Then there are the kind of people who guard themselves against all sins, venial as well as mortal, but this cannot happen without divine grace. They truly live. They do not lack the divine inflowing, which is so powerful that it flows over from the soul to man's outer faculties so that by it they realize the splendour of the divine clarity. By the same outflowing of God they return to God and with the same clarity which is God Himself. And through this clarity they are preserved from mortality. Just as the sun produces fruit, generating all things among creatures, so the divine sun brings forth all truth in the soul. But its generation is so wonderful that no one save God perfectly knows it.

No one has ever been so naturally wise that he could understand even the slightest action that God immediately performs in a pure soul. And this is why one should never judge a holy man. A genuine holy man is hidden from all natural men. Such a man, however, should not let his goodness be known, especially to those who are prepared with natural words but no life. Because of their natural notions they fail to understand what God performs by grace in a pure heart. That is why they too frequently consider good to be evil and evil good.

The generating of the divine sun is wonderful. As the natural sun generates the fish in the water, the divine sun causes all the works of the senses to be fruitful, for by the water is to be understood the senses. As the water is unstable and fluctuating, so also are the senses. If, in their movements, the senses turn to virtues and perform them, they become fruitful. And this is caused by the divine sun which has fertilized them.

The sun generates the beasts of the earth and makes the earth fruitful. In other words, when the body performs good works its action brings forth fruit for eternal life. As Christ says: " He that shall drink of the water that I will give him, shall not thirst for ever. But the water that I will give him shall become in him a fountain of water springing up into life everlasting."[17] The living water is the divine light which pierces the soul and causes her to flow over into all virtues so that she may attain to eternal life.

The sun also generates the bird, and by the bird is understood the thought of man. Just as the bird flies hither and thither, so man's thoughts wander and are restless. But these are also made fruitful by the divine sun. Should they turn from earthly things to contemplate the Passion of our Lord, and thereby enter into

the Godhead, they will bring forth countless fruits. And this
is caused by the divine light which enlightens the thoughts and
directs them to God.

5

THE SPEECH OF TRUTH

By the air is understood the reason of man. Just as the sun
generates various things in the air, such as foliage and grass,
so also does the divine sun generate various wonderful truths
in the reason. The reason is adorned with this truth and
experiences such an unutterable joy that no mind can conceive
nor mouth express it. St. Paul found himself in this ecstasy
when he said: "I know a man in Christ . . . that he . . .
heard secret things which it is not granted to man to utter."[18]

He who talks about what he perceives in himself proves that
he has not yet discovered in himself the real divine truth. And
it frequently happens that they who talk the most have the
least pure truth. For divine truth does not consist in talk but
in silence, in remaining within the heart by long suffering.

St. Paul says that we should be silent on these things. All
that can be said consists only in images and these images are
quite apart from them. Human reason perceives truth, but it
can never fully embrace or hold it, since truth always outruns
reason. By this running ahead it entices reason after it and,
should reason direct its course to the peak of perfection, then
it seizes the truth and this seizing is eternal life. Only then
does it find rest and satisfaction.

But man will not find this on earth, because as long as man
lives in time he must move on and develop. Hence he cannot
find perfect rest. But if the soul parts from the body and enters
into eternal life, then her object becomes the pure truth and
in it she finds rest and satisfaction. In this way the reason is
radiated by the divine light.

The sun also generates the phœnix in the fire,[19] and grants
it life without means of other creatures. Because it is not

born like other creatures through the influence of creatures, it is the noblest creature that is born under the sun. In the same way the divine light generates the will and causes it to fructify many virtues. By the phœnix is understood the will, for, as the phœnix is the noblest creature, so the will is the highest power of the soul. And just as the phœnix revivifies itself in the fire, so also does the will in the divine fire.

The phœnix holds the first place among living creatures; the will holds the first place among the faculties. Since it has the first and noblest place, it also has the best fruit. And just as the phœnix is born by the sun without a mediary, so also the will is lifted above all things and in this way bears its fruit. When it is empty of all things that are not God, the divine light shines gloriously and makes it fruitful. And when it is wholly separated from all things and united with God, it produces with God that which He produces. Now the fruit that the divine light produces in the will is essential, for God's being is granted to all creatures, only each receives it according to its receptive capacity.

A perfect will desires a perfect good, since the good is the object of the will. And it desires this same perfect good for all creatures that are receptive of the good, such as souls and angels. Only souls and angels are receptive to an essential good; all other creatures only to an accidental good. The essential good, which alone is God, is distributed to all other rational creatures by a perfect will. Hence a perfect will works essentially in all creatures. Its fruit and action are essential. And this essential fruit is brought forth by the divine sun in a perfect will. The will, however, that is good, though not perfect, only issues forth accidental fruit. Nothing can operate beyond its own powers. For this reason, then, the will cannot perform a perfect work if it is not itself perfect. And for this reason also its fruit is neither perfect nor essential, but only accidental.

CHAPTER III

THE PERFECT WILL

****

THE perfect will is an abandonment of all that is not God. If a man has not done this in action, he must do it in the will if he wants to be perfect. What he lacks in actions he must put aside and cultivate a genuine detachment. If he does this and has fully performed accidental virtues, he gains the essence of virtue. Into this the will penetrates and thus performs an essential work, for, where two things are united, they have but one action.

1

THE ESSENTIAL WORK

If the will has gone completely into the essence of the soul it also has but one action with this essence. Each thing operates according to its quality and hence this essence operates essentially and the will along with it. This action, however, is not brought about by the movement of the faculties. Rather it is motionless, a standing still. It is also godlike, for God works in this manner and in the same way an essential work is brought forth.

But how can the will perform an essential work when it is a movable force and what is movable cannot perform anything essential? I reply that the will has two trends. One is towards time and the creature, the other towards God. When the will turns to time and the creature and to the body, it is movable and is unable to foster an essential act. Nothing can operate beyond its power—since time and the creature are unstable, the action of the will is movable if it is united to them; an essential act is immovable and he who wants to perform an essential act must have his will separate itself from time and the creature.

The other trend which the will has is towards God. When it turns towards God it becomes immovable with God, for movement is only in time and in those who are burdened with accidents. If the will is lifted above time into eternity, if it is freed from all accidents, if it penetrates into the essential good, which is God Himself, then behold all that God does the will also does with God. Because God's works are essential, the works of the will are essential and immovable. When an imperfect thing is united with one that is perfect, it will not act according to its imperfection but according to that with which it is united—such also is the proper order which is held in the works of the will.

In itself the will of man is imperfect and so of itself it has an imperfect work. But if it elevates itself above itself towards God, then it also has a perfect work with God. For that which is one has also one operation. If, then, the will is united with God, it has one operation with God and the divine light produces an essential fruit in the will.

And what is an essential act? An essential act is when the essence of the soul is one and simple, when it is placed in utter silence. Through simplicity it has communion with all things, since what is most simple is also most universal; it imparts itself to all things while remaining undivided and unmoved in itself.

To communicate and share with all things is called an essential act and in this action one work is all works, and all works are one work. Just as God beholds all things with one glance and acts without any movement on His part, so also does an essential will. It beholds all things in one glance and in this one glance it performs all acts and all acts are only one glance. Now the divine light performs this in the will, for a perfect will is so dear to God that He grants it all gifts and makes it fruitful in all things.

If God did not give all things to a perfect will so that some things of His own might remain with Him, God would not have fully rewarded the will and it would not experience satisfaction. God must give to the perfect will all, that is, Himself. As St. Augustine says: "If God gave me all things without Himself, it would not satisfy me, but if I have God I have all things and with that I am satisfied."[1]

Let him who desires to work in pure tranquillity be certain that he has a perfect will in which God generates all virtue and all truth, and in this way he will grasp the essence of perfection. As Solomon said: "I have sought rest in all things."[2] Man finds rest in all things provided he practises virtue in such a way that he seizes the essence of virtue, for then he rests and becomes silent, leaving God alone to do the work. And without any effort on his part all truth will be poured into him. Virtue and truth flow into a pure being so that he lacks nothing, for there is no defect where there is a pure being.

A man, then, has nothing more to do than to put himself aside, and when he has done this and kept himself purely passive, he will have all virtues and truth in this purity. He need not seek virtue or truth here or there, since he has them within him. All save the perfect, pure and poor spirit are lacking in virtue and truth. He alone has them and the divine will has worked this in his perfect will, and this essential working endures for ever. And because he is in time he has an increase in essential truth—he penetrates continually into the essential good which is God. Whether he sleeps or wakes, eats or drinks, he is always moving on. The perfect will cannot stand still; it is always hurrying towards God. This is the supernatural power by which the will is led, and as God, who leads the will, is eternal, so also is the direction of the will eternal.

One may object to this, for just above it was said that the will was immovable, and now I speak of a direction of the will. Is not this direction a movement? I said above that if the will turns away from all things and unites itself with God, it becomes immovable. And this is true. Now this immovability is to be understood as meaning that it no longer moves according to time and the creature, since it is elevated above them. Nor is it moved by time or the creature. It no longer turns to this or that but it wills only and always *one*—and that is God. It clings to Him without ceasing, without any going back. That is why it is called immovable; it does not suffer itself to be moved away from God.

When I speak of the will as continually hurrying on, this means a never ceasing advance into God and His eternal immobility. And by this immobility of the will is meant its stability in God. Creaturely movement is to this and to that, but the perfect will is different. It leans continually towards God, penetrates into God, and this penetration is its course. This course has nothing in common with creatures, and therefore it should not be considered as a movement. It should be considered as being immovable in a godlike way, for in this sense the will never moves outside God, rather it dwells continually in God, and its course is its indwelling. The more it hurries the more certain and stable is its indwelling; the faster its course is in God, the more thorough is its silence and immobility.

Now how can a man attain to this in time? How can his will become immovable in time—for he is hardly so perfect that he does not notice how his will leans now to this and now to that? And since a man is born in time, does he not have a movement with time?

My answer is that man is made of time and eternity; hence he must have an influx from both. The body is receptive to the temporal influx, and this he must endure because he lives in time. Out of bodily necessity the will leans to the body so that it may try to fulfil the need. In this way the will is movable and it leans now to this and now to that so that the body may obtain its needs. If a man directs bodily things with discretion and gives the body the needs that pertain to it and which it utilizes in God's service and in accordance with the teachings of our Lord Jesus Christ, he is against neither truth nor perfection. Nor is this really a movement. It is only a movement of the will when it turns from good to bad, but here that is not the case. The will merely grants to the body what it needs, sincerely and truthfully, and what a man does not need the will does not grant.

If a perfect will always lives in truth and perfection, if it refuses to allow itself to be led astray, it is rightly called immovable. Whatever movement may occur in a perfect man is more a movement of the senses than the will. When a perfect will *wills* only God, it suffers the senses to seek what is otherwise only its bodily needs; and this is not done for the comfort or pleasure of the body but for God's glory. When the body takes its need, the will takes the power which the body has received from the food and transfers it to God so that it disappears in Him. Thus is the will immovable. And movement that takes place in it is for the sake of virtue, for it is not moved by any evil. So it always remains there in truth, never allowing itself to be moved. And this immobility is caused by the divine light which encompasses the will and which contains no untruth.

Some say that men who are poor in spirit rely too much on their own will and like to follow it, and that this is a fault. But a truly poor spirit is wholly submissive. He has renounced his own will. He never exercises his own will. No, instead he always fulfils the will of God to whom he has resigned himself.

2

THE RESIGNED WILL

What is one's own will? And what is a resigned will? One's own will is nothing else than a self-possession of either bodily things or spiritual things. A person who has not detached himself from temporal things, inwardly as well as outwardly, still has possession of his will. For one of the characteristics of the will is that it leans towards time and the creature, and so he who is burdened with creatures continues to keep his own will.

He who wants to be free of ownership must part from creatures inwardly and outwardly in so far as discretion permits. It may be said, of course, that there are many good people who preserve many excessive possessions and yet internally retain no sense of property, since they do all for the glory of God and would even abandon all things if they knew it was God's will. Yes, but when a man is inwardly empty of all property and selfhood he is also detached outwardly, for one is outwardly the same as one is in his heart, whether it is good or evil. If one is really empty inwardly, this would show itself outwardly. Indeed, one might be quite empty within, but if one knew that certain external things separated one from God, one would forgo them and turn to a life of detachment. No, to say that such are perfectly empty within is not true. They may, no doubt, say that they would forgo all and assume detachment, if only they knew that it was God's will to do so. But it is God's holiest will, and it is His will which makes us truly perfect, as St. Paul says: "This is the will of God, your sanctification."[3]

The highest perfection rests in spiritual poverty and for this reason it is also the will of God that we should become spiritually poor, for Christ Himself says: "If thou wilt be perfect, sell whatsoever thou hast and give to the poor . . . And come and follow Me."[4] Were it not the will of God, He would not have said it. Indeed, he who desires to disown his self-will should also empty himself of all excess property.

To retain personal ownership in spiritual things is also an aspect of self-will. For instance, a man adopts an external work that obstructs him in his perfection, yet he will not abandon it but perform it according to his own opinion thinking it to be good though it is obvious to others that it is not good. Gladly would he advise others to abandon such a work for something better, but he himself will not follow suit. This is simply from man's self-will and it obstructs his perfection.

Furthermore, if one has a false view yet regards it as true and will not let himself give it up, it is again a sign of self-will. Even if his opinion is half right and another understands it better, he will refuse to listen to the better opinion but insist on having preference given to his own more ignorant view. And should his opinion really be a true opinion so that an opposing view cannot be entertained, this man will boast of it, despise others, regard them as ignorant and consider himself the wisest of all. All of this springs from an overbearing will which is indeed unfortunate.

On the other hand, if a man is more humble in his opinions, if he does not despise others, but at the same time is pleased at thinking that he has made such a great penetration, this hinders his perfection which goes beyond all that is merely human. For the highest perfection cannot be seized by the senses; one must be lifted above the senses into pure silence. The reason must finally forgo its images, become peaceful and at rest, and in this way one will perceive that which is perfect. He who does not accomplish this according to discretion and a proper order still retains his own will.

St. Dionysius says: "Still yourself that you may be at rest from all contest."[5]   One single view of pure divine truth is better than all the outer works that holy Christendom performs one with another. Christ says: "Take no thought how or what to speak: for it shall be given to you in that hour what to speak."[6] By this He means that man should not busy his heart with imaged thoughts and use them as intermediate things between God and the soul. Rather he should always remain silent and let God alone speak. The divine Word teaches him more in real wisdom as to what he should say, if necessary, than if he were to study and seek what he ought to say. David also said: "Blessed is the man whom Thou shalt instruct, O Lord."[7] When a poor spirit retains silence God teaches him, and God alone speaks to him. It is this speaking that makes him blessed and instructs him in all truth.

Let us suppose that all that a man understands is true, but he places little value on it and takes no joy in it. Instead he finds more joy in that which is beyond all images, in that which is pure, divine truth. And if he has to perform external virtues that necessarily pertain to him, but does not give himself properly to this work because he considers himself too pre-occupied with God to bother about external things even though he wants to be free of them—I say that this man still retains self-will.

3

THE REAL MEN OF PRAYER

Is it not better that a man should attend only to his heart and let God work in him, than bother about outward works? Yes, but there is a difference. For in such a case it would be necessary that a virtuous man be no longer able to perform an external virtue even though it were to please him. And this may happen in two ways.

If a man has utilized all that he had on virtue to the extent that he no longer had anything on which to exercise virtue; if he would gladly do something, but cannot since he has nothing, is poor in spirit and is so attentive to God that he cannot separate himself from God for a single hour; if he is weak in body so that he has insufficient strength to perform external virtue, then he is excused from this exercise. And if he turned to external things he would in this case be in error.

Virtue must now operate in the will alone and the will is now more pleasing to God than the external act. It is not an obstacle to his self-abandonment that he does not work this, for it is a proper self-denial that he has emptied himself of external works and that God can operate in him without obstruction. Such are the real men of prayer, who pray in spirit and in truth. In spirit because, without hindrance, they allow God to operate in them and perform all virtue inwardly in the will; that is, in the intention. The virtue which they then perform is essential. For the accidental has fallen away and only a pure essence remains. Virtue now operates in this core and for that reason it is called essential.

Such men can perform all virtue in a single moment. Their being is so simplified and so purified that it penetrates into the

centre of every virtue. And this virtue which they perform
is almost equal to the divine virtue, for as God fosters and
performs all virtue, while remaining in Himself immovable
and at rest, so do such men foster virtue. Before virtue is performed, it is first fostered in a pure heart. And a pure heart
arouses more virtues in love than all men can possibly perform
in external actions. And such a heart also fosters virtue while
remaining immovable, and for this reason it is similar to God's
virtue. Men who have this essential virtue can let accidental
virtue fall away without committing a fault, for they have
abandoned their own will.

But the man who clings to temporal things, who has not yet
directed all to virtue, must eventually work out those virtues
necessary to his condition. Even if God were to work in him
inwardly, he must nevertheless break off from the internal work
and exercise himself in external virtues. He must do this if
necessity requires it; he must do it if he wants to be humble.
And if he fails to do it he commits a fault, that is, he neglects
to do it out of self-will rather than through God's will. Since
he is still weighed down with selfhood he cannot yet have the
essence of virtue, and for this reason it is necessary for him
to practise accidental virtues until he is free of all accidentals.
And when this happens, he is then free from the need to practise
this kind of virtue, but henceforth performs it essentially.
Should there be no reason for such a work he must, of course,
omit it; but if there is one he should certainly do it.

4

THE FINAL ABANDONMENT

Man is humble if he performs virtue to the point where it
becomes his very nature, and only then can he omit accidental
virtue. But he who has not acquired virtue to where it has
become his very being, still possesses a property in his will.
He may say that he is willing to abandon all and do all that
he is requested to do, he may even believe that he possesses

abandonment and has denied his own will. This may be all well and good. But the final abandonment lies in virtue. The more a man has virtue, the more abandoned he becomes and the more he has denied his self-will. If a man has all virtue, he is always abandoned; if not, then he does not resign himself and is not poor in his own will, regardless of what he says.

Now man's abandonment of himself whole-heartedly to virtue is brought about by the divine light. It radiates the will and enkindles in it the fire of divine love, which drives him on to increased virtue. And it never lets him rest until he has obtained the essence of virtue. He who follows this light is abandoned, and no one else. One may certainly display self-denial, but this display hinders a man from true abandonment more than it helps him.

Worldly people, for instance, frequently assume abandonment and say to others that they will sacrifice. But in most cases they only sacrifice in so far as they give away a few temporal things and perform certain virtues—no further. But the man who turns in upon himself and beholds the divine light follows all that is revealed to him by God. This is the abandoned man, for he has departed from self-will.

Some might protest that this light is doubtful, and men are frequently deceived and proceed to regard a natural or devilish light as divine; hence it is better that one should depend on another who has more light. Yes, it is well for a person who is in doubt to permit himself to be led so that he may be shown what it is best that he should do. He should, however, not just stop at external teaching, rather he should carry it into the light of his heart and see what he finds good there and follow it. Above all should he follow what he learns there. Nevertheless, he should always compare his findings with the witness of Holy Scripture and the general teachings of the Church. In this way he will never go wrong.

Nor is it necessary that he should always accept what his guide says and directs, rather he must accept what God commands of him within. This he should follow above all and through it arrive at true abandonment. He cannot arrive at this by the advice of men only. Man can only advise what is human and this alone does not bring about perfection. God's advice is divine and does bring about perfection. And he who follows God's counsels attains to the highest perfection. As David said: " Blessed is the man whom Thou shalt instruct, O Lord."[8]

There are some who will say that the teaching of a truly wise man is from God, and hence it should be followed. Yes, the teaching of a truly wise man is from God, but it is still intermediary and as long as one remains in this he is not immediately touched by God. To be so touched he should follow only God, not a fellow creature. God reveals a light by which he cannot go wrong. God gives him sufficient to do with himself so that he may forget creatures. That is why the Philosopher of Nature, Aristotle, said: " He who is touched by the first cause must follow no human counsel, but Him who is above all human counsel."

And how is man to know if he is touched by God? By two things: When God enters the soul He reveals Himself with a new light which she has never previously perceived. This light bursts out with warmth in the body so that by bodily experience man is made aware of it. The very warmth of the light assures him that it is from God. For the light of nature is cold, the divine light is hot.

Again, when God reveals Himself to the soul there is so much certainty that man cannot doubt it. Even though others were to say that it is not from God, this man would not be affected. For he has discovered a truth in himself that no human can grant—only God. Natural light, however, is doubtful and full of conjecturing. But the divine light and experience are completely lacking in doubt and conjecture. And this experience fosters a perfect awareness. Those who have experienced this abandonment know that what I say is true; those who have not experienced it cannot know it.

PART III

How a Man Shall Attain
to a Perfect Life

CHAPTER I

FOLLOWING CHRIST'S LIFE
AND TEACHING

****

THE third part of this book deals with how a man shall attain to a life in which he acquires the highest and most intimate perfection. It also deals with the things a man should consider in order to become poor in spirit.

Man should first attend to the teaching and life of Jesus Christ, for He has taught spiritual poverty and lived it. He should also, if he wishes to be perfect, follow this teaching and life, because Christ says: "If any one love Me, he will keep My Word."[1] The love of our Lord, in the lowest degree, is that we keep the Commandments which are necessary for eternal life. The second degree of love for Christ is that we keep His counsels; that is, His teaching of the Holy Gospels in which He has counselled us to follow Him in a spiritually poor life, as when He goes on to say: "Whoso cometh after Me, let him deny himself."

1

THE TURNING FROM THE NATURAL TO THE SUPERNATURAL

Now if a man wishes to follow after Christ, what must he deny in his very own selfhood? Man's selfhood consists in four things. First, his weakness, and his tendency to fall into sin. This he must, of course, put aside; he must die to his failings and sins, and mortify himself. Secondly, he is inclined to creatures. Man is inclined by nature to his like, and he should subdue nature and withdraw from creatures, for God and creatures are antagonistic. He, then, who wishes to have God must detach himself from creatures; for the soul is so narrow that God and creatures cannot live together in her. Hence, if God is to live in the soul, creatures must remain outside.

Man should next forgo sensual pleasure, for he must die to this and mortify it in himself if he wishes to have the pleasure of God. As St. Bernard says: "The pleasure of God is so noble that no one receives it who seeks pleasure elsewhere."[2] Fourthly, a man should, if he wishes to follow Christ, forgo natural intellectual pleasure by realizing the difference between supernatural and natural knowledge.

Through his reason man turns from natural things to religious images and forms, and so orders them that he forms a rational distinction which gives him great pleasure. This pleasure is natural, but it is superior to all bodily pleasure. However, he who lingers long with this natural, rational pleasure, hinders himself from the supernatural pleasure which God in His grace grants to the soul. Frequently man regards this natural joy to be the working of grace, but he who takes that to be grace which comes only from nature is grievously fooled. Now although this pleasure of the soul does not blind as much as bodily pleasure, it should nevertheless be shunned, for it is an obstacle to perfection. To be sure, this pleasure attracts the heathen to the knowledge of natural truth. But the person who stops in this is like the pagan, and not like Christ, and he is by no means a poor spirit who follows Christ.

How, then, shall a man deny himself so that these four things may be mortified in him? Well, to begin with, man should mortify sin in himself by putting on virtue; for to the extent that man is removed from God by sin, so is he brought close to Him by virtue. St. Paul says: "As you have yielded your members to serve uncleanness and iniquity unto iniquity: so now yield your members to serve justice unto sanctification."[3] Because man has an inclination in his nature to sin, he must exercise himself in virtue if he wishes to conquer feebleness.

But let no one believe that he is free from sin unless he has acquired all the virtues.

You will, of course, ask: Who knows if he has all the virtues? I answer with St. John, who says: "Whosoever is born of God . . . cannot sin."[4] In the same moment in which God the Father begets His Son in the soul, all sins and all unlikeness vanish, and all the virtues are born in her in a likeness with God. In the same instant man stands there in all the virtues and stripped of sin.

Man also possesses all the virtues if he utilizes all his faculties towards virtue, so that he acquires virtue in a perfect will, no longer accidentally but essentially. However, no one can attain to this except a pure, poor spirit, one who has stripped himself of all things for the love of virtue, one, in other words, who clings to God only and who performs virtue in God.

Can, then, a man have virtue so that he needs no more? We must say something on this, for it may be understood from different points of view. Now if the outer man has virtue, he can never have so much that he needs no more in number, greatness and purity. He must always practise more and more virtues, and so long as he lives on earth he must continually grow in greatness, so that his virtues may become greater and greater—and also in purity, so that his virtue may become purer. So must he strive even to the end.

But if the inner man has all the virtues, he needs no more in number, for he who possesses one virtue perfectly has them all. In the unity of his will he possesses all the virtues so that none is further needed by him. His love of virtue, however, must increase; it must always become greater and greater for each virtue. It must also grow in purity, so that the virtue may be always purer and purer. He should grow in this way until he overcomes sin—until death.

The next thing that a person must forgo is his inordinate love for creatures. Poverty of spirit is an abandonment of the self and of everything earthly. Hence, he shuns creatures, is shunned by them, and is thus liberated. A spiritually poor man accepts nothing from creatures; but he accepts all from God

M

whether it is bodily or spiritual. Only God will be his Giver.

Surely, he who accepts something from other than God alone is hardly a poor spirit, for one can give nothing to a perfectly poor spirit, except it come as a gift from God, in which case it is also good, since God alone is the Giver. A poor spirit can happily abandon all things in order that he may receive from God alone. His friends withdraw their natural love from him, and the love that they continue to show him comes from grace. In other words, the gift to a poor spirit has a very great reward, for everything is given to him through grace. Furthermore, his life is fruitful, since all who show him love harvest a reward. Not only does he himself come into heaven, but he also brings others with him.

However, to him who possesses many temporal things, all is given out of a mere natural love, and he is only loved from nature. The giver harvests no reward, nor does he who accepts; the gift is lost for ever, since no action of man is rewarding unless it issues from grace. St. Augustine says the same: "He who gives his gift, but not rightly, does wrong." But you do not do rightly if your gift is given where it is not needed. This is why Christ says: "Give to the poor." He certainly does not mean the rich.

The other aspect of selfhood that a person must forgo is fleshly lust. And this may be accomplished by consistent inner contemplation of the Passion of our Lord.

If a man steeps himself in the Passion, he is purified, and a light is kindled in this purity, a light that burns and consumes all luxury of the body. A spiritual divine ecstasy is granted which surpasses all bodily rapture. Indeed, he who desires this divine joy, must take to himself the wounds of our Lord. If he continues to do this he will overflow with a joy so divine that he will wonder where this great grace comes from. The wounds of our Lord are full of sweetness, and all men, if they only knew it, would turn to His Passion. If a man did not do this for God's sake, he would do it for his own, since all men desire comfort.

But seek it where you will, nowhere shall you find it as in

the Passion of our Lord. Those who do this have heaven here and yonder—and if God were not to give them heaven in any other way, He would give them sufficient to reward them for all they have endured for His sake.

2

THE GRACE TO BE FOUND IN CHRIST'S PASSION

Many of you say: I have no grace. Nothing can be blamed for this save that you do not seek it in the right way. If you seek it in the Passion of Christ, you will always find grace and comfort. It may at first be bitter to you and give you no pleasure, but this is merely a sign that you are still weighed down with bodily luxury which must be uprooted in the bitterness. If bodily delight is chastened, it disappears, and a spiritual, divine joy greater than you have ever felt is born in you. But if you try to escape from this bitterness, you will never be free of this luxury. Man should therefore gladly endure a brief bitterness in order to be free from that bitterness which endures for ever.

A man who seriously attends to the Passion will not be deprived of its fruit. He ascends the tree of the cross whose fruit calls him on, if he is willing to have it. All on the cross is full of fruit; yes, more than all tongues could in truth proclaim. Not even angels' tongues could describe the abundance of grace that is hidden in the Passion. Blessed indeed are those who have found this treasure; but unhappy are those to whom it is not revealed or who do not turn to it in order that it may be revealed to them. It is the living fruit of living paradise.

He who eats of this fruit shall never die. Had Adam eaten the lawful fruit and not that which was forbidden, he would have remained deathless. The same thing occurs to us. If we eat the fruit of the cross, which is granted to us, and shun that which is forbidden, that is, all natural lust, then we shall become deathless. If, however, we disregard the fruit of life and take the fruit of death, we become truly mortal and shall be deprived of paradise. Those who have tasted this fruit always long to eat more and more; they are always hungry for it and are never satisfied as long as they live in time. In order to satisfy this hunger they hurry with great longing to the Sacrament, and their hunger is so great that God could not satisfy them with His whole creation, but only with Himself. Nor can they ever be satisfied while they live in time, for they always long for more.

Priests should have great care for such a hungry soul. They should give her God's Body so that she may not perish from hunger. It is often said that he who permits a man to die of bodily hunger, when he might have assisted him, is guilty of that man's death. Far more is a man guilty towards souls when he permits them to die of hunger. For inasmuch as the soul is nobler than the body, so are you guilty, if you permit the soul to suffer hunger.

These persons who suffer this kind of hunger are often strongly criticized because they go frequently to receive the Body of our Lord. But in truth if one were readily to see their hunger, one would not criticize them. The person who criticizes them is unwilling to acknowledge his own blindness and his low degree of love. He acts like a man who sees another sitting in his own tree, from which hangs ample fruit, and who finds fault with him because he eats his own fruit. For this is what these holy men do; they sit in their own tree of the cross, which has an abundance of the noblest fruit of the Body of our Lord. The Sacrament of the Body of Christ is the fruit of the holy cross, and he who wishes to eat its fruit in a profitable way must break it off from the cross by a persistent inner contemplation of the Passion. Others pass judgement on this simply because they cannot endure it, and their sins are to blame for this.

But let him who wishes seriously to give thought to the Passion go cheerfully to the table of our Lord, for it will be a great benefit to him and he will become rich in grace. Indeed, if he could lead all men to it, they would be saved and become perfect. It is in this way that men surmount bodily lust; and not only bodily lust, but all things that are not God. Regardless of how great it may be, there is nothing which does not pass off into nothingness if it is brought into the Passion of our Lord. It is a glowing fire in which all inequality disappears and is consumed. As Christ says: "I am come to cast fire on the earth."[5]

Now the fire that our Lord casts is the heat of divine love, which He draws from the wounds of His heart. Let him who thirsts hold his mouth to it, and he will take such a drink that he will never again thirst for temporal things.

This man has little need for preaching; he has need only to come and remain here. For if he enters whole-heartedly into the Passion, he is seized in such a way that he cannot turn away from God. Those who have learned this give thanks to God, for God has chosen them from among men, as our Lord chose St. Peter, St. John and St. James, and took them aside from the other disciples to a special place, and pointed out to them the secret of His Passion, and said: "My soul is sorrowful, even unto death."[6] This was a sign that He loved them more than the other disciples.

Likewise, those who occupy themselves with the Passion of our Lord are loved by God more than others. For they take their drink at the source from which divine love continually flows, and they rejoice in such a way that they are unable to please themselves. They abandon all outward and inward things in order that they may be able to give a comparable love to God in return.

3

SINKING INTO THE GODHEAD

The true lovers of God are those who love God with their whole heart. Those who love God with their whole heart abandon everything for God's sake. Now the heart is bodily; hence when they turn their heart away from all bodily things towards God, this is called loving with the whole heart. These persons also love with their whole soul, that is, when they surrender their life for God's sake. For the soul gives life to the body and it is this life which they surrender wholly to God.

They love God further with their strength; that is, they direct all their faculties in accordance with the highest choice. They direct all of them to one end, and through this striving they penetrate into God. Here all the faculties keep silence and rest, and when they are thus passive and allow only God to work, it is the highest action that they can perform.

The true lovers of God also love Him with all their mind and this is when their mind rises above all created things and penetrates into the uncreated good, which is God Himself, and then loses itself in the secret darkness of the unknown God. It loses itself in Him and breaks through Him so that it cannot return.

To illustrate this, let us consider a man who throws a stone into a bottomless sea. As the stone must continually sink, yet never reach ground nor be brought out again unless it rests somewhere (and this is impossible since the sea is unfathomable), so it happens with the mind which has thrown itself into the unfathomable Godhead. He sinks continually, but finds no stopping place. No one can bring him out again and he has no final ground where he can stop and rest. He has broken away from the created; hence no creature can reach him and he thus lives for ever in God. He can no more come out of the Godhead than the stone can rise again to the surface by its own force.

Because sensuous men cannot understand this, they say: As long as a man lives in time he can always fall. This is quite true. But the men we have spoken of do not live in time, for their " dwelling-place is in heaven ",[7] as St. Paul says. He who enters this dwelling must remain there. For example, if a man is bound by bonds so strong that he cannot break them, he cannot, people will say, become free unless he is helped. It is in this way that the mind is bound by God. Even if all creatures united their strength, they could not break this bond. And the mind has become so powerless over itself that it is unable of itself to break the bond.

One will immediately say: If this is so, then the freedom of the will is taken away. My answer is that the freedom of the will is not taken away from but given to it, for the will is quite free when it cannot endure anything except what God wills. We say that a king is free who conquers all his enemies and rules mightily in his kingdom. He who is conquered by his enemies and forced out of his kingdom, is not called a free king. Now the will is a free king when it surmounts all its enemies and rules mightily, that is, in God, in whom he can do all things, as St. Paul says.[8] In this way a man subdues all in the Passion of our Lord, in which everything must necessarily disappear into nothingness.

When a man clothes himself with all the virtues, a spiritually poor life, and with the Passion of our Lord, he arrives at the third degree of perfection in which he hears, in a silent utterance, the eternal Word which God the Father utters in the ground of the soul. This utterance drives out all created images, so that man throws off his selfhood in all natural, intellectual pleasures, which consist in attractive creative images and forms. He will hear only God's eternal Word and he will know and love God in a most perfect way. Hence Christ says: "If any one love Me he will keep My Word,"[9] that is, when God speaks to him and he endures it. For man to endure God and not hinder Him in His action is indeed the highest work he can perform.

4

GOD'S INWARD AND OUTWARD ACTION

Now what is God's action? There are two kinds of action in God—an inward action and an outward action. The inward action is God's very being and nature. The outward action is in the creature. And in the same manner that the creature has flowed out of God, so must it again flow into Him. In other words, God works in souls in order that He may bring them to the prime origin from which they have flowed, for they cannot re-enter by their own actions. For this reason it is of the utmost importance that a man should attain the point where he can receive the work of God, so that by this work he may return to God. As Christ says: "One thing is needful, without which no man can come to God."[10]

But if man cannot by his own actions come to God, what, then, is the use in his striving? I reply that man by his self-action much more hinders than furthers his coming to God. For all that man does by himself is incomplete and it is never enough to bring him to God. Since the creature is defective, its actions are defective. If man is really to attain God, he must empty himself of all self-action and permit God alone to act in him. Christ speaks of this when He says: "If any one abide not in Me, he shall be cast forth . . . and shall wither."[11]

The best thing, then, for man to do is to empty himself of all self-action. If he were wholly empty of this he would be a mere tool of God, and God would act in him without hindrance. Now all that God wants from us is that we cease self-action and allow Him to be the master workman. If we did this thoroughly we should become perfect men. For all that is good is the work of God, and if God does not perform the work, it is not good. Yes, and if a man prays without God working in him, it is not really the best prayer. As St. James says: "Every best gift and every perfect gift is . . . from the Father of lights."[12]

The question, of course, arises: How is a man to know if his action is of himself or from God? In brief, let it be said there are three supernatural divine virtues, Faith, Hope and Love. Now whatever increases these virtues comes from God; whatever lessens them is an indication that it is the work of man. And he who views these things inwardly knows that it is true. For that which man does of himself, he applies to himself and to time, and hence fails to increase the supernatural virtues. But that which God does, draws a man out of himself towards eternity, and this increases Faith, Hope and Love.

What is the divine work? The work which God performs in the soul is twofold, one the work of grace, the other essential and divine. By the work of grace man is prepared for the essential. God works in man through His grace when He leads him away from sin and on to virtue. If man turns from sin and practises virtue it is a grace of God. God makes man agreeable by grace; it leads him away from all deficient things and on to virtue, so that man ascends to a perfect life, in which he knows the most divine will of God and lives in complete accordance with it.

The second work that God performs in the soul is essential. When man reaches the point where he has acquired all accidental virtue and obtains the essence of virtue, then God performs all virtue in him in an essential way. In other words, the heavenly Father begets His Son in the soul and this birth elevates the spirit above all created things into God. The spirit is now above grace, since grace is a creature, and the spirit is elevated above all creatures. Grace, however, does not forsake the man but it directs and orders the powers of man to await the birth that God brings forth in the essence of the soul.

God's action in this sense is an essential work, a work raised above all grace and reason, a work in the light of glory. Grace is thus transformed into the light of glory, and this man becomes known as a godly man. Then the essence sees essentially and essence gives essence, and the spirit does all things with God in an essential manner. Her work is the work of God, and God's work is her work. For when two are one they also have one work. The reason cannot grasp this work through images, as it is beyond them; it is wrapped in the very Godhead.

The reason certainly recognizes that this action is a work elevated above all created things and that it is the noblest work whereby the spirit can be blessed. The reason is for ever reaching and, if possible, trying to grasp and to know this essential action. But she will never fully grasp it in time, for if she did, this action would grant the fullness of heaven in time. Although reason cannot understand it in time, she nevertheless always stretches after it and refuses to rest until death.

Through this endeavour to strive after the divine work, reason empties herself of all created images, and, aided by a super-natural light, reaches out for the mystery of the hidden God-head. Beyond this knowledge she cannot know, and beyond this love she cannot love. This means that the spirit no longer knows in a creaturely manner, and that she no longer loves with her own love, but according to the love of God, of which St. Paul speaks when he says: "I live, now not I: but Christ liveth in me."[13] The spirit is now dead to creaturely ways and henceforth lives according to godly ways.

He, therefore, who spurns the reason does a great wrong to her. For all things crave life, and when the reason compre-hends that all temporal things are deadly and that only God is life, she must necessarily direct her attention to God, for she naturally craves life. It is certainly much more natural for reason to turn to God than to creatures. For creatures cannot satisfy her—only God can do this. Hence, it is obvious that she should turn to Him who gives to her, rather than to that which detracts from her.

It is no fault of reason that man should choose the earthly and abandon God, for if reason were properly utilized this would not happen. That which the creature chooses instead of God is done by sensuality and not by reason, and so David said: "Be ye not as the horse or as the mule, which have no understanding."[14] He who chooses the creature rather than God is not a rational man, but is like an irrational beast. If, however, reason adheres to created things and clings to images and forms, it is because she realizes the eternal God in created things, as St. Paul says: "In visible things the invisible are seen."[15]

That which hinders the reason from reaching God through created things is simply the pleasure attached to created images. This is a natural pleasure which blinds her so that she cannot see the divine truth. And this pleasure must be abandoned.

It is, however, often surmised that this pleasure is from grace and hence many linger in it. These men are usually considered natural, rational men, and yet they do not possess true reason. True reason seeks God, and eliminates from creatures, whether they be bodily or spiritual, all pleasure accompanying them. And he who attains to this true reason is a proper rational man, whose intellect is brilliantly filled with a divine light by which he perceives the Godhead and forgets creatures. And he who surrenders himself to this has a joyful experience and foretaste of eternal life. This joy leads the spirit away from all natural pleasure towards God in whom she receives her true joy, as Christ says: "Who eateth Me hungereth not any more,"[16] that is, after creaturely pleasure.

One must understand how the spirit in this condition is lifted above grace and above reason, and even above all pleasures in God, and how she thus stands in naked poverty of all created things. In this state she has only one vision of the divine Being, which is lifted above all grace and above all reason, and she comprehends nothing of herself nor of anything created, but of God only. Now man attains to this perfection if he follows the teaching of our Lord Jesus Christ.[17]

CHAPTER II

THE PERFECTION OF VIRTUE

✳✳✳✳✳✳✳✳✳✳✳✳✳✳✳✳✳✳✳✳✳✳✳✳✳

THE second way that carries a man to a spiritual, poor life is the perfection of virtue.

1

WHEN IS VIRTUE COMPLETE?

Virtue is never completed, nor followed to its utmost, except when a man strips himself of love for temporal possessions. Nor is it completed until he exercises himself in all the virtues, loses the image of virtue, and arrives at the point where he is no longer able to perform any virtue accidentally, but only essentially. In this way virtue is brought to its highest fulfilment. The result is that all things become small to such a man, and virtue alone great. He easily turns all things to virtue; he exercises himself in all the virtues until he can do no more and becomes so poor in spirit that no one desires any more virtue from him. Thus free of guilt, he is emptied of all accidental virtue; then he can attend wholly to God without any obstacles, which was not previously possible.

As long as a man has, he must give. And when he has nothing more, he is free. This freedom is far nobler than the former giving, for he no longer gives in accident but in essence, and he no longer gives one gift, but all gifts, and he no longer gives to just one man, but to all men. His gift is similar to the gift of God, as a teacher also says: " It is good when a man shares his property and comes to the help of his fellow-men;

172

but it is far better to give all and follow Christ in a poor life."[1]

Never will you possess virtue in its most perfect degree until you have abandoned all for the sake of virtue. Take, for example, the case of mercy. The person who is utterly merciful keeps nothing; he who keeps something is not perfectly but only partially merciful, and in a fragmentary way. And he who desires to be perfectly humble must exercise himself in every humble action that is required; he who fails to do this is not entirely humble. Let men look upon virtue, then, in this way: he who desires perfect virtue should abandon himself to virtue until he is spiritually poor in all creatures and possessions, and until no one requests anything further of him. Thus the perfection of virtue consists in this poverty of spirit.

2

DOES BODILY NECESSITY HINDER VIRTUE?

But if a man is naturally weak and retains the things that are necessarily required, does this prevent him from the perfection of virtue?

My opinion is that if the man is weak in such a way that he requires this, and retains something that he needs, this is not against virtue. For virtue demands a sense of proportion because it has an order, and if a man gave away this necessity he would act counter to order, and that which he obtains for his own needs is as right as if he gave it to a poor man.

If would, of course, be more perfect if he were so strong that he could strip himself of things to the point where he had nothing when he became weak. The perfection of virtue consists in utter abandonment; hence, we should happily surrender all so that we may possess all virtue.

CHAPTER III

DYING TO SELF

✳✳✳✳✳✳✳✳✳✳✳✳✳✳✳✳✳✳✳✳✳✳✳✳✳✳

THE third reason why a man should give himself up to a spiritual, poor life is that he may die to himself and all creatures, and that only God may live in him. Such a life is living in dying, and in this dying there is blessedness. as St. John says: "Blessed are the dead who die in the Lord."[1]

1

ONE MUST CONTINUALLY DIE

We should make ourselves poor in spirit in order that in our very ground of existence and in this dying we may be made alive again. Christ says: "Unless the grain of corn fall into the ground and die it cannot bring forth fruit. But if it die it brings forth much fruit."[2] This is actually so. He who desires all the fruit of life must endure all manner of death. Yet no one save a poor spirit can have all manner of death. As a teacher says: "He who lives after the Gospel has a cross and martyrdom."

Only a man who is poor in spirit can have the fruit of a true, perfect life, as Christ says: "If thou wilt be perfect go sell what thou hast and give to the poor."[3] Now this selling implies man's self-denial; the giving is virtue; the following of Christ is to die in one's ground, so that, dying altogether to himself, God may live completely in him. A spiritually poor life, then, is useful in order that we may continually die. He who does not wholly die cannot wholly live.

174

How is it possible, then, for such a man wholly to die, for he still is seen to live like other men and he is even seen to be happy? To this I answer that a true Christian always dies. Whether he eat or drink, or wake or sleep, all is for him a dying. That it should happen that he lives much like other men is because it is simply a directing of the outer man, according to which necessity he cannot attend to God, and this is his dying. So far as the inner man is concerned he would prefer to occupy himself continually with God and abandon all things.

Furthermore, if he is cheerful and happy, this joy has nothing in common with time, nor with creatures. It issues only from God, and hence it is without blemish and does not hinder the dying of the creature. Although a poor spirit would perhaps gladly help himself so that he might not altogether die, God will not let him. For his future lies in his dying, and what he possesses he possesses in dying. His deaths are countless since he dies in each moment.

Blessed is the man who can die all manner of deaths. But his dying is of such a nature that no man can really comprehend it. No one can fully comprehend death except he to whom God has revealed it.

Why must one continually die in order to be blessed? There are two reasons: One is that, since Adam's fall, man's nature is full of feeble inclination, and this inclination must be uprooted. Since this can never be absolutely uprooted, one must always die. It is indeed possible that a man may die to his rational will so that he wills only what God wills. As St. Paul says: "You are dead: and your life is hid with Christ in God."[4]

But the sensuous will, following its sensuous tendency, can never absolutely die in time. The rational will must constantly kill this tendency, so that sensuality may remain under the control of the higher faculties, and these ordered to God. He who does this stands in the justice in which God created Adam, and he who stands in this justice is free of mortal or venial sins. This, of course, can never happen unless God leads man

to it. Hence, a man cannot be entirely without defects, and
for this reason he must always die.

Another reason why man must always die is because of
the ceaseless attacks of the evil spirit and the world, which
strive to make man fall. Regardless of man's state in life,
he is always attacked, and none is free of this in time.

We must, then, continually fight against this and die in
order to overcome the world, for he who does this shall, as
St. Paul says,[5] be crowned. The deaths that we die in this
struggle are countless, for the evil spirit surrounds us with
many traps, and we must always be on our guard to resist
him. It frequently happens that an image is granted to man
which he fancies comes from grace, though it is from the evil
spirit, as St. Paul says: "Satan himself transformeth himself
into an angel of light."[6] He grants this image to us in a pleasing
light; nevertheless it is evil in itself.

Those who are occupied with images and visions are very
often fooled in this way; for they are for the most part from
the evil spirit, and now in our time more than ever before.
Truth is revealed and laid open in the Holy Scriptures, and
it is therefore unnecessary that truth should be revealed to
us in another way. He who accepts truth otherwise than
from the Gospel is weak in faith, and little is to be thought
of his life, for our life is only from the Gospel, as St.
Paul says: "Our Lord hath begotten us through the
Gospel."[7] He who is begotten elsewhere is not a legitimate
child.

Yes, the evil spirits have frequently granted man an image
that appeared good in order that he may accept false, un-
reliable truth to be the real truth. Man must die to this. The
reason why God formerly revealed Himself in visions was
because the truth was concealed, and this was necessary.
But it is not necessary now and hence it rarely happens from
God.

We must continually die to that which is not like simple
divine truth. Simple divine truth is a pure contemplating
of the spirit on God's being and reality. And we must die

to all that obstructs the spirit in this. He who is brought into it by a way other than the teaching of Christ is a thief and a murderer, and is a follower of the Antichrist. Therefore, let him who does not wish to be fooled cleave to the teaching of Christ; then, let others teach what they will, nothing can hurt him.

Men are often judged to be relying on their own selfhood when they say that they would happily live according to the teaching of Christ. These men should not ostracize themselves on this account, for it is only fair that they should be so judged. He who does not really live on the highest ground of Christ's teaching stands on his own selfhood. Let him become as humble as he will, yet he is not truly humble, and his humility is more an attachment to himself than a self-denial. True self-denial rests only in the Gospel, and he who does not live most intimately with it is never altogether humble, nor does he wholly die to his selfhood. Let every man, then, look and see how much he lives in the Gospel, for to this extent is he promoted in humility, and to this extent is he dead to himself.

2

THE VALUE OF THIS DYING TO SELF

What is the actual value of this dying continually to self? There are at least five uses involved. First, man comes closer to his first innocence. He was created sinless, but when he fell, he became burdened with all kinds of sins. This feebleness must be uprooted by dying; the more he dies to it the more he approaches his first innocence. And if he enters into this nobility, he is without infirmity.

If man had not fallen his nobility would have remained immortal and he would have suffered no pain. Those who have died the most to their selfhood are the most exempt in this, for in that death and denial of self a new joy arises; the death that man endures opens up a secret happiness. Christ

N

says: "Take up My yoke upon you and you shall find rest to your souls."[8]

The second use is, that in each death a new life grows up in man, and with this life there is each time a new love, so that man becomes flooded with grace, and his reason is filled with divine light.   He grows continually so that he becomes wealthy in grace and his reason becomes so clear that no false light can further confuse him, and he can perfectly distinguish all truth in so far as it is necessary.   He is so inflamed with divine love that no one can further separate him from God.   St. Paul was in this state when he said: "Who then shall separate us from the love of Christ?"[9]   He means, of course, no one.

He who wishes to be receptive to God's gifts should always remember this business of dying.   Let him endure all kinds of deaths and to him will come all gifts, for he receives a special gift in return for each death.   They who thus die also become so wealthy that no one can count their spiritual riches.   Oh, if we only knew the value that lies in dying, we would hurry to it as if the greatest worldly honours were about to be granted to us.   But we seem to fly from that which is most useful to us, and we always seek that which is most injurious.   It is said that they who are in heaven, before they would relinquish the smallest part of the reward they have gained and which they have received through their suffering, would return to earth again and suffer till the Judgement Day.

Next, if a man is really pure, he is emptied of all infirm accident, and is receptive only to God.   God is present in all things; if all things are worked out, then God alone remains. But this purity must be sought by dying, and if the soul is liberated from everything else, she is ripe for issuing forth the Son of God within her.   As God the Father begets His Son in the Godhead, so also the Son of God is born in a pure soul, and she is again born in God.   Hence Christ says: "Unless a man be born again, he cannot see the kingdom of God."[10]

The fourth use of a continual dying is that by it God is born in the soul.   In other words, when God transports the spirit from the soul and throws her into the darkness of His God-head, he transforms her with His Godhead so that she becomes like God.[11]   She loses the shape of creatureliness, and is formed into the formless image of the Son in the Godhead; hence, the man becomes a son of grace in the way that he is a son of nature.

Fifthly, if the soul is lifted into God, she reigns also with God, as St. Paul says: "If we die with Christ, so shall we also reign with Him."[12]   The spirit can now do all things with God; she orders all with God, she directs and leads all with God.   What God does, she does with God; she performs all things with God.   And we attain to this unutterable perfection through spiritual dying.

3

AS IS THE DYING, SO IS THE GROWTH

Does all this mean, then, that no one can fundamentally die without external poverty?   No, but as long as a man is attached to temporal things, he uses them without dying to his nature. If he is poor in temporal things, outwardly as well as inwardly, all is changed into grace.   That which previously was natural to him is now of grace, and he continually dies, for he who always increases in grace must always die to nature.   However, all things are not of grace to man; so if he has not yet freed himself from those which are not of grace he does not always die.   Truly, no one can entirely die except a man who is pure and poor in spirit.

If a man has all his necessities, this does not kill sensual nature; but if he has little and must ask for more, this may kill nature and increase grace.   In other words, he who always suffers want can always die.   Poor spirits are so rich in grace that they do not know it, for their deaths are countless, and the grace that God then secretly grants them is beyond measure. It frequently happens that a man believes that he is abandoned by God as well as by creatures and that he is without grace.

But want and self-denial kill nature, and he is filled with an unutterable grace. As is the dying, so is the growth in grace, and blessed are they who have chosen God in a dying life, for their wealth in grace is exceedingly great.

If spiritual poverty had no use other than that man should always die and hence receive countless graces, it ought to be performed for this reason alone. He who does not love it gives indication that he has no divine love. Were he a possessor of divine love, he would also love the image of our Lord Jesus Christ. And His image is spiritual poverty and misfortune. He who does not love spiritual poverty does not truly love God.

According to this a man should be able to know if he belongs to heaven or to hell simply from his love for the poor or the rich and whether he prefers to be with the poor rather than the rich. As Christ says: "The kingdom of heaven is for the poor in spirit." He does not say it is for the worldly rich; in fact, He says a rich man can hardly enter the kingdom of heaven. Indeed the man who is poor in spirit finds the presence of his own kind more pleasing than that of the worldly, and he who frequently busies himself with worldly people fails to show that he is a spiritually poor man. Like loves its like. He to whom one is closest, he loves, clings to him and happily walks about with him.

CHAPTER IV

THE CONTEMPLATIVE WAY

****

THE fourth reason that urges one towards a spiritual, poor life is the perfection of a contemplative way of living.

1

WHAT IS A LIFE OF CONTEMPLATION?

As long as man is bound to temporal things, he must have an active life, for he has much to do. And as long as this operation lasts he must work. But he who would free himself from it before he has brought these external works to a proper completion, would have an imperfect self-denial and fail miserably. For to be against God and the truth by such a neglect of virtue is laziness. Regarding this a certain teacher says: "He raises his hands in vain to God who does not offer them, if he could, to the poor." Neither true freedom nor contemplation takes place in the possession of temporal things, for to the extent that a man possesses in temporal things he is lacking in eternal things. Temporal and eternal are contraries and he who has the one must depart from the other.

A contemplative life is elevated above all that is temporal and is an enjoyment of eternal things only. He, then, who desires to lead such a life must necessarily depart from all that is temporal. If a man has turned himself towards the best, towards God, then God is his sole object. He enters into God and detaches himself from all creatures so that no one can speak either evil or good of him, since he is completely hidden in God.   Such a man is a real friend of God.

No man can hide himself in God except he who is truly detached from creatures, for he who still clings to the creature is also known to it.   But if you are detached from the creature, then only God knows you and the creature forgets you.   When these men of contemplation sink themselves into God and hide in Him, they become strangers to all the created; they contemplate God without obstacles.   But those who still cling to earthly things cannot do this, for they would be too much hindered in it.   Hence, a perfect contemplative life is a spiritual, poor life, emptied of all that is temporal.

2

THE DISSOLVING OF LOVE WITH LOVE

Some say that if a man abides in a contemplative life and realizes God without mediation, yet sees that his neighbour is in need, he should abandon his contemplation and come to his neighbour's assistance.   Now if they still possess temporal things they must do this, for if they do not their contemplation is of no use—in fact they do wrong.   But they who are wholly free from temporal things and hence have nothing with which to help their neighbours are also set free from this external work.

This freedom is far more noble than employment with creatures.   Christ praised the passiveness of Mary, for our Lord only goes about with passive creatures.   And this going about is simply the dwelling of the lover with the beloved.   God cannot dwell anywhere except in a soul that is detached from earthiness.   They who possess this freedom go about with God, and God with them.

Solomon also says in the Book of Love: "He kissed me with the kiss of His mouth."[1]   The soul is kissed by God when she is elevated above all temporal things and beholds only

God's countenance. God then inclines His countenance and kisses her, and His kissing is simply a dissolving of love with Love. One gazes at the other and neither can do anything without the other. By love are they bound together. And of this love St. Bernard says: "How sweet is this bond of love; it makes the poor rich, but the rich who do not have it are poor."

Is it possible for worldly rich people to be bound by this bond of divine love, and can they too participate in a life of contemplation? Hardly, for as long as a man clings to creatures and to time, he does not possess divine love. The bond of divine love breaks every bond with creatures, and he who is still held by these creaturely attachments shows that he is not yet clothed with the divine bond, as St. Augustine says: "If the heart is seized hold of by divine love, in that case the vanity of creatures finds no place in it."

True love is a following of the beloved. That which the beloved directs and advises is accomplished by true love; it omits nothing but executes everything. Now these worldly people do not have this true love because they do not follow the counsel of our Lord. They may certainly display acts of love, but these do not spring from the ground of love. If these did spring from it they would easily perform one and all acts of love. To the God-loving man nothing is too difficult, for, as St. Paul says, he can do all in Him who strengthens him.[2]

Such people are incapable of all acts of love since they do not possess divine love. Divine love is such a fountain that he who holds his mouth to it, overflows with love, shuns creatures and clings only to God. Again St. Augustine says: "To souls that love God all creatures are too narrow for them." Yes, it is the nature of divine love to forsake creatures and cling to God.

St. Peter wished to prove his love for God when he said: "Behold we have left all things and have followed Thee."[3] In no other way could he give witness to his love. And if we would truly love God we must also abandon the earthly and cling to Him. He who departs most from what is earthly most loves God. He who does not cannot say that he loves God. All who love God, all who are thoroughly inflamed by the fire of divine love, can give witness that this fire destroys all that is not God.

There are some who say that a man may keep temporal things provided he does not let his self-will cling to them but to God's will. This is only a light statement which evades the real issue. He who properly loves the will of God does not love it according to his own opinion but according to the teaching of Jesus Christ, who best knew the will of God.

If we desire to fulfil God's will we should follow the teaching of Christ. And His teaching was to abandon all and follow Him; he who does not do this has not yet struck real root in the ground of divine love, as Christ himself says: "Whoso loveth Me, keepeth the words which I have taught him."[4] A real lover fulfils the counsel rather than the commandment of his beloved, whereas the misdirected lover stops at the commandment and lets the counsel by-pass him.

Others say that if our Lord Himself were on earth He would not even ask me to give up external things which were not necessary for me. But my reply is that if He were on earth He would say the same thing that He said to His disciples. He said: "If thou wilt be perfect go sell what thou hast . . . and follow Me." No one is excluded from this request and he who fails to accept it should not lay claim to any perfection.

Divine love is a power which elevates a man above all things to the highest level of perfection, and he who stands on this highest level has true love. But no one can attain to this unless he first pass through the lower levels. The very lowest level of divine love is to forgo excess temporal things; the second is to shun the self, the third is to forgo all things bodily or spiritual which mediate between God and man. Only in this way does a man attain to true perfection. He who has not surmounted the first level cannot arrive at any of the others.

What acts of love do those rich people perform if they do not possess divine love? Their love may be of two kinds—natural, which has no reward, or the love of grace, which truly has a reward, though it is not perfect since it can increase and decrease. Perfect love continually increases and is never otherwise. But only they who are detached from temporal things have this love. Temporal things are changeable. He who clings to them is also changeable, and, since there is no perfection in that which changes, he cannot have perfect love.

Neither can the man who does not have perfect love live a life of true contemplation, for a perfect love is only begotten in a pure contemplation of the divine Being. Whatever he lacks in this contemplation he also lacks in true love, for it has its source only in the Father or the Son. If this eye of reason is pure and directed away from all that is not God, then he can perfectly contemplate the divine Being. But if this eye is impure and anxious about temporal things, it cannot contemplate Him, for "the light is unbearable to a sick eye", as St. Augustine says.[5]

He who is weighed down with temporal things cannot lead a contemplative life, for his eye is impure and sick. But he who desires to attain this life, which consists in the best, must detach himself from external possessions and live a spiritual, poor life; hence, he arrives at the highest level of perfection. He who quits a spiritual, poor life also neglects the contemplative life, for contemplation and spiritual poverty stand on the same level.

Among all things there are only two: God and the creature. He who is poor in creatures is rich in God, and these riches consist in the contemplation of God without mediation. Indeed, our entire blessedness rests in this, that we know and love God without the mediation of creatures.

3

CONTEMPLATION HAS MANY USES

Should one abandon all things in order to attain to a contemplative life, what, then, would be its use? Ah, its real use is one which is beyond words, as St. Paul says: "I have seen such things which it is not granted to man to utter."[6]

However, I will mention, among others, several uses which the contemplative life has. First, one performs all works without much labour; labour only results from being overburdened with earthly things, and he who is free from them is also liberated from anxiety. When a truly contemplative man is liberated from all that is earthly, he is also freed from this labour.

Next, that which others perform accidentally the contemplative performs in essential divine truth; he performs all works in this truth. But they who are weighed down with creatures perform their work in natural accidents. Thirdly, that which others perform only in part a truly internal man performs entirely. He accomplishes all acts in one, and one act in all, since he is united with God. Hence, he has one action with God, and as God accomplishes all in one act and one act in all, so does such a man. All good works are proper to him as if he himself had performed them, for Christ says: "All that I have received from My Father I have given unto you."[7]

Again, that which others first acquire from an active life, the contemplatives have already a foretaste of in time. Since their spirit is lifted above time and all things earthly, the pleasure and the ecstasy of everlasting things are manifested to them. This overflows from the spirit so that it covers the body, and hence they have a foretaste of eternal life, as Christ says: "From your body will flow living water, flowing into everlasting life."[8]

Fifthly, he who comes to a genuine contemplative life is drawn by God into Himself and God reveals His divine being to him. In other words, God holds him so that he shall not slip away from Him. Had Lucifer been drawn in this way to where he could have had a true knowledge of God, he would not have fallen. For the being of God is so pleasing that he who truly knows it in the light of glory is unable to turn away from God. Yet God grants this only to the person who will live for ever with Him. He who falls into sin has never known God in this light, and therefore Christ said of St. John: "So I will have him to remain,"[9] and of Mary: "She has chosen the best part, which shall not be taken away from her."[10] He to whom the best part is given possesses it for ever, since it is not an accidental but an essential gift that dwells eternally with man.

Next, the contemplative life brings to one a never ceasing entrance into divine truth and an essential increase in divine love. Now the very being of God is beyond comprehension and no creature can fully comprehend it. He who has been drawn into it eternally sinks, never reaching a ground or sounding; the spirit lives in God as the fish in the sea and the bird in the air. Seventhly, new mysteries, ecstasies, joys and truths are always being discovered by the contemplative, for only God fully satisfies his spirit. The more he contemplates God the more he desires Him, and the more he gazes at God with the eye of his intellect the purer he becomes and the more clearly he knows God.

Lastly, if the spirit is lifted above all things in essential truth, all unlikeness leaves her. The spirit is placed in a likeness and in this she enters into God in such a way that she realizes nothing except God since she is embraced by God. She loses her very name, so that she is called God rather than spirit. Not that she is God, but only godly; hence she is called God more than she is called spirit.

David wrote: "I have said, ye are gods and sons of the Highest."[11] He says *gods*, not *God*, by which he implies that we are not God by nature, but only godly through grace. Through God's speaking we are sons of the Most High, for as the Father looks to His nature so He begets the Son by nature.

It is similar when God utters His Word in the soul. Thus we are gods and sons of God. He who prepares himself for this birth, which God the Father begets in the soul, is for the most part God's son through grace.

4

THE POOR SPIRIT IS A TRUE CONTEMPLATIVE

Since spiritual poverty, then, is a preparation for a contemplative life, do all men who adopt a truly spiritual, poor life have it? Yes, for he who has rightly and closely followed spiritual poverty is a true contemplative man. Spiritual poverty is simply a lack of all that is not God; if one is liberated from all this, and if all means have vanished, then he has God's Presence. In this Presence one contemplates God. God is then present in all things; when all external roughness and artifice are removed, only God in His nakedness is found. Hence spiritual poverty and contemplation stand on the same level.

But not all those who take up a poor life are poor spirits, and hence not contemplatives, as Christ says: "Not everyone that saith, Lord, Lord, shall enter into the kingdom of heaven, but he that doth the will of My Father who is in heaven."[12] It is the same with each man. Not everyone who says, I am a poor spirit, or who appears to be poor, is a poor spirit. Only he who performs the real actions of a spiritually poor man is poor in spirit. And he is also a contemplative man.

Some, of course, say that spiritual poverty and contemplation have no actions since they both imply an emptying of all actions through a pure dying in God. That is true. But in the beginning and progress of a spiritual, poor and contemplative life, one must have actions which prepare a man and which liberate him so that he can realize true spiritual poverty. And he who undertakes the right action arrives at a life truly poor in spirit.

On the other hand, he who undertakes the wrong action—

and this frequently happens—never arrives at true spiritual poverty nor at true contemplation. For example, if a man on a journey, wishing to reach his destination, takes the wrong road, he goes astray and does not arrive at his goal. It is here the same; many who have the intention of arriving at a perfect life of spiritual poverty take the wrong way. They go astray and never arrive at the real goal of a poor, contemplative life, in which man attains to the highest level of perfection.

PART IV

---

*How to Live
a Contemplative Life*

CHAPTER I

THE FIRST WAY: DETACHMENT

****

WHICH are the right paths that lead to a spiritual, poor life? Generally speaking there are four paths which men may pursue in a poor and perfect contemplative life. And the first is that one should have a perfect will to detach oneself from all that is contrary to God—in other words, all of which God is not the direct cause, all that is not God Himself.

1

PUTTING ON VIRTUE

To begin with, detachment implies a forgoing of sin, and then the causes of sin, such as excess temporal goods, intimacy with women, and so forth. It also implies a removal of all that enters as a hindrance between God and man, such as spiritual images and forms by which one can no longer realize God. A man must gain victory over all things with a perfect will, he must willingly practise virtues that pertain to him until he gains the summit of virtue so that none escape him until he has acquired all. He who neglects one virtue wanders from the path of a poor, contemplative life.

Spiritual poverty consists in a detachment from all obstacles and an attachment to all virtues. And this contemplative life is nothing else than an active life. He who lacks virtue also lacks spiritual poverty; he who lacks an active life in detachment and in virtue, also lacks a contemplative life. For only when a man has arrived at the highest point of an active life does a contemplative life really begin. And no one contemplates the divine light except the man who acquires virtue with all his faculties. Then this power may detach him from and raise him out of himself and the darkness of created things, into the divine clarity in which he will realize the purity of the divine Being. He who lacks this power must wait here below. For nothing can operate beyond its capacity.

2

THE JOY OF A VIRTUOUS MAN

Since man is by nature feeble, he cannot by himself rise above himself. This must take place through the divine power of grace which issues from virtue. It is easy for the virtuous man to go into himself and make room for God to work within him, and this working is full of joy. On the other hand, it is very difficult for the unvirtuous man to go into himself and make room for God to work in him, because he is not receptive to God's co-operation. He is still lacking the power of grace which issues from true detachment and virtue. Such men rarely observe a meal time before they turn to external things in which they take more delight than in the inward turning.

The meal time for a truly virtuous man always seems too long and he always wants to go without eating so that he may attend to his heart, which is more pleasant to him than all eating and drinking or all outward pleasures. His joy is wholly within, not without. This is how it is when a man is dead to himself, when only God dwells in him. For where God is, there is joy and ecstasy without affliction.

People frequently imagine that a virtuous man has much distress—not realizing that all is well with him. For every virtue and good action fosters a particular joy, and he who has the most virtue has the most joy. What, then, does our Lord mean when He says: "Blessed are they that weep and mourn, for they shall be comforted?"[1] But observe here that the joy of virtuous people does not spring from creatures. It springs from God. Since they always possess a divine joy, to that degree is creaturely joy bitter to them, and our Lord means that they are happy to whom the creaturely is bitter and to whom only God is sweet. As St. Gregory says: " If you taste the divine spirit, all bodily things become bitter to you."[2]

He who advances on the path of virtue surely arrives at the goal of a perfect contemplation. Every virtue prompts him forward and aids him in his advance, since he cannot go there by himself alone. And when he gains all virtue, he is brought forward to the highest degree of perfection.

CHAPTER II

THE SECOND WAY:
THROUGH CHRIST TO THE GODHEAD

※※※※※※※※※※※※※※※※※※※※※※※※※

ANOTHER path to spiritual poverty, in which man contemplates God's wonderful riches, is by walking in the footsteps of Christ and following Him in every possible way. By this path one receives all the divine light and all the light of grace necessary to lead one on to a perfect, contemplative life. As Christ says: "Who wisheth to come to the Father must enter through Me."[1] In other words, one should enter through His humanity and into the Godhead. And this may take place in two ways.

1

THE OUTER FOLLOWING OF CHRIST

One may clothe himself with the outer image of our Lord. In this he is shielded from all sins. For Christ's image is a new bringing forth of man in all the ways from which he had fallen and from which he might fall. Our Lord did not take sin upon Himself, but only that which uproots and atones for sin. And this was accomplished by suffering and adversity through which He brought us back to an innocent life. This, however, does not aid us unless we clothe ourselves in the same garment, unless we forgo sin and surrender ourselves to the sufferings of our Lord. Thus are we brought back to an innocent life.

Were I not willing to endure things as our Lord endured

them, I would not be greatly benefited. But were I to suffer through Him, as He suffered through me, His suffering would make mine fruitful and would lead me to eternal life. This is why Christ said to His disciples: "If they drink My cup they will come to everlasting life."[2]

Thus the suffering of our Lord helps us on to where we cannot bring ourselves and this is because all of us have a tendency to fall. If one is to be elevated it must be according to our Lord's image, and he who turns away from this image lets himself fall. No one can stand by his own strength but only by the power that springs from our Lord's work. He, then, who wants to have this power should seek it in the likeness of the image and the actions of our Lord. As St. Peter says: "Christ has suffered through us and left us an example, that we may follow His footsteps."[3] In the person who adopts the image and actions of our Lord there will grow up the fruits of His works and these will separate him from all unlikeness by fostering in him a purely poor life in which he will realize God.

In this way Christ is known by the fruitfulness of His works. The fruits which are in the works of our Lord will spring forth in man and reveal to him that Christ is God and man. As St. Paul says: "I know Christ and Him crucified."[4] This means that he knew the fruit of the cross in himself, and to him from whom the fruit of the cross and the works of our Lord are concealed, Christ is unknown. Every tree is known by its fruit. Christ, too, is known by the fruit of His works when a man adopts the works of our Lord. Christ cannot be really known in any other way. The true men of Christ are those who believe perfectly in Him, and no one can separate them from Christ, for the fountain of grace has overflowed in them so that they can flow only into Christ.

When it is said that a man comes to the knowledge of faith, this is simply the fruit of faith bursting up in him through grace and revealing to him in a clear manner that Christ is both God and man. On this St. Paul says: "I know Christ only." This was because Christ revealed Himself to him in the fruitfulness of His works, and killed all that was not God so that only Christ remained known to him.

Now we attain to such a knowledge by following His image and actions. The more one follows Christ the more one becomes like Him, and the more one is like Him the more one knows Him. Everything is known by its like and he who is most godlike most knows God. God is a pure Being, and he who would know God must become pure and stripped of all unlikeness. This purity and nakedness comes from the image of our Lord and he who most adapts himself to this image is the purest and best knows God. In this way a man is prepared in the image of our Lord for a spiritually poor life in which he contemplates God in all His clarity.

2

THE INNER FOLLOWING OF CHRIST

A person may also enter through the humanity of Christ into the Godhead when he has clothed his outer self with Christ's garment in such a way that he now occupies his inner self with a continual contemplation of the actions and the Passion of Christ. By an outward practising of the image of Christ and by an inner dwelling on His Passion, one becomes so inflamed with the fire of divine love that all unlikeness to truth is readily consumed in him. Truth then appears to him in all its nakedness and he contemplates it in its utmost purity.

Through Adam's fall all in man has wandered away; the senses have wandered, the faculties of the soul have wandered, and none of them is obedient to another. And if all this is to be corrected so that one faculty may be obedient to another, as they were when Adam stood in his first innocence, it must pass through Christ. Just as Adam was a cause of falling and of mortality, Christ is the cause of resurrection and life. St. Paul says: "As in Adam all die, so also in Christ all shall be made alive."[5] All that is in man must be made pure, and this takes place in Christ. Therefore each must do the best that he can and convert himself so as to render himself capable of receiving.

Now if the senses of man are to be made pure they must be directed to the outer man of Christ. They must be formed and guided after Him, for in this way they will also be purified and reordered in the inner man. Without the image of Christ the senses never die to sensuality so that the inner man may become unobstructed by them. If a man is to be called free from sensuality it should take place through Christ's image. The more he turns his senses and governs them according to that image, the more they will die within him. This is why the external senses should be directed towards Christ so that they may be restored to the condition of their first order.

Just as the external senses are purified and ordered according to their first nobility in Christ's image, so also should the internal faculties of the soul be purified and ordered by an earnest dwelling upon Christ's actions and Passion. He who fails to do this will never properly be ordered in the inner man. He will remain in disorder according to Adam's fall. Nor will his reason become enlightened with divine light.

Christ is the true Light which enlightens all the faculties of the soul. As He says: " I am the Light of the world."[6] Hence, he who desires this light of truth must place his reason in Christ, for he who becomes enlightened elsewhere has more a false than a true light. On this Christ says: " Beware of false prophets, who show themselves good, but inwardly are ravening wolves."[7] The false prophets are the lights that are not radiated from Christ and His teachings, His actions and Passion. They appear very good, but inwardly and secretly they are false. We should guard against them and turn to the true light which is Christ.

Let no one be guided by a light unless it is similar to Christ, and let those who want to travel the road of an undeceived life turn their reason away from things towards Christ's action and Passion. Let them sink themselves in it, for then they will be born again as a newly born child craves milk to drink; then will the eye of reason be anointed with the oil of divine grace in which, pure and clear, it will apprehend the naked truth and in which false light can no longer deceive it. Reason immersed in anything other than Christ's Passion is not anointed with the oil of divine grace. It remains dark and cannot perceive divine truth. That is why many are fooled by many false lights, accepting the false to be true, and the true to be false. This is simply because by themselves all men err and are blind. If they are to see they should leave darkness and turn to the light which is Christ. Then the eye of reason will be enlightened by divine truth.

Man's reason is naturally dark and like the night. When the sun sets, night falls; when it rises, day breaks. And when the divine sun rises in the reason, it becomes clear as day; when this sun fades it becomes dark. Now the light fades away when the reason turns to creatures and forsakes Christ. It is rightly said that the pagans attained to a great natural light. But I believe that all their light was night compared to day, when confronted with the light which the genuine Christian receives when he focuses his reason on Christ. All unlikeness of light dies in him; he becomes all light. But with the pagans all unlikeness did not die, and that is because they did not have the pure light. And it is still the same with those who have been greatly taught by nature but who have not been born from the Passion of Christ, and the wonderful distinctions that the latter comprehend are derived from Christ's action.

It is true that natural men detect truth from images and forms which they draw from their reason, but godlike men who are united with Christ in His Passion keep the truth in silence. The truth they hold is elevated above all images and forms in a pure experience of the divine good of which no one can speak. Yes, they are silent, and that is why they are often considered devoid of reason.

And this is as it should be, for they do not give it to be understood what they know; they cannot express it with words. Were they to speak of what they inwardly see they would have to lie rather than speak the truth. They remain silent in order to refrain from saying something false. St. Dionysius says:

"All that you can speak of God is rather untrue than true, for God is inexplicable."[8] It is quite the same with the reason which is purified by the Passion of Christ and enlightened by the divine light.

Regardless of what one may say of the divine good it is always something other. St. Paul says that it is not lawful to speak of it. These men are recognized by their silence. Many give evidence by their talking that they are nothing, whereas others give evidence by their silence what they truly are. He who talks much proves that the simple divine truth has never been perfectly discovered in him. But he in whom it has been discovered is not interested in external words except when they are necessary for his neighbours, and this he must allow. Unless it is necessary, he does not speak. He is intimate with no one, rather he retains a continual contemplation of the good that he has discovered in himself. In other things he finds no rest since they always drive him back to this good.

People accuse this man of lacking charity, but this is because he busies himself only with that single divine good which renders all that is manifold uninteresting to him. Always would he cheerfully be alone, and that no one may hinder him he passes over many accidental charitable works. But all that he omits in external charitable works he performs immediately in God. Indeed, such an action is a thousand times more noble than any accidental work since it is an essential action. The other is accidental and hence not as noble.

He who performs all acts in immediate love is truly abounding in good works for he performs all works in one. All are essential to him and they also bring an essential reward. These men are often criticized. People say that they are inactive and that they will not perform any good works. They are also accused of passing over the commandments of Holy Church; but if they are perfectly detached from all that is external, they perform all the commandments of Holy Church in God.[9] Because external men cannot understand this they always criticize them.

But this is to be expected, for these critics are blind. Nevertheless, it is foolish for a blind man to want to lead men who see. Such men require no leader. They have the right opinion and they cannot go behind another, for they have the true light, which comes from the Passion of Christ and which does not let them fall under any false light. Christ's Passion destroys all falsehood in the reason and enlightens it with truth. And this is how the reason attains to its first nobility—through the contemplation of Christ's actions and Passion.

3

THE INESTIMABLE TREASURE

The human will is also completed in Christ and in His actions and Passion. Without Christ all men wander away; with a blind will they wander towards a false good and pay no attention to the true good. This is also to be expected, for temporal things are in themselves blinding, and all who choose them are so blinded that they miss the true good which is hidden in the Passion of our Lord. Should man turn his will to Christ and His Passion, then Christ will come to meet him with every true good and bless him with gifts so wonderful that they far surpass all the gifts of creatures.

When the will accepts these gifts of grace it forgoes all earthly gifts and clings to Christ so that it may receive from Him alone. Christ says: "The kingdom of heaven is like unto a treasure hidden in a field; if man findeth the treasure he hideth it, and from joy he runneth away, selleth all that he hath and buyeth the field and also the treasure in the field."[10] This is the most holy fruit of our Lord's Passion. If man gives his entire will to it and there seeks, he discovers a treasure beyond words, for from every wound special gifts issue, and these streams of grace which flow in the richest measure are six thousand six hundred and sixty-six.[11]

When a man enters this field where these living streams burst forth, he opens his mouth and drinks, drinks so much that he is intoxicated with joy. He can no longer control himself under this overwhelming rapture. He runs off and sells all that he possesses, all that is not of God. He abandons all and buys the field in which the streams of grace burst forth. More and more he seeks for the original source of these springs until at last he finds it hidden in the heart of God. And there he drinks the secret wisdom of God which no one knows except the person who has received it.

This divine fatherly wisdom flows continually through the Passion of our Lord into panting, thirsting hearts which are burned up by the divine fire of love. This fire so dries and burns them that they are seized with an excessive thirst, and in this thirst they run with a flaming desire to the streams and to the wounds of our Lord from which all grace flows. To these they hold their mouths and drink. Oh, what a lovely drink they have! The Giver as well as the drink are priceless, for Giver and drink are one! It is He who gives, and He, too, is what He gives. Oh, if all men only knew what a treasure is hidden in this field they would certainly seek it. So much would they discover that they would crave nothing more in time, for this field is full of riches.

That we are weak in grace is a sign that we have not yet come rightly to this field. He who rightly comes to it and digs will not go away empty. Oh, how foolish so many are for not seeking this inestimable treasure! If one could find a penny he would seek for it, yet here he leaves this wealth— Christ and His Passion, upon which blessedness depends— untouched. For he who seeks blessedness outside the Passion of Christ loses far more than he seeks. The wounds of our Lord are the streams from which blessedness flows. Let the man who seeks blessedness seek it in the Passion. There he will certainly find it, not elsewhere.

I can find nothing better for man to turn to than the Passion of our Lord. What he is there advised to do he should do, for thus will he most assuredly gain entrance into God. He who would know of the noble fruit that grows in this field would cultivate it day and night and never leave it. He would put a fence around it, build a tower on it and live there and also make a wine-press. The fence would be his senses, which he would guard against all luxury and which he would turn to the Passion of Christ. The tower would be his spirit, rising above all created things and where he would dwell in the un-created Godhead. And the wine-press would be his heart where the delicious new wine would continually flow so that he would be quite intoxicated with it. In the field of the Passion of Christ grow corn and grapes so that he may have food and drink at the same time.

They who enter this field and eat and drink here are full of divine graces. As the prophet says: "Eat the grist and drink the new wine, and be ye drunken, ye most beloved."[12] Oh, what a noble food they eat, what a good wine they drink! It is indeed a wonder that they are not satisfied with this feast and that they are not inebriated from the overflowing sweetness of this wine. Neither hail nor frost can damage this fruit and wine which is harvested in winter as well as in summer. One can always gather the fruit and press the wine. It is always harvest and vintage time. He who desires this wealth, only let him build a large silo and a spacious cellar and store them full. For the more they can hold the larger is the supply of fruit and wine.

Yes, if all men's desires were turned to the gathering of this fruit and wine, think how many wealthy people there would then be on earth! When a person's will seizes these riches it sinks itself in them, eats and drinks and is content, seeking nothing more from creatures but everything from God. God abundantly blesses him with all gifts. And with these gifts He overpowers the will and renders it submissive to His own. He liberates man so that he is free from all attachment to creatures, and so that he clings only to God. The fire of the love of God is enkindled in him and it makes him loving and entirely swept away in love—a love that is God's by nature but now his by grace.

Thus he attains to the condition of his first innocence where the will is no longer his will; it even loses its name and is now called God's will. It is really for this that the man's will was created, and this is brought about by the noble fruit of the Passion of Christ. It delivers him from all creaturely entanglements and floods him with a godlike sweetness. It overpowers him, kills all otherness and integrates him. In his simplicity he is elevated to where he may realize divine wonders, and on through these wonders he is led to where he beholds the wonder of wonders—God. He is now absorbed in God's wonder; all other wonders leave him. And when he discovers that he can never come to the end of this wonder, he falls silent and abandons all to God, for all that God then does is realized to be good.

Thus the will reaches its highest penetration and God gives this poor spirit such an incalculable wealth of divine goodness that he is completely overpowered and can do nothing else but good. This is obtained in the Passion of Christ in which bitterness becomes sweet, and all the worldly sweetness becomes bitter. Only here is true goodness revealed, which is God, and this goodness empowers one to will only what God wills.

4

THE WORK OF A PERFECT WILL

How shall one know that his will is overpowered by God? Well, there are six signs: First, if a person does not indulge in any sinful action but always resists it. Man's will cannot of itself do this, as he who lives according to his own will can never live without sin. Secondly, if a person prepares himself for virtue and practises each virtue as God requests it of him. Man cannot of himself do this, as Christ says: "Without Me you can do nothing."[13]

Thirdly, if he does not escape all the deaths that come to him, but endures them gladly through God. No one can do this except through God, as St. Paul says: "I can do all things in Him who strengtheneth me."[14] Fourthly, if a person puts aside all that mediates between himself and God, whether it be a bodily or spiritual mediator. And God Himself must accomplish this in man and remove all media from him, and this is the highest work that God can perform in man through grace.

Fifthly, if his object in all his actions is only God's glory—that is, if he always chooses the best for the greatest glory of God. For the light of glory has burst forth in man when he realizes that the only desire in him is that God's glory should always increase and his own decrease. There are, it is true, many who say, I wish that God's glory might be fulfilled in me and in all. This is easy to say, but it is the rarest exception when this can always be, and no one can really do this except a perfect man who stands in essential truth, unmoved by accident, whether it be weal or woe, so that he always remains at peace in every circumstance.

Sixthly, if a person standing in essential truth continually penetrates this essence to the secret, unknown will of God and wholly loses his will in it so that he becomes entirely will-less, not willing good, not willing evil, but willing no *thing*. Hence Nothing becomes the will's object. This takes place because he then knows no *thing* other than God's naked will. Thus is he delivered from all willing, permitting God alone to will. This is the highest union of the human will with God's will.

All of this is accomplished through Christ's Passion in which one raises himself and delivers himself from all that is not God. Thus by the great good that is hidden in the Passion of our Lord is he bound to God, and thus does he arrive at the highest level of perfection. What he asks of God, God grants, for he has accomplished all that God would have of him. He who desires that God should always hear him must first listen and hear what God desires to have from him. St. Gregory says: "God's hand is never empty of gifts when the ark of the heart is full of good will."

A perfect will accomplishes as much with one good action as an imperfect will with many good actions. It accomplishes as much in a single moment as another in a long time. This is because God does not consider the quantity of number, nor of magnitude, rather He considers everything according to the perfection of purity. The action which is perfect and pure is dearer to God than a thousand that are impure and imperfect.

Since only a perfect will can perform a perfect action, then a single one of these actions is worth a thousand others. This is also why the actions of a perfect will are better because a perfect will fulfils all good actions in one—not only those that it might do, but even those that all men, saints and angels do. In one action the perfect will does all that it can, and if it could do all as that one, it would gladly do it.

Yes, if the man with a perfect will could do what God does he would not neglect it. Hence, he merits essential reward in all good actions. This is because he loves them, and where love is, it merits reward and the action answers to perfect love. This is not what an imperfect will accomplishes in its imperfection, rather the action answers as if perfection had been performed.

That which is lacking in a good action must be made up by him who performs it, but he who loves has no drawback in his action, for it answers to the perfection with which he loves it. Hence, it merits reward. The perfect actions that Christ performed, and that all the saints in heaven and all the perfect men on earth accomplish, now answer to a perfect will, as these actions deserve a reward according to their perfection.

Should this man of love fall short of perfection, he suffers much. He would gladly desire to be perfect according to God's dearest will, and he would do all that he could to become perfect. What is now lacking to him God fills with His perfect acts. For God greatly loves a good will. His desire is that it should lack nothing, that it should continually embrace the best, and He will provide it with every good.

5

THE UNION OF THE HIGHEST POWER OF THE SPIRIT WITH GOD

Even the highest power of the spirit, which is called *synderesis*[15] [the integral thought power] is brought back to its first nobility by Christ's Passion. This power was originally created by God without a mediary, but through the fall of Adam it was brought under media and this must now be banished through Christ so that the spirit may be completely stripped of media. This may take place when all the faculties of man, external or internal, pass through Christ's action and teachings and accomplish all that they can. (See Addendum B, p. 287.)

Such an exercise in Christ purifies the faculties and this purity is enkindled by the fire of divine love so that each faculty directs itself towards what it was ordained—in other words, towards the highest power which attains to God without media. God then reveals Himself in the centre of the soul, draws all the faculties to Him and unites them with Himself. Hence all that is in man hurries towards God and seeks Him. God shows Himself and permits him to try on His cloak, and when the faculties taste how sweet God is, they find such a relish in this sweetness that they always follow and hurry after Him.

As a hound dashes after game as soon as it picks up the scent, so all the faculties dash after God when they track Him in the centre of the soul where God is. He lifts and embraces them and they embrace God. Each sits down to table and craves to eat, and each invites the other to eat and drink, which they do, and all are filled in common. Each permits himself to be moved by the other—what one wills the other wills, and all are in accord. As Christ says: "And I, if I be lifted up from the earth, will draw all things to Myself."[16]

Thus when this highest power of the spirit unites itself with Christ, it is drawn up with Christ, drawing all things with it. Each thing comes to the first origin from which it came. When the highest faculty of the spirit establishes itself on the most perfect level for which the spirit was created, all the lower faculties of the will and intellect are obliged to stand on the highest perfection for which they were ordained. For when anything fails in the highest, it must also fail in the lowest.

This is how it is known if a man is right or wrong. If the inner man is well-directed towards that which is best, the outer man must also be well-directed. For all that the spirit receives from God it gives to the lower faculties and just as God orders it, it orders them. Hence, the inner man is known by the outer man, for if the spirit is inwardly formed according to Christ by grace, then the outer man is determined by this. Christ says: "Even as the Father hath sent Me, so send I also you, that you may go and bring forth fruit."[17] A disciple of Christ can be known by his likeness to Christ.

Now nothing makes us more like Christ than the consideration of Christ's actions and Passion. For Christ worked and suffered to eliminate all unlikeness in us. We should, then, form ourselves according to His actions and Passion if we really want to lose our unlikeness. For as truly as Christ has redeemed us in no other way than in His life, working and suffering, so doubtful is it that one can be blessed and made perfect unless he accept His teachings, actions and Passion. He who is most preoccupied with this is happiest and most like Christ.

The actions and Passion of Christ are full of blessedness and hence our mind should feed on them. As the bee flies to the flower and sucks sweetness from it in order to make honey, so also ought we to fly to the wounds of our Lord and be refreshed, for then we shall overflow with divine sweetness. In this way only do men gather this priceless honey; all that belongs to man will so overflow with divine goodness that he will want nothing else. The bee which flies to the most distant flowers in the field brings home the most honey, and what comes from it is all honey. The man who flies the most towards the wounds of Christ, the loveliest flowers of the field, accumulates the most honey. His soul is full of divine glory and what issues from him is simply the glory of God which is for ever revealed to him.

As Christ has established for all time the glory of His Father, so these men establish the glory of God. The wounds of our Lord overflow with grace, and he who drinks of them always drinks internal graces, and they overflow into all his actions and into all that he sanctions, and renders all to God's glory.

God protects him from whatever is contrary to His own glory. As a master permits nothing to cross his servant that would be contrary to his own honour, even out of love for this faithful servant, so also God permits nothing in His servant that would be unworthy of Himself and the servant. God does this out of special love for those who cling to His dear Son, to those who embrace His Passion and diligently consider it.

The man who clings to Christ and considers His Passion is as little unable to leave God as the Son is able to leave the Father. When a man turns to the Passion of our Lord, God opens the fountain of His grace, floods the man's mind with it and overpowers him so that he can do nothing outside grace. That which now flows from God is love and grace. Oh, spread your wings and fly away to the field where the flowers bloom —as Solomon said: "I am the flower of the fields"[18]—and suck the sweetness of the flowers and gather honey! So great an abundance of honey shall you receive that you will be able to share it with everyone!

Why do people think that God permits sinners to live, rather than slay them? Because good men who hold their mouth to the wounds of our Lord and consume all its grace, go to God and pray for these sinners. As grace compels one to pray, so one compels God to listen. Christ said to Zaccheus: "This day must I abide in thy house."[19] Just as God's grace compels men to do what God wills, they compel God to do what they beg. Under the old covenant the overflow of divine grace was not so perfect and God slew sinners instantly. But now the overflow of divine grace is perfect; it floods every pure heart, compelling it in genuine love to cling to God, and thus is God also compelled by them.

6

THESE MEN ARE UNKNOWN

How wise one would be who knew these men and was close to them! If they requested God should do anything, He would do it wisely, for what they ask of God He grants. But they are really known to no one save those who are like them. Their treasure, which they carry within, is hidden as gold in the earth. The heart overweighed with temporal things cannot know these men.

They also cannot be known because what they have they carry in the innermost depths of their soul and the man who is attentive to external things cannot observe them. They are unknown because their treasure is lifted above all images and forms and they cannot be recognized by one who conceives truth through images. What they have they received from Christ's Passion and he who does not understand this does not understand these men. They cannot be known because they have received all that they possess in a pure state of rest. But the impure and disquieted know them not. They are unknown because there is nothing singular about them, and those who persistently strive after notorious and singular things know nothing of these men. The best men are usually the most ignored, the least loved, because people do not love what they do not understand.

They are not known because their property is beyond all words. Those whose love of things is measured according to words are frequently deceived. Hence it is the highest wisdom to know holy men. True wisdom is not studied in Paris but in the Passion of our Lord, and he who converts his reason to this learns all divine wisdom.

But no one is hidden from these men. They see all; for as Christ has communion with all things, these men, when in communion with Christ, also learn all things. Christ is the measure of all men, and the man who knows the measure knows all men. He is full of grace and truth; to the man who receives the grace that is in Christ all mediation disappears and all things become immediately known to him.

The reason we do not know all in truth is because we still have mediation. Were we free from this we would certainly know the pure truth. Its purity we receive in Christ and His Passion, which is like a grindstone, and to the man who grinds his mind to it all rust falls away. The Passion eliminates all from the mind so that one comprehends purely and no more unlikeness remains. Thus the spirit becomes a vessel of God; God can now work in her without obstruction.

Now God works in the soul without obstruction when her highest power looks deep into her and drives out all that is harmful. What does not belong to this house is not allowed in; all is shut out so that no storm may cause damage. God now rests in it and invites His guests, namely, all the faculties of the soul. He leads them into the house, to the very centre of the soul. They must all be there and then He gives to each his special dish. Each receives his own and takes what is his due, as Christ says: "Pay them their hire, beginning from the last even to the first."[20] The last is the highest power and the essence of the soul; this is the last in the divine service but the first to be rewarded. The lower faculties must begin in God's service and each must do what he is capable of.

Thus the lowest faculties are gradually brought to the highest, but the highest is brought to the soul's essence where God lives. He first produces His Son in the essence of the soul since this alone is capable of supernatural birth. And all the other faculties receive their special gifts through this birth. God grants light to the reason, love to the will, strength to the memory. The lowest faculties also receive their reward: from the sight God eliminates all that is contrary to Himself; He draws the hearing to Himself; He turns the feelings away from bodily luxury; He withholds from taste all that is unwholesome; He directs the smell to Himself, and so each receives his own.

But these lower faculties clamour because they are not endowed first, and this disturbance occurs when a man begins to turn to God. Man wants to know all truth at once, to have immediately perfect love and deliverance from all that is contrary to God. And when he does not find this at once, he becomes angry with God. Yet he cannot embrace all until he attains to the point where the Father begets His Son in the soul. Then every perfect gift is granted him by the Father of Light in whom there is no shadow or change. God always draws the weakest to Himself, and yet He first blesses the best. For if He were first to endow the lower faculties, they would be too weak and could not retain the gifts. And these gifts lead the spirit to the highest degree of perfection, in which she sees truth in all its purity, and which is God Himself.

Now all this is accomplished by the fruitfulness of the actions and Passion of Christ. The spirit overcomes all things with it, receives true peace and enjoys God without media. She is then established in wisdom and freedom, and what she wills takes place, what she commands is obeyed, what she asks is received. Why? Because the spirit and God are one, and what God wills she wills, what God orders she orders, and hence all things must take place as she wishes, and all things must be obedient to her. This is the second way by which one may attain to a poor, contemplative life.

CHAPTER III

THE THIRD WAY:
THE ACCEPTANCE OF SUFFERING

****

THE third path to a spiritually poor life in which one inwardly contemplates God is abandonment of self and the acceptance of all that kills one spiritually. This implies being so spiritually dead that one is often spurned, judged and condemned by creatures. If a man really wants to die to his nature he should not try to escape this. For he who does goes astray from the path of the poor in spirit and from a pure life.

1

WHEN DESPISED BY OTHERS

One wanders astray from the path of the poor in spirit because one has through sins fallen into despising God, and this must be uprooted by a similar treatment of oneself on the part of creatures. He who is most despised in his repentance of sins will most certainly be forgiven. In that man seeks the admiration of creatures he departs from divine love, for creaturely love and divine love cannot subsist together.

He who is naturally despised is spiritually loved by God. No really poor spirit is ever loved by creatures in a natural way, nor does he love anyone by nature. He always dies to the creaturely in him and in others, and hence no one finds anything to love in him by nature. It is proper that natural men who centre their lives on their bodily nature should despise

him. Like loves its like, and hence he who desires never to
be loved unrightly should be sure to die to his nature in himself and in others. That which is then loved in him is God.
It is a sign, then, that he who is loved by natural men is not
yet wholly dead to his natural leanings.

Natural men love the luxury of nature and when they do
not find it they do not love. It is a good sign if a man rejoices
when he is despised, for no sinner can feel this. One should
abandon all likeness with mere natural love, and his aim should
be that he may only be loved through divine love.

No one loves another unless he finds in him some likeness
to himself, both by nature and by grace. When the likeness
of nature has disappeared, only the likeness of grace remains.
Hence, he who dies to all natural likeness has his efflux in
divine love and his influx also in divine love. Sometimes men
not dead to themselves frequently fancy that their natural
love is a love of grace, and when they are warned of this they
are disturbed and angry. This in itself should tell them that
their love is natural. Genuine divine love is everlastingly
patient, it endures all, accepts all and allows itself to be despised. But it hates no one and it renders all things for the
best. On the other hand, men not dead to themselves are
always disturbed in contradiction and distracted from their
peace.

2

WHEN JUDGED BY OTHERS

One should also suffer all judgements that fall upon one,
for this too prepares one for a spiritually poor life. If a man
is to be delivered from all the judgements which he has
deserved, he must be judged, and by patiently suffering the
judgement, God's judgement is removed. For those who
belong to God it is necessary that they should be prepared
by many judgements. Christ says: " It is necessary that
scandal should come, but woe to him through whom it
cometh."[1]

It is necessary, in other words, that virtue should be guarded by contradiction and judgement. He who is not judged shows that he has never exercised real virtue, for the highest virtue that man can perform is subject to the attacks of criticism. To flee from criticism is to flee from virtue. In truth, the person who desires to live most perfectly must be judged by humanity since humanity is not established in the same closeness to perfection. Every man praises his own and what is unlike his own does not receive his praise. Instead, he tends to judge all that is not like him.

Let no one neglect a virtue because it brings forth criticism. Let him not say, I will spare my fellow-creature and not be a stumbling-block to him. Let him not say, I will leave virtue for God's sake. I say that a virtue is never a stumbling-block to anyone, rather it is a cause of placing them upright and guarding them from falls. He who falls through virtue is like a man who dies from a physician's medicine. A man who does not improve himself by good actions can never improve himself by bad actions. The very neglect to perform a good action is in itself wrong. No one is improved by the omission of pure virtue.

He who neglects a virtue because of the criticism involved fears more the bodily harm to himself than the spiritual harm of others. Genuine virtue never causes harm; it is always useful. The man who omits virtue out of fear shows that he never obtained true virtue, which springs from divine love, for "in divine love there is not fear",[2] as St. John says.

The man who is dead to creatures exercises virtue even if the pains of hell were to fall on him. Neither out of fear of hell nor for the reward of heaven does he perform virtue, but only out of a pure love of God. Gladly would he suffer all that falls on him, for it is the greatest joy for him to suffer in this way, as the twelve disciples rejoiced that they were to suffer through Christ. No, he who has divine love omits no virtue; he suffers all others to judge him as much as they will. He looks only at what pleases God rather than at what pleases people.

When a man still keeps an eye on other people and on what pleases them, his eye is not clear. Hence, his actions are not pure, for the creature blinds whereas God gives sight. He who wants to see perfectly must turn his eye away from all creatures and to God alone. Then all his actions will be pure virtue, and whatever happens to him will be for the best. No one should be guilty of leaving his best and following the best of others, for when a man follows his best perfectly, he does what is best for all perfectly. As Christ says: "I, if I be lifted up from the earth, will draw all things to Myself."[3]

He who is elevated with Christ above all things earthly draws all things with Him to where Christ is, and this is the best for all men. It is a man's own fault if he does not take his best into Christ, as one is then unworthy of Christ. But no one should neglect virtue for any unworthy object, and if he were to do so he would fall into unworthiness. God's glory does not lie in my omission of virtue for the sake of my fellow-creature, rather it lies in my fulfilment of all virtue, and I should suffer whatever judgement may fall on me— that is the glory of God. For these judgements make me a powerful judge at the Last Day, a judge over all who now judge me. As Christ says: "Judge not, that you may not be judged."[4]

Now he who judges another here in good actions, gives him power to judge himself. As St. Paul says: "He who judges his brother heaps judgement on himself."[5] Let no one be afraid because he is judged, for all his weaknesses are thus removed and he thus becomes sorry for his defects.

3

THE PRECEPTS OF LOVE

Can a virtuous man in any way give occasion for the falling of his neighbour? Where genuine virtue is perfectly accomplished by divine love there is no cause of falling. And whatever judgement it receives is simply a revelation of truth and justice. But the good action that springs from fear or mere natural causes, natural likeness or an unprepared ground, is impure. And the greater the impurity the greater the cause of falling to fellow-creatures.

He who overthrows his neighbour with such actions is guilty of his fall, and such good actions must often be omitted for the sake of helping one's fellow-creatures. This is because these good actions are altered into bad actions through an improper attention, so that they are no longer good but bad and hence must be omitted. Good actions that spring from divine love are entirely pure, nor are they a cause of our neighbour's falling. Hence they should not be omitted.

Could not, however, an evil action spring from love so that, though the intention is towards God, yet the work is evil? I reply that all right actions of love are good, not evil. St. Paul says that "charity works no evil".[6] But there are many who fancy that they act out of love when it is not love, and hence their actions are frequently wrong.

Divine love is ordered according to a necessary aim, and when a man performs acts of love without order or necessity, love loses its name and a loveless action takes place. Such actions merit no reward, as St. Paul says: "If I lack charity, I am nothing."[7] Therefore, it is very necessary that men should know how they should perform acts of love and how they should drop actions which lack charity. Few men can be found who know the art of performing acts of love perfectly.

Now a true love-act has four kinds of precepts: The first is the law of Holy Church; the second is the natural law, and these two precepts meet in one law and their law is a measure which applies to outer actions, and he who does not use this measure in his acts of love spoils them. Now this measure is a *mean* between little and much and he who always hits the mean in his love-acts has them well-ordered according to divine love.

It is not a love-act to give to a man who does not need

it and the giver does not exercise himself according to the
mean, which is here necessity. Necessity is the object of gifts
and their mean. Hence it is not a virtue for a rich man to
give to another rich man. It is like giving food to a man
who is full, or drink to a drunken man. Give to me and I
will give to you—there is hardly any virtue in this. God gives
no reward for this since it is not an act of love. Nor is it a
rightly ordered act of love when a man fasts beyond the power
of nature so that his nature is harmed by it. Nor when a man
should eat beyond his need.

A mean should be kept in all things and he who observes
this mean in all his actions keeps the commandments of Holy
Church as well as of nature. As William says: "The best thing
that a man can do is to keep order in nature and spirit."[8]
All things have an order and he who removes the order from
things also removes their being. He who breaks the right
order in his love-acts transgresses divine love and his actions
are more evil than good. As Christ says: "None is good but
God alone."[9] Therefore nothing is good unless it is done in
God, and nothing is done in God unless it is in accordance
with order.

The third precept according to which a love-act should be
performed is that of the Holy Gospel, and the fourth precept
is divine. Now these two precepts have one aim—God. For
the Holy Gospel counsels external freedom from all that is
not for God, and the divine precept counsels internal freedom
from all that is not in God.

He who keeps both these precepts properly in his actions
always acts without mediation—for God and in God. This
is because a perfect man who lives according to the Gospel and
according to the divine order is stripped of all creatures,
inwardly and outwardly. God is his object without mediation.
All mediations are removed and hence all his actions are
without mediation for they are performed outside and above
all creatures in God. As Christ says: "Whoso leaveth not all
cannot be My disciple."[10] He says "all" and not to leave
only part and keep part, as this aims at natural means. He

says we should abandon all excesses and retain none, and this aims at God without mediation.

A man is a true disciple of God if he goes only to the divine school in which he learns all truth, and if God, who instructs him how to perform all actions according to divine order, is his only teacher. Christ says: "Whoso doth not leave father and mother and sister, and all other things is not worthy of Me."[11] In fact, he whose selfhood clings to a thing which is not in God, regardless of how small it is, renders himself unworthy of God. Worth subsists in likeness and he who clings to his selfhood is unlike God.

4

RECEIVING THE BLESSED SACRAMENT

The holy Sacrament of our Lord is God and man. The person who wants to receive Christ here worthily should as far as possible become like Him. As His humanity is pure so must the person who receives Him externally be pure from all temporal things, and as God is pure, so must the spirit be emptied of all that is not purely godlike. In this way the Sacrament may be worthily received. As Christ says: "He who does not leave all, is not worthy of Me."

Only a poor spirit receives the fruit in a most perfect way since he has nothing in himself that can keep him from this fruit. He can go every day and receive his own food, and only he can do this properly. To refuse him this food would be to remove from him his fatherly inheritance which Christ has left for him through His death so that he may feed on it and satisfy his desires. He who goes to God's table otherwise than with proper intention does not go as a child of his fatherly inheritance. And he is withheld from this sinless inheritance until he has been chosen as a true child of the covenant.

Such people must hold themselves back from the Holy Sacrament until they are sufficiently prepared.[12] They should consider the judgement of others when it is not yet their proper inheritance, and because of this, they must be judged. If they go to receive they disturb the people, and they are to blame for they take what is not their own.

But the true children of the covenant, whose inheritance it is, need not go without it for the sake of anyone, unless in their own depths they do not consent to it. They should turn to their Father and wait for their inheritance. They disturb no one when they use their inheritance, for they not only use it themselves, but share it with all who desire it. They need not observe any judgement, for no one can deny their privilege. They must insist upon their inheritance and if they let it be denied to them they prove a lack of love for their Father and by that they would make themselves illegitimate children.

He who would let the Blessed Sacrament be withheld from them would be like the man whom a householder invited as guest and offered him food and drink. But the guest refused to partake, drove the host from the table and spilt the food and drink. Thus both host and guest had to fast. A wise and earnest householder would not pardon the guest and if he were to do so, he would be a fool who was void of a manly character and unworthy to eat his meal.

He, then, who knows that God feeds him with Himself, let him eat and drink without fear. Let everyone gossip and judge as they please, he does properly by himself, by God and all men. Should he neglect it because of gossip and judgements, he shows that he is no child of the covenant and that he does not properly eat his food.

Some people suggest that one ought to consider one's neighbour and omit the Sacrament for God's sake. But he who goes worthily to our Lord's table gives alms to the whole of Christendom, and to each one is given according to his worthiness. He who neglects it gives nothing and lets men go hungry. To criticize a good man for receiving the Body of Christ renders one unworthy of all of the good of the whole of Holy Christianity. The highest good of Holy Christianity is that good men receive the Body of Christ. The man who sins and makes himself unworthy in the highest, also makes himself unworthy in little things. To treat God with dishonour is also to dishonour all the saints. Because of this unworthiness of his critic, no one should neglect the Blessed Sacrament so that all men should not have to answer for it if one sins.

Should one neglect it when he ought to receive it, he will fall into the same unworthiness of the one who criticizes him. To do this is to follow the critic more than God; it is to have more likeness with him than with God. He who stands on a weak tree which is shaken by a ferocious wind must fall and, if he does not fall with the first gust of wind, he will fall with the next. But if he must fall it is better that he should fall with the first. However, there is no occasion of falling when one receives the Body of Christ. The cause of falling is only in one's own internal weakness, and if it is not revealed in this, it will be revealed in something else, for one cannot escape.

That such people should be helped is proper, for it is the greatest work to receive Christ's Body and man in his weakness cannot prepare himself for it. Hence he should be helped so that he may sooner become worthy. God permits judgements to fall on him, and these judgements purify him so that he may become worthy of receiving the Body of our Lord. To flee these judgements is the same as refusing to let oneself be prepared for it. Therefore it befits a spiritual, poor life that a man be so judged that he may be set free to commune with God immediately and exercise each virtue perfectly.

5

GOD COMES WITH LONG-SUFFERING

Now one should also endure every hardship which prompts him towards a spiritual, poor life. Through Adam's fall man is full of feeble tendencies which retard him from the best. These inrooted tendencies and man's defects must be uprooted by sufferings. He who does not conquer Adam through sufferings never attains a pure, poor spirit, and that which gives him reason to suffer helps him towards this end. God does not will that anything should be uprooted in man without sufferings. All that is false must vanish through them. Nor does He grant gifts if the ground for them is not purified by sufferings.

St. Augustine says: "No evil remains unpunished and no good unrewarded." When evil is uprooted by suffering, then all good is granted and for this reason Christ wished to suffer so that through His suffering all evil might disappear and all good be granted. He who endures the most in his sufferings, also benefits the most from the Passion of our Lord. But he who escapes this, flees from his eternal blessedness, as through nothing else does man come nearer to blessedness than through long-suffering. It purifies one as fire purifies gold. It is the same with man. He who endures most becomes the purest also. He who is the purest is closest to God. This long-suffering is the greatest gift that God grants here in time, for through it one comes closest to Him.

No man is worthy of suffering except he who endures all in the highest degree of divine love. He who does not have this is not guided by love. God permits sinners little suffering upon earth. Good men, however, must suffer much, and it is the wise and holy man who accepts suffering with more joy than if he received all the riches on earth. Temporal goods rob man of eternal happiness if he joyfully lingers in them. But they give him suffering if he suffers through love.

The fool is the man who leaves the good and chooses evil. Yet many fools are found on earth who crave and seek temporal goods while escaping from sufferings. They are, perhaps, the wisest in the eyes of the world, but the most foolish in God's eyes. Were God to grant sufferings to worldly men, He would do like one who would kill his friend and keep his enemies alive and give them what they desired. Nothing brings increased life into the soul more than the acceptance of suffering. It uproots all that causes death to the soul and, when this mortality is removed, only life remains. Thus the most severe suffering may foster the greatest joy, for joy springs from suffering.

Which kind of suffering is better—that which man brings upon himself or that which others or God inflict upon him? Just as it is infinitely better that God should bless man than that man should make himself happy, so is the suffering that others or God cause infinitely better than that which he brings upon himself. Furthermore, that suffering is best where the greatest patience is called forth. And patience is greater when one suffers at the hands of others than when it is self-caused. It is easy for a man to endure himself, but it is not so easy to endure others.

But if the suffering that is inflicted on us by others is better than that which we inflict upon ourselves, is it not better that we should not seek suffering but allow it to come to us? And if this is true, then is not the suffering of worldly people better since they do not seek it, than that of poor spirits who do seek it?

My reply is that that suffering is best which is endured in true love, and it is certainly greater love to accept suffering through love than to escape it out of fear. Worldly people, however, try to escape from sufferings whether self-caused or caused by others. Since they are much more liked than despised, no one does them much harm except themselves. On the other hand the man who is really poor in spirit lets himself face every suffering; he flees only from sin.

One's own proper suffering comes from one's own sins and he suffers quite rightly who lives in sins, and each sin fosters a special spiritual suffering. Worldly people who suffer in this way merit nothing unless they avoid sins. But should they live in sins they must endure severe sufferings. This kind of suffering is similar to the suffering in hell, for the more one suffers there the worse one becomes. This happens to sinners; the more they suffer through sin the more wicked they become and they fall more and more into sufferings in their effort to escape. The more they try to escape from external suffering, the more they are internally punished. Even if they have no external punishment, they are yet tortured internally by their sins and they complain of their great sufferings. They think they ought to merit by it because people say that suffering is good.

But this suffering is more a beginning of hellish torments than a penetration of heaven. Just as good men have a fore-taste of eternal joy, sinners have a foretaste of eternal torments. Just as eternal joy is fostered in virtue, eternal torment is fostered in sins. Hence that suffering which is patiently endured for love and truth's sake alone brings merit. It is this suffer-ing which is sought by good men, and that is why their suffering is so pleasing to God.

Nothing brings man closer to God than the acceptance of suffering. Why? Because it uproots all that is ungrateful to God and thus man stands empty of all ingratitude in his love for God. Therefore the Lord speaks through David: "I am with him in tribulation; I will deliver him and glorify him, I will give him a long life and show him my salvation."[13] "I am with him in suffering" means that one always has God present.

No, God even comes with long-suffering and cannot better come to man. Thus is he delivered from all that is not God. He clings to God alone and God enlightens him with the light of His glory and fills him with eternal blessedness—Himself. This suffering is like a wine-press in which grapes are pressed. If the grape is pressed, what is in it flows from it; if it is sweet, sweet wine flows, if sour, sour wine flows.

It is the same if man is pressed by suffering, what is in him flows from him. If he is a virtuous man, only godlike sweetness which is hidden in him comes forth. It shows itself so that he gives good, noble wine to drink to all men, and he can say, "Come all to me who thirst, you shall all be filled and satisfied with my wine."[14] This sweetness now flows into all things; he makes them good and he receives the best. He disturbs no one and no one disturbs him. If he remains quite

Q

immovable in the mind, he gains likeness with God. As Christ says: "Blessed are they that suffer persecution for justice's sake, for theirs is the kingdom of heaven; blessed are you when men hate you and persecute you; rejoice and be exceeding glad, for your reward shall be great in heaven."[15] "Blessed are they that suffer persecution for justice's sake," He says, and this is because persecution, hatred and contempt bring salvation to man, and he who does not suffer these when they come does not find happiness.

No one can bless himself. If man is to be blessed he must be open to this, and this rather than his actions blesses him. Christ says: "Rejoice in the days of adversity, for your reward is great in heaven."[16] In other words, such a reward will be given to man as he could not have merited by his actions. Let no one, then, be sad in his suffering, for it really removes all sorrow and secures peace. Good people have the most sufferings, and this wine-press causes the hidden joy to overflow. It is truly a noble life when man always rejoices and is never sad!

6

"BE YE JOYFUL!"

Now our Lord also says: "My soul is sorrowful unto death."[17] How, then, can the poor in spirit always be happy? There are two kinds of sorrow. First, a sorrow that springs from our sins; but Christ and perfect souls do not have this sorrow. The other sorrow is one of compassion, and this springs from man's love. Christ had this and also all the saints. This sorrow subsists well with divine joy, and he who most loves his fellow man and has compassion for him, has the most of divine joy. Even though the good man must feel sufferings on account of his defects, this springs from divine love, and his suffering is not like that of the sinner in whom the pains of hell are always born. Rather his suffering springs from love and fosters divine joy.

He who does not rejoice in suffering proves that it is not fruitful. St. Paul says: "Rejoice in the Lord always."[18] And again: "Be ye joyful! " Now, "Rejoice in the Lord always," means that man should remain in eternal joy in the Lord, but a joy springing from a pure conscience. He who has this joy proves that God reigns in his heart, revealing Himself in love and joy. Good souls cannot display much sadness, for God has removed it from them and has put Himself in its place. And where God is there is everlasting joy.

"Be ye joyful," means that as often as a man confronts suffering he should always have a particular joy. For this indicates that God answers him in all things and continually comes to meet him with new gifts. Every suffering endured out of love and with joy brings new gifts, and he who always rejoices in suffering shows that God is always giving to him and that no gift passes him by. New gifts bring new joys, and the joy is known by the gift. No one rejoices if you take something away from him, but only if you give to him. God gives continually to spiritual men, and so they continually rejoice.

But if spiritual people always have joy, what then is their suffering, for suffering cannot subsist with joy? Man is composed of body and soul, and each has its separate work. But when the body rejoices in temporal things and sins, then the spirit becomes sad. Such joy and sadness belong to sinners. Further, when the spirit rejoices in God, the body saddens in time, and this joy and sadness belong to spiritual people. The suffering of the body which they have in time brings them to eternal life. And the joy that they have is the fruit of suffering, and this suffering and joy subsist together, and the greater the suffering of the body, the greater the joy of the spirit. That they can rejoice in suffering proves that they belong to eternity.

No one ever had a divine joy in suffering if he belonged to hell. This is why all sinners have a perpetual sadness in their joy. The fruit of their temporal pleasure is more false and imaginary than true. Nor is their joy really true, rather it is a torment. The more external pleasure these men have the more they are inwardly tormented, and this indicates that they do not belong to God. For good fortune in time implies ill fortune in eternity.

He who tries to lift himself with temporal fortune is like the thief who is pleased when he is led across a green field. As long as he is in the green field he thinks all is well for him, but as soon as he has crossed it and they begin to hang him on the gallows, all joy disappears. It is the same with the sinner who indulges in this short span of time and is afterwards hanged on the gallows. This is as it should be, for they are thieves and steal from God what is His own. All that they have really belongs to God and they return nothing to Him, and so they are rightly judged. He who is conceited over his good fortune is conceited because he is a thief, and he has to be judged. Good fortune in time is a source of hell and ill fortune and the acceptance of suffering a source of joyous eternal life.

CHAPTER IV

HOW THE FRIEND OF GOD SUFFERS

✳✳✳✳✳✳✳✳✳✳✳✳✳✳✳✳✳✳✳✳✳✳✳✳

SINCE there are many spiritual people on earth who suffer little, must they then merit less reward? My opinion is that he who is a true friend of God is never without suffering. He always suffers. And this takes place in four different ways. He suffers in his actions, and he suffers in his will; a third suffering is in his spirit and a fourth in God. And each suffering fosters a particular joy.

1

SUFFERINGS IN ACTIONS

The first suffering that a friend of God endures is from external accidents. For instance, God inflicts sickness or condemnation on a man, or He permits a man to fall into poverty so that he is exposed to hunger, thirst, misery and insult. And all the other sufferings he endures, he endures through God. A friend of God is rarely without such suffering. Were it withdrawn from him he would wander away from the kingdom of heaven. For whether he realizes it or not, he must endure suffering in several ways.

On God's path one must always journey by one's own strength and yet no one can do this unless God assists him and gives him power, and power always flows into the soul through suffering. To lack suffering is to lack strength, and he who lacks strength cannot make this journey. Yet he who does not make this journey wanders from God's path.

Friends of God must always suffer that they may have

strength, and yet their suffering may be both secret and open. It frequently happens that they are secretly despised and that ugly things are said about them. Such sufferings prepare them and this brings them great reward. As Christ says: "Rejoice in the day when ye are hated, for your reward shall be great in heaven."[1] What he says of the day is said of the light of truth. For as the sun enlightens the day, suffering enlightens the reason with knowledge of truth. As Isaiah said: "Suffering gives understanding."[2]

Those most tested by suffering possess the most understanding. And this is because it causes one to know everything as it really is. It reveals the secret nature of things and what is revealed is also known. Voluptuous pleasure and temporal luxury darken the reason in the darkness of creatures, so that it becomes blind and loses its natural discretion. But suffering draws into itself the soul from all things that are not God. It loves the truth in the light which is in the spirit, which is God-in-the-spirit, and in no other way can one better know truth than in suffering. The sweetness of temporal things covers the reason with darkness, but their bitterness removes all darkness from the reason, since the knowledge of truth is a separation from all natural things. The sweetness of material things causes the reason to cling to them but their bitterness causes the reason to turn away from them. This is how suffering fosters detachment and the knowledge of naked truth.

Let him who would be truly wise attend the school of suffering. For there each thing reveals itself as it is. As St. Gregory says: "Whatever was hid in man, when suffering comes, it is revealed."[3] And this is also how man attains to a knowledge of himself and all things, as St. Paul says: "Through much tribulation must we enter the kingdom of God."[4] This kingdom of God consists in our knowing God within us and ourselves in God when all that is not God is driven out of us by suffering and when God alone remains known in us. Hence, as St. Paul again says: "He who wishes to live intimately with Christ must suffer persecution."[5]

Suffering is driven out by long-suffering, and when man has accepted all suffering with love he is delivered from it and lives intimately with Christ. That is, in true quiet and peace of heart. But he who tries to escape suffering is never free from it because the ground of his heart never becomes clear and hence it is always disturbed. All disquietude must cease with suffering, and therefore God's friends must always have some suffering in order to remain pure. As long as a man is in time he cannot be without certain weak tendencies and these must be uprooted, and he who most endures this proves· that God loves him most and especially removes his sins and purifies him from sinful accidents.

Suffering is a noble plant that quickly heals man's wounds. But this plant does not have a pleasant odour to fools, who turn their noses from it and run away. Hence they must always be fools, disturbed, poor, unhappy and reprobate. The richer they are in time the greater fools they are. Hence God's friends must always endure sufferings so that all folly may disappear from them, and so that their reward may be granted to them. A wise man says of this: "These are they whom we held as fools and mocked at them, but now they are counted among the sons of God."[6]

2

SUFFERING IN THE WILL

Friends of God must also have suffering in the will, and what fails them in actions must be accomplished in the will. For instance, when a man turns into himself and beholds in the light of faith the love of our Lord, which obliges Christ to suffer great martyrdom for him, then an answering love issues forth in man who out of true love for our Lord would make good all that He suffered for man's sake. Thus the will falls upon all the sufferings that might occur to him and he is willing to suffer these through and for Christ. His desire for suffering then becomes greater than his desire for everything in time, and by this true co-operative love he discards all that may bring him temporal pleasure, comfort and delight. He accepts a spiritual poverty of all bodily rapture and comfort and creaturely pleasure, so that he may repay Christ for a part of His sufferings. This beginning of spiritual poverty is a reliable path to a perfect contemplative life. And after a good beginning, a good middle journey and a good end readily follow.

How wonderful it is that these friends of God are never abandoned by God! Their beginning is in love, which is Christ, and He must uphold them and keep them with Him for eternal life. Now nature will attempt to seduce them, but the will bound to God with the determination to give up all things is able to resist all temptations. These men are God's disciples. The only thing that can cause the good to fall short is a will that is not in earnest, for when a man stands on merely his own satisfaction he must fall.

But he who earnestly takes upon himself the repayment for the sufferings of Christ is helped by God, who lifts him to godliness and never lets him fall into a mere individuality. An earnest determination can therefore resist deadly falls. For example: A king who has an enemy tries to capture him, and if he gets him into his power he punishes him, takes his goods and possibly kills him. It is the same with the human will when a man relies on it unaided. It is the enemy of God who tries to arrest it. He sends forth scouts and these are the men who pronounce the word of God and the warnings of conscience which He gives. If through the light of reason the man is led to recognize as evil all that he had previously sought, he becomes determined to run from all that is evil and from all that is a cause of evil. God now persecutes him, punishes him with mental and external sufferings, takes all his goods, that is, his voluptuousness. He slays him, that is, removes from him all that is mortal and not of God so that all earthly attraction is crushed and overcome. Men who thus die in God are indeed blessed. As St. John says: " Blessed are the dead who die in the Lord."[7]

All that which is kindled by the burning fire of the Holy Spirit through the sufferings of our Lord causes a great love. And this love compels the will to suffer all pains that are forthcoming in recompense for the One who loved man so greatly. And this love causes all things to bring suffering upon him, and that which it does not bring upon him externally, it brings upon him mentally. The will then attends to all the sufferings endured by our Lord, all endured by the saints, and even all that men must yet endure. The friend of God integrates himself in this with whole-hearted affection and the desire to suffer all or more.

Such a love makes the will receptive to all the advantages which are to be found in the Passion of our Lord and the sufferings of all the saints and devout souls. Concerning the holy St. Martin it is said that, although not executed with the sword, he nevertheless did not lose the martyr's crown because he suffered in the will what the martyrs suffered in the flesh, since it gave him pain that he could not suffer bodily.[8] In this way many friends of God are able to be companions with the martyrs when they have willed to accept all their martyrdoms. But they should also remember that, when they walk in the footsteps of Christ and the saints, they must endure in the love of God all that crosses their path, no matter how cruel, and with a determined will to accept more if necessary. Thus can a friend of God share in all suffering.

The man, however, who asks for suffering and yet always tries to avoid it in action does not take on the form of Christ. And this shows that his desire was not whole-hearted. As long as one is able to perform actions he should perform the action which God assigns to him. First, when he has accomplished all things and desires nothing more, God works instead of himself. Then the godly work really begins because the man is actually delivered from his own actions; though without sin he nevertheless continues to experience suffering.

And what he is able to suffer he suffers. Love makes others' sufferings its own, not one, but all. Should God grant him less than all suffering, He would not justly reward him.

But this is to be understood as essential and not as accidental reward, because essential reward implies an understanding and love of pure truth. If the will has a perfect and unlimited love of absolute truth and since absolute truth is the greatest reward, then the will gains an essential reward. Since the object is simple, the reward is simple.

Some say that when a man has attained to pure truth he cannot increase it since pure truth is simple and he who has it wholly lacks nothing. Yes, so far as the increase in quantity is concerned one cannot increase it, but one can increase it in its simplicity and purity while one lives in time. The simpler and purer one is, the more one is able to understand absolute truth. If in his effort after absolute truth man does not first see the highest summit of pure inward simplicity, he cannot immediately comprehend the truth. Yet as he increases in this singleness of purpose his reward will also increase. Since his will essentially detaches itself from things and turns to the one unity, which is God, it therefore increases in absolute reward. The spirit increases in pure sanctity to the extent that it is united with God.

And when the will attains to where it increases in reward, man then undertakes all good actions with love, perfecting all virtues and sufferings with perfect charity. He draws forth the best fruit with love and keeps it, for it is God the source of all things. With this love he forces God to regard him essentially as a co-operator in all good works. Were one to realize what a hidden treasure he would obtain by a humble and devoted will, he would not rely on his own will, because with this love he attains to a point—that beginning without end—which even the reason of angels does not reach. The beginning of God, which is really without beginning, no one can know except God. The human will can only love God in this way, and therefore God must reward as if he had always been and as if he had always loved.

St. Augustine said: "What one does not understand one does not love."[9] Love issues from the understanding. Hence, if God's eternity is beyond understanding, is it then impossible

for the will to love His eternity?   My reply is that love is twofold.   One aspect comes from the understanding and with this
the will cannot love God in His eternity.   The other comes
from faith and loves God for the sake of eternity.

As we can and should believe that God is without beginning and without end, so also can the will love Him completely from the light of faith as an ever-present and eternal
God.   And to the extent that the will loves Him so will He
reward it.   God loves it as if it had been an eternal will, and
the reward will be comparable.   As Christ says: " With the
same measure that ye measure out, will also be measured back,
and a heaped up and overflowing measure will be given into
your lap."[10]   Equal measure is equal love.   God gives no less
to the soul than she loves Him.   And He measures out to her
according to the peak of His love.   The heaped up, overflowing
measure is God Himself, and when the soul understands God,
then more than she can comprehend remains for her.   The
soul has more delight in this divine abundance than in that
which she already comprehends.

But God rewards the will with external love, for the will
does not stir itself to love God, rather the Holy Spirit is now
the love by which the will loves.   Since the Holy Spirit is
without beginning and without end, it loves God without
beginning or end.   And the will only loves God in this love
of the Holy Spirit when it is elevated above the beginning and
end of the created world.   When this is so, then the will goes
out into the eternal God with whom there is no beginning or
end.

The friend of God now loves essentially and is comparably
rewarded.   All suffering that has been accepted or is yet to be
accepted, he desires for himself.   And he adds his own sufferings for the sake of Christ's sufferings so that the suffering and
recompense may be perfect.   St. Paul had this love when he
said: " Who is weak, and I am not weak?   Who is troubled,
and I am not troubled?   Yes, I am all things to all men, that
I might make you all holy."[11]

3

SUFFERING IN THE SPIRIT

The third suffering of a friend of God occurs in his soul when the spirit is seized by the divine spirit. God's garment of love is so wrapped around her that she relies on it and this bond becomes so pleasant that she finds everything else unpleasant. If the friend of God then meets anything which does not spring from the Holy Spirit it causes him pain. And all that he sees and hears, all that is not divine, pains him and causes him suffering.

When Solomon said: " The righteous will not be troubled,"[12] he referred to temporal things which trouble one and make one impure. But this suffering of a pure soul is caused by all things that are not God and hence it causes the soul to purify itself and keep this purity. When a sinful thing falls upon the spirit it must necessarily be met with bitterness and this bitterness casts off this degrading attack and protects the soul in its purity. If the soul is delivered from impurities she establishes herself in a godlike form and then finds herself in the righteousness in which she was first created. She has attained to this through grace; she is not disturbed, for she has journeyed beyond the point where sorrow can reach her. She has united herself with that which is all joy and ecstasy, and in this no sadness can touch her. This is what Solomon meant when he said: " The righteous will not be troubled."

Again, it should be said that nothing can trouble the righteous unless God were stolen away. In other words, only the tearing away of his righteousness could disturb him. But man will always be persecuted as long as he lives in time; he will always feel this trouble and bitterness. This trouble does not harm the righteous, rather it secures him in his righteousness.

Moreover, man will not be troubled when he lives in the full enjoyment of his righteousness. This, however, cannot be completely ascertained in time—only in eternity. As long as man is here below, so long must his soul be troubled with the suffering of desire because he has insufficient capacity to enjoy his righteousness. This is not destructive, rather it compels him towards this perfect righteousness. As Christ says: "Blessed are they who hunger and thirst after righteousness."[13] Where hunger and thirst exist there is also affliction.

The righteous man will not be afflicted when his soul is abandoned to God, when all worldliness has disappeared and only divinity stands before him. But should he cast a glance on his fellow creature and perceive his misery, he must then suffer with him. Such an affliction does not hinder the righteous, for their righteousness really springs from charity. It is written of Christ in the Gospel: "Jesus shuddered in spirit, and was troubled."[14] This was simply compassion which He had for us.

Nor is the righteous soul able to be disturbed when all created things are removed and when she is preoccupied in the uncreated, which is God, for only there does she find peace and satisfaction. But when she busies herself with created things, which detract her from God, then the spirit is troubled since her sanctity is not fashioned and formed in that shape. And that is why such a man is not able to be quiet in spirit. But even this affliction of the spirit is not destructive, for she gradually casts off all that is not God until at last only God dwells with this man. Should we have, however, a momentary peace through the preoccupation of reason, it is only a natural peace and by no means complete.

Pagans had this peace. They drove away all earthly things in order to enjoy bodily peace and although the spirit experienced happiness through this, it was not its true joy. This mere natural joy should be surmounted and joy should be sought only in God. They who rely on this joy are more like the Gentiles than like Christ. It is of course possible, and it frequently occurs, that a man drives everything away in order to have peace of spirit without hindrances and it is somewhat difficult to distinguish these pagan men from true Christians. Both avoid earthly things, both have a similar way of life. They love spiritual poverty and they bestow full glory on the Creator. Both attempt to imitate an external image of our Lord.

But the difference lies internally. Objects and forms are the aim of natural men and in them they find their joy. The godlike, on the other hand, seek their joy in the humanity and the divinity of Christ. They come from Him and they return to Him. Let no one try to find the difference between these two men unless he has the divine light and unless he is guided in spirit, for he may easily attribute sins to holy people. Always the best side should be considered in every attention and no one should be called wicked of whom the wickedness cannot be clearly understood.

Now if one loves a natural man as though he were a godlike man, will God equally reward him? It is of course better that one should love a man who bears the name of Christian, good or bad, than that one should dislike or despise him. God prefers any kind of love to no love at all. Love, however, should be universal, not particularly directed to only one person. He who loves a worldly man with particularity and at the same time keeps God in his intention has a love which is more incomplete than that which merits full reward, for all attachments foster mediations.

On the other hand, he who loves all his fellow men equally, without personal attachment, has that true love which God fully rewards. If one were to love another as if he were good when he is not, it would not be right for God to reward him. Since love springs from understanding, an unjust understanding implies a similar love, and hence God cannot reward him. It sometimes happens that a man loves another because he considers him good though he is considered bad by others. In this case God gives more reward to those who thought him bad, if they were right, than to the man who thought him good.

To the degree that love is lighted by divinity it becomes better, and the more it is drawn away from that light, the more it decreases in value. It frequently happens that one is attracted to another by blind love, considering him righteous when he is not. But one who is enlightened does not hold him with a blind love, but loves him universally according to his being. This love is really nobler than blind love and accordingly God's reward to it is more complete.

Another view, however, may be held, since love does not spring wholly from the understanding but also from faith. Hence, if one man has more faith than another and loves him through faith, because he regards him as good, will not God reward him more than another who does not have so much faith and who does not love him as much? A man has only as much true faith as he receives from divine light. To whom the light fails, faith also fails. He who has learned best to know divine truth also has the truest faith. But only the man who has comprehended essential truth knows this and only he loves with an entire faith. And his love is the most worthy and useful.

It sometimes happens that a man trusts another, thinking him righteous and loving him, but he does not really understand why he loves him. Another has no trust in the man, does not think him righteous and does not love him, yet understands what he should believe. This indifference is nobler and more useful than the other love, for God does not reward a false faith when someone believes something that is not true. It is more akin to faithlessness and weakness than to perfection, and love which springs from faithlessness is not rewarded by God. As Christ says: "Take heed of false prophets that come to you in sheep's clothing, but inwardly are ravening wolves."[15]

False prophets are they who consider themselves respectable, but who are really bad. To regard such men as good is unrighteous rather than righteous. Our Lord counsels us to guard ourselves from them and so they are unworthy. On the Last Day false teachers shall rise up and preach, but he who believes in them shall prove that he is not right. He who likes the superficially good man and considers him good, proves that he himself is not righteous. He is, as a teacher says, "a fool that believes anything or everything".

One might say here that the light of faith is beyond all understanding and that one requires no reason with faith, for he is lifted above it. Men without understanding truly believe; hence God gives them the same reward as the enlightened. Is it, then, not necessary to understand in order to believe, since faith is simple?

My reply is that understanding is twofold; one is necessary for faith, the other is faith itself. The first is that a man should understand the articles of faith and the teachings of Christ. He who knows the teaching and lives accordingly has revealed to him the fruit of the doctrine by which he will be known. The tree is known by its fruit. And if he attains to understanding he immediately begins to believe and it is then certain that his faith is true. On the other hand, the man who has not lived according to the teachings of Christ does not know the fruits of His teachings and hence he does not know whether his faith is right or wrong. Because he believes only from hearsay, his faith is incomplete, and he is apt to err easily. Since his faith is incomplete, his love is also incomplete.

The other understanding which friends of God has is one with faith. When a man acts according to Christ's teachings, brings all things into one, and this one into unity of knowledge in the light of faith that is God, he penetrates into the hidden darkness of the pure divine Being. His understanding then consists in suffering, but his faith co-operates with God. And this faith in God operates on the understanding with burning love. This love experiences it, and this experience is its understanding; all that is beyond it is true faith. This man is then a genuine Christian. He, then, who is not guided by the teaching of Christ, and by all virtue, until he enters into this oneness without any distinction, lacks true faith. His faith is manifold, but not altogether true. And his love, which springs from it, is also untrue.

Now the best and only way to come to that true faith which promotes all love, is to become immersed in the teachings of our Lord and live an honourable life. To know this vivifying spirit and believe it, one should be filled with

Christ's doctrine.   And this faith implies that one should love without attachment, loving not men alone, but also the life and image of our Lord, and this love is always good and meritorious.   Even if such a loving person continued to be bothered with defects, he would not lose his reward.   Christ says: "He who taketh up a prophet in the name of a prophet will receive the reward of a prophet."[16]

He, then, who finds a man walking on Christ's path should love him as a follower of Christ.   And he will then receive the reward of a disciple of Christ.   But one should attend not only to the image of Christ but also to His life, for it is of great importance.   The man whose love does not include Christ's life has a worldly love.   This is defective and wasted. And that which is not a pure love and truth is a suffering to the spirit.

One must so strive that his spirit may be emptied of all falsehood and that it may be inflamed by the love of the Holy Spirit in order not to be deceived by pseudo-lights.   If the spirit establishes herself in purity everything reveals itself in its true light.   If good, the spirit abides in peace; if bad, it loses its peace.   Hence, spiritual men recognize all things through peace.   Nothing can err in a pure heart.   Evil must show itself, for such a heart is like a spotless looking-glass in which one sees everything that is held before it and as it really is.   So is it with the spirit united with God.   God permits nothing to approach which could mar the unity; He throws away all that is of no value.   It is not necessary for pure men to see things with differences of form, for appearances cause distraction if one concentrates on them too long.

Falsehood penetrates all external forms and the evil spirit clothes himself in them.   One should then observe his heart in all simplicity and permit God to work without any external images.   Thus will the eye of reason remain pure and unmixed, and it will not err.   It is this purity that the evil spirit dislikes, and he will run from it.   The pure man remains untempted by evil, for God works in a pure soul by illuminating it with the flame of divine love and by directly imparting His

R

love to it. When the evil powers sense this they flee it as a thief flees from the light in a house where he intends to steal. The sorcery of the devil is simply a mixing with sense, worldliness and creaturely images. If these are avoided, if one casts off all creaturely images and attachments, the enemy will find no room.

Should one, however, turn again to the senses, he will be tricked by the evil spirit. And one who lives a life of the senses cannot continue long without falling, for there is no refuge where one can stay. God is the refuge of all men and He does not work in the senses nor in images. In fact, He withdraws the senses and throws off all images, and then He becomes man's dwelling-place and his refuge against mortal falls. Those who do not stand apart from their sensuality and stripped of all images are in danger of falling.

Indeed, it is a wonder if these men manage to stand upright. That is why it is necessary that the senses be drawn into the highest part of the soul where they may penetrate into God. For only there can one stand without mortally falling. Were it possible for the senses to be always drawn into the higher reason and the reason directed towards God, one so established would always remain untouched by mortality, without venial sins, and placed in that original justice in which God created the first human.

Now the spirit that is elevated above all things into God lifts the senses with it and turns them in the direction that she is turned. She subjects them to herself as she is subjected to God. As long as there is obedience the spirit has rest in God. But when the senses are rebellious in disobedience the spirit is disturbed and deprived of peace. And this is a real suffering for the spirit.

4

SUFFERING IN GOD

The fourth suffering that a friend of God has is a suffering in God. This takes place when all unlikeness falls away from the spirit through grace. She is placed in a likeness when she is receptive to God's work. God works in this receptivity and the spirit suffers that work.

Now there are two kinds of work in the soul, one is of reason and grace-like, the other is essential and divine. The reasonable work is when the reason penetrates all things with the distinction of images and finds God in all things. God is a good that flows into all things and thus man offers himself to serve all in order that he may find God in them. The reason is then called an " inworking reason " and it grants to each thing the property that belongs to it and so finds God in all things.

He who accepts things in the order in which they have been ordained by God finds God in them. If we do not find God in all things it is because we seek things without order. It is in disorder that we lose God. As order is a means of finding, so disorder is a means of losing. If the reason seeks all things in proper order it finds an ever-present God. And when it finds God it forgets things and clings only to Him. It perceives that all things are disquieting and that perfect rest is alone in God. Hence, reason raises itself above all things and seeks God outside things, and this happens through the working out of the images which it has drawn into itself from creatures. It strips and frees itself from all creaturely images and, as the reason previously drew in the image of creatures in order to find God in them, so it now strips off all these images in order to find an unveiled God. And this is called a " stripping-off-reason ",[17] since it strips away all things so that it may be free from working and that only God may be the master workman. Now all of this is of grace in an angelic light.

It is now that the divine work takes over. When reason has stripped off all creaturely images God enters the soul and takes the place of the working reason and there performs His work. The reason is then called a suffering (or passive) reason, for it suffers God's work. All the works are then performed in one work, and as all things are enveloped in God, so He encloses all in the one action that He performs in the soul. The soul has received the eternal Word when she is delivered from all things and if she has penetrated the divine heart with ardent burning love, she begets the Son in the Godhead.

However, this divine birth in the soul is twofold: internal and external. It is internal when the soul penetrates into the divine heart; then her heart and all her faculties become a nutriment of the divine heart so that she loses her heart and her faculties. But God gives His heart and His powers in return; and the heart of the soul is now no longer merely human but godlike.

Thus the heart always lives in an ardour of the divine fire and is penetrated by it so that she becomes weak through love. Her human powers are so insufficient that all the members become weak. All this is necessary, for wherever the divine power works human power must fade away since its tendency is towards error. Once this defective power is absent, God can pour His power into the soul without obstruction. He sends the fire of His love into the heart so that all evil may be consumed, so that all disorderly forces may be ordered, all defects healed and all unlikeness removed. Things then lose their proper form and are changed into god-like forms, as Christ says: "Behold, I make all things new."[18]

This happens when God lives in the soul, for then He orders everything as He wishes it and makes the old new. Hence, St. Paul says: "Put off the old man and put on the new man which is shaped like God, in holiness, justice and truth."[19] Now this old man is put off and the new man put on when God the Father begets His Son in the soul. By this birth He makes new all that was defective, and all returns to its first nobility. Hence, man is created after God in holiness, justice and truth and is called a new man. Christ says: "If you do not become as little children you cannot enter the kingdom of God."[20]

In other words, unless a man is reborn as a child of God he cannot enter into God's kingdom. And as he is reborn

within so he will be reborn without. The outward man takes
on a new being so that he is transformed in a godlike way.
Before he had used his members as instruments of luxury;
now he turns them to the service of God in justice and holiness.[21]   As everything is new within so it becomes also new
without. When the divine fire inflames the heart and inwardly
consumes all unlikeness, it passes throughout the body, consuming its sinful tendencies, and converting it to virtue and
good actions. Thus it attains to its original justice, and so he
who is created in righteousness according to God's likeness is
called a new man.

Friends of God suffer in this birth and God works all in
them. This is why Christ says: "None is good but God
alone."[22] No man's work is good save that from God and by
God. It is also the best thing when a man is delivered from
all self-work and when he lets God alone work and when he
makes himself suffer it. When God is the working and man
the suffering being, then all is made quiet within him.

God's working in the soul is essential; it issues forth from
the divine essence and is fulfilled in the essence of the soul.
All evil that was ever exercised in the soul is uprooted by this
divine work. Man is absolved *a poena et a culpa*, that is, from
punishment and guilt, for, when God reveals Himself to the
soul, all must give way to let Him in. Nothing can reign there
save God.

CHAPTER V

THE PROTECTING SPIRIT

✳✳✳✳✳✳✳✳✳✳✳✳✳✳✳✳✳✳✳✳✳✳✳✳✳

IS it possible for a friend of God to be protected from
venial sins? Yes, as the following ways will indicate.

1

HOW MAN MAY BE PROTECTED FROM FALLING

First, man is overcome with a divine power through which
all his faculties are strengthened. If the divine birth is fulfilled in the essence of the soul, it moves on into all the faculties.
Each receives divine power to resist all that is contrary to God.
It is necessary that this divine power work in us, for no one
can resist sins by mere human strength. And one receives
this divine power when all his faculties turn to the divine birth
which occurs in the centre of the soul. If each faculty seeks
to perform its work without turning to this birth, they cannot receive its power. He who wants to receive something
from another must get close to him; so all the faculties must
be united and in a state of waiting for the divine birth.

What causes good men to fall is that they attend too much
to unnecessary things, and thereby scatter their powers. The
more they do this the more the divine power escapes them;
hence they must fall. Holy Scripture says: "The just man
falls at least seven times a day"[1]—that is, one does not constantly realize the divine birth in the soul. Were the faculties
persistent they would continually receive the divine power and
they would be protected from falling.

Another way to be protected from venial sins is for the lower faculties to become subordinated to the higher. This keeps man in his original justice as Adam was. He fell because the lower faculties turned away from the higher. And this is still the case. When man turns to sensuality without attending to the higher faculties he falls. Were he to perform an external action while attending to his reason he would not fall nor would his action be wrong. Though such action is exercised by the senses, the reason has a greater part in it. Hence it is called a reasonable action and is virtuous.

Let him who does not wish to fall attend to his reason in every action, inward or outward, and then his action will be virtuous and more godlike than human. Man's actions are sensual when blindly exercised without reason. Since it is through these that he falls he ought not to have them. Hence, as a teacher says: " It is right that a man be free of all actions, namely sensual actions which are sinful." Such actions are man's own, but virtuous actions are God's. He alone is the source of all good, and whatever good must be performed must begin in Him and end in Him. If the senses are subordinated to the highest faculties, and are thus reduced to God, they can receive the divine power necessary to resist all falls.

Thirdly, man is protected from venial sins when his will is wholly united to the divine will and when the reason always hears that divine will and lives in accordance with it. Through this abandonment of one's own will one is able to receive all the divine gifts and these strengthen him for resisting all that is not God. God only bequeaths His own will in us and what is not His will does not receive any gifts. Should God's will live wholly in a man and if man has wholly abandoned his will, he is able to receive all gifts. What he asks of God he will receive. If he requests God to guard him from all sins against His most holy will, so it will be. But if he continues to fall into faults, it is through God's will but not as though God's will consented to faults. No. God permits it so that man may learn to know his defects and be made humble, through which he can alone keep his footing against every fall.

It is indeed harmful if a man find his will without the will of God and if he complacently considers himself to be somebody. If God permits a man to fall it is in order that complacency may be killed and man gain a knowledge of his own weakness, and that he may be protected from a greater fall. When man is completely dead to his own will, God becomes his life. Not he lives, but God lives in him, and protects him from injurious falls.

Fourthly, a man is protected from venial sins when he persistently uses the right proportion in all things. He who always observes the right proportion in his words and work will not fall. Faults and sins arise from doing too much or too little. God is always present to him who does what he ought to do, who omits what he ought to omit. The Gospel speaks of this: " Jesus stood in the midst of His disciples."² Jesus, that is, salvation, stood in the midst of His disciples or, in other words, the disciples reconciled by grace received their salvation from the midst of the Godhead. He who has proper order and discretion, who always takes the right proportion in all his words and actions, will always find God.

Yet it is said that we must approach God with mediation. This approach to and finding God is twofold. One lies in the creatures and in its actions, and here God is found in mediation, for God is in the midst of all creatures and he whose actions bring him there finds God. The other finding is of God only, wholly detached from all creatures in His simple being. But only the man freed from all creatures and their actions finds God in this way. The pure, detached spirit penetrates beyond all mediation and casts himself into that pure, immediate, divine Nothingness, and he knows nothing of creatures and their actions. If, on the other hand, man preoccupies himself with creatures and their actions in creation, he must keep proportion in their midst. Thus he approaches God through God. And this he must observe if he wants to be without defects and if he wants to find God within and through all things.

Fifthly, a man is protected from venial sins by inward and

outward voluntary detachment. Men who are really poor in spirit suffer, and should they fall through a fault, their suffering quickly removes it. St. Gregory says: "Do not criticize the defects of poor people, for what lacketh in them, is cancelled again by poverty."[3] Spiritual poverty protects one especially against certain faults, for if anyone begs a poor man for a gift, he cannot give it, and he does not commit a fault in refusing the beggar. But if they who have many temporal goods refuse a beggar, they sin. They evince a hardness and a need of pity, and this is defective.

Spiritual poverty is good against sin, for excess temporal property presents many sinful occasions. And since poor men are free from property, they have no such motive for sins and cannot commit them, as Aristotle says: "When the cause faileth, the work also faileth."[4] Nothing is without a cause, and nothing can seduce a man who has no cause.

Now spiritual poverty really protects a man against sins, for when a man has parted with all things he has a perfect will to virtue, and he who wills all virtue also opposes vice. A perfect will has the power to resist all vice; it performs all virtues and at once denies all sins. If a man still falls, it is not his will and therefore no sin, for sin occurs only with the will, as St. Augustine says: "If there were no will, there would be no sin."[5] Hence he who has not abandoned all things has not the power to will all virtues, for as long as man is obstructed by material things he cannot exercise virtuous acts. He, however, who has converted all to virtues, obtains this power of the will. That is why they who possess things cannot at once will the virtuous nor at once cast off the unvirtuous.

Sixthly, a man is protected from venial sins by his own heart when it burns with the fire of the Holy Spirit, for it consumes all unlikeness and purifies man of sin. Love and hatred cannot subsist together. If a man would love, he must part from all that fosters hatred. And he lives without sin just as long as he continues to love. St. Paul says: "Charity is a consuming fire."[6]

2

THE LOVE OF THE HOLY SPIRIT

Some say that they who have received the Holy Spirit live without sin, since the love of the Holy Spirit destroys sin and this gift that the Holy Spirit grants remains for ever. St. John says: "He who is born of God cannot sin."[7] My opinion, however, is that man must be seen in two lights according to his inner and outer man. The gift of the Holy Spirit is received by the inner man and protects him from falling. The outer man, however, is not receptive to the gifts and because he refuses them he is never without venial sins. He is somewhat similar to time, and time is changing and defective. Hence his senses are defective and tend to sin. The outer man can only live without sin when his senses are drawn into the inner man which is established in God.

As long as this continues man is without external and internal sin, for any defects the actions may have are consumed by the fire of love. Were it possible for the senses to be always drawn into the inner man, he would always remain united with God and without sin. This is so because sin is nothing else than a turning away from God and an inclination towards creatures. If the whole man is turned to God, no sin occurs while this continues. Should he return to his selfhood and the service of the senses, he will probably fall. When one does not attend to the spirit, one forgets his obligations and commits faults and sins. Were one to perform all his internal and external actions according to the precepts of his reason, enlightened by the divine light, he would rarely fall. He would direct all his working and suffering to the glory of God.

All this is caused by the ardent love of the Holy Spirit which completely inflames him, drives out all darkness and enlightens him so that he can do all for God's glory. It gives him the power to do all things, abandon all that is contrary to God, and attain to all that is holy. The goodness of the Holy Spirit blesses him so that he refers everything to that goodness. And when this goodness penetrates his heart and fills all his members, all that was bitter and coarse in them disappears. Only goodness remains and this goodness protects him from the bitterness of sin.

Now should such a man realize that he has committed a fault out of forgetfulness, he suffers far more pain than one who has actually committed a venial sin. This is so because he who has tasted sweetness is more disgusted at bitterness than he who has not tasted it. To the man who really loves God all things are bitter in comparison to the great sweetness of the Holy Spirit. What is pleasant for another is painful to him. Nothing is dearer for him than to love God perfectly—all else is bitter. And this bitterness fosters greater purity and greater love, and God sometimes causes men to hesitate in order to bring them to a greater purity and to love Him more ardently.

St. Paul says: "Where sin abounds there doth grace abound."[8] He also says: "All turneth to good to them that love God."[9] One gives the best to the person he loves. God loves them who love Him and He always gives them the best.

But should such a man fall into sin, it does not happen through this that is best, as though sin were good. Rather it reveals to him his weakness and makes him humble. Nor is it because sin enlightens man to self-knowledge; it is because what is hidden should be made known. The light enlightens the darkness of sins and thus man attains to a knowledge of his feebleness, resigns himself humbly to God and to men for God's sake. He stands in his humility well protected against a relapse which would cause him great injury.

All this is caused by the love of the Holy Spirit. All man's weaknesses are revealed to him through it; it bows him down before God and protects him from faults. In this way, then, man must suffer and patiently endure and accept all if he truly desires to attain to a contemplative life.

CHAPTER VI

THE FOURTH WAY: PEACE OF HEART

✳✳✳✳✳✳✳✳✳✳✳✳✳✳✳✳✳✳✳✳✳✳✳✳

THE fourth path that leads to a poor contemplative life is when one has exercised himself in all virtue with meditation on our Lord's Passion, and attains to true rest and finally to peace of heart. And this fourth path to a perfect contemplative life is nothing else than a diligent watch over all that happens to man regardless of whether it is bodily or spiritual, so that he may accept it in such a way that the spirit does not suffer injury, but always finds herself immediately in simple purity.

1

THE INTERIOR EXERCISE

To fulfil this aim man should turn himself away from external exercises and exercise himself within. Exterior actions pass over to creatures, the interior to God. He who truly desires to find God should enter into himself and seek God within. To seek God without may certainly result in finding Him with creatures, but true blessedness does not lie in this.

He who seeks God within finds Him apart from creatures in His pure, simple essence. It is in this that true blessedness lies. St. Augustine says: "Lord, when I first knew Thee, I knew that Thou art a good that entered into all creatures, and I surrendered myself to the service of all created things in order to find Thee in them. But while this seeking lasted my heart was always in unrest. Then when I knew Thee better, I knew

252

that Thou art a good that is detached from creatures; I withdraw myself from them in order to find Thee alone outside creatures. Then was my heart quiet; for it is disquieted except it rest in Thee, for Thou hast created us solely for Thyself."[1]

All things are changing and unquiet. The heart of the person who preoccupies himself with things is always in unrest. We do not find God in unrest, for He abides only in peace and he who wishes to find Him must have peace of heart. St. Augustine says: "There are many who seek God, but there are few who find Him, for they seek Him without where He is not."[2] Some say, however, that, since God is everywhere, why should we not find Him? The reason for this is that God is within, but we are without.

God is a spirit, but we are in the body. God is detached from all creatures, but we are encumbered with them. God is pure, simple good; we are changeable. God is the Light, we are darkened through sin. God is Love, we are still spotted with hatred. It is this unlikeness that prevents us from finding God. To find Him we must have likeness in order to seek Him. Since God is within and in the spirit, detached from creatures, simple and pure, the clearest light, which is Himself, full of ardent love, we too must be this way if we would find Him. We must enter into our heart, turn away from all external actions. We must have a pure mind, empty of all images and forms, clear, simple, enlightened by the divine light, inflamed with the fire of the love of the Holy Spirit. It is in this likeness that we will discover the pure Godhead, who grants us that peace in which He is immediately experienced and enjoyed. It is then that man stands in real spiritual poverty where he can behold God.

If man turns to himself in this true purity, observes the state of his heart and seeks God in it, all that makes one like God will spring up in him. If he had previously been outwardly focused, he now becomes inwardly focused; if he was materially minded, he now becomes spiritually minded; if he adhered to creatures, he is now free; if darkened, he is now enlightened; if cold in divine love, he is now inflamed with the fire of love. To find the right treasures which enrich him with God's gifts, he must seek all inwardly. To neglect this inward seeking is to neglect the gifts of God which He freely grants.

The senses are not receptive to the best gifts, for they are changeable whereas the divine gifts abide for ever. God does not grant them to the person who is always fluctuating. Hence, to be receptive to these gifts, the senses must be gathered into the inner man which has a likeness with God. It is here that the Father of Light imparts the best gifts,[3] and with Him there is no shadow of change and all His gifts are unchangeable. One must also accept them in unchangeableness; yet the senses do not have this since they have a likeness with time. Only the inner man has this property since only he is created in the likeness of God in holiness, justice and truth. He receives God's unchangeable gifts and God gives him His best. A master does not gladly give his property to a spendthrift who can neither care for it nor protect it. Neither does God gladly give to the spendthrifts who squander all and save nothing.

One should never entrust a perfect good or a perfect gift of God to external sensual men, for one would be deceived. God finds no receptive place in them, and even if God would gladly give His gifts to sensual men, He cannot because He would not find a place prepared for them. He who would build a house on flowing water would be a fool. Like flowing water, the senses are also unstable and fluctuating with time and so God does not give to them His best gifts.

No doubt externally good men can gain reward in heaven through their good works, but they can never in time receive God's perfect gifts which He grants to those who turn within and listen to Him. As David said: "I will hear what God the Lord saith to me. He will give peace to His people."[4]

2

CONTROLLING THE SENSES

There are some who mortify their senses, fast, keep the night vigil and flagellate themselves. This may be good, but he who truly desires to annihilate his senses must first cast aside all material interests. He must live within, and when he gains victory in the inner man, he can annihilate his senses, or rather subordinate them to obedience. Man then turns in his deepest spirit and truly sees God. He becomes receptive to the divine power in whose obedience the senses are always resigned, for they cannot be controlled in any other way.

Man only receives this strength inwardly and then gathers in and controls the senses. The senses remain uncontrolled when this divine power is lacking. And we observe this with many men who, after striving much, fall in the end because their senses were not controlled in the way in which the divine power controls them. Real strength fails them and they fall. Had Adam relied on his inward control rather than on the senses, he would not have fallen. Since he obeyed his senses his fall was certain, for he lacked the divine power that keeps a man upright. It is the same with all who act in this way— they must fall.

But why does God create man so that He permits them to fall? Had he wished to hold men back He would have formed them otherwise. Having a body and soul, with free will to direct himself as he wishes, man turned himself towards his weakest side, to the senses, and hence encountered the most dangerous result—mortality. Had he turned himself to the inner man he would have seen the truth, seized it and been prevented from falling. Since he followed the senses, he could not see the truth and so he fell; the senses cannot receive divine truth, only the inner man can do that, for he is fashioned like God in truth.

Now all this happens to those who surrender to the senses. It is right that they should fall and no one should wonder if God permits them to fall and lose themselves. It is God's justice that permits these men to fall if they do not turn themselves from the senses to reason. Then God must assist them, for they are then receptive to His aid. Were the senses the better vessels for the divine gifts then surely all men would readily become great saints and would easily resist all sins, for all their dexterity would be utilized to suppress them through the senses.

This, however, is not the case. Rather they fall and, the greater the sensuality, the greater the fall. It is also the justice of God that sensual men who persistently live and remain in sin should be condemned. God wants to give them everlasting blessedness, but they do not want to receive it, since they are like death and will die, and are not receptive to life. Death and life cannot exist together.

The man who desires to receive everlasting blessedness must receive it inwardly in the inner man which is fashioned like God. As Christ says: "He who believes and is baptized, is saved."[5] In other words, when faith is seized by the reason and not by the senses. What one hears takes a form, but it is the reason that receives the light of faith. Such men are baptized in the waters of repentance and are twice born in the spirit of truth. They who rely on their sensuality cannot have faith. They may, of course, say they have faith. Many people say: I have a hundred pounds of silver, when they have none at all. They are like pagans and are only Christians by name, and this certainly does not make them blessed.

Christ also says: "Not everyone who saith to Me, Lord, Lord, will enter the kingdom of heaven, but the one who carrieth out the teachings of God."[6] Not everyone who says, "I believe," but the one who does good works, for "faith without works is dead". The senses cause death, faith is our salvation and brings everlasting life. Hence it must be received in the reason and not in the senses. All that the senses pick up they lose. That is why it is necessary that the essence of faith should be impressed upon the reason, for it alone holds and keeps faith. When the senses are under the control of the inner man, then he receives the impression of divine faith which fosters blessedness.

3

UNITY WITH THE INNER MAN

If the senses are unable to receive the most intimate truth why should they be gathered into the inner man so that he can seize the truth? Where it is necessary for two to receive a gift, the weaker must always submit itself to the stronger. That which is defective in the one must be corrected by the other. Man is body and soul, yet they have but one movement. Since the soul cannot operate without the body, she cannot receive divine gifts if she is hindered by the senses. But these hindrances are removed when she completely detaches herself from all sensual activity. Only thus can she receive perfect truth and this reception she divides with the senses. The senses do not receive it as independent sense-faculties, but as faculties wholly resigned and controlled by the inner man. And there within, truth penetrates them and obliges them to follow it.

The best bond with which to bind the senses is when they are wholly gathered within and bound together with divine truth for the glory of God. No one can protect himself from falling without this union. And why, one might ask, should the inner man be receptive of divine truth and not the senses? Since the inner man cannot receive divine truth unless the senses are united to it, then the answer is because there is only one God and one faith.

Man must also attain to this unity, for only in this unity is he receptive of God, since oneness truly believes in God. Were there more than one God and one faith it would be impossible for a man to be inwardly united. However, since there is only one God and one faith, man must become one if he wants to be a vessel of God and of true faith. To the extent that he falls short of this unity, to that extent does he lack God and true faith, and must further gather in his senses into unity.

The more the senses are turned outwardly the more scattered

s

they become in their operations. And the more dissipated these interests are, the more the inner man is hindered from receiving the divine simple truth—God. It is impossible for God to be united in the fluctuating, outward sensual man. It is impossible for God to be received in what is disunited. He can only fully enter into unity.

It is written in the prophets: "I will lead thee in the desert and speak to the heart"[8]—that is, in the desert of inner unity where all foreign beings and all things are united in one, where alone the eternal Word is spoken from the fatherly Heart. Only in this silence of unity can He be heard. Should God utter His Word to the man preoccupied with external concerns He cannot be heard, for if two speak at the same time one cannot hear them. One of them must be quiet. When God speaks to the soul all creatures and all things must become silent to the listener. Then and only then will his spirit hear the Word of God.

When a master speaks the servant usually listens. But if the servant is disrespectful, the master becomes angry. When God utters His Word, all things should become silent in man and he should listen to the divine Word through which wisdom is acquired. The person who disturbs God is really disrespectful to Him.

Now a man disturbs God when he preoccupies himself with the senses without attending to God's counsels. If sensual men never attain to the love of God, it is because they continue in their disrespect for Him. The greatest honour and love one can show God is to listen to His Word. But they who favour the senses cannot hear It and hence cannot love Him with a true love.

CHAPTER VII

UNION WITH DIVINE LOVE

❊❊❊❊❊❊❊❊❊❊❊❊❊❊❊❊❊❊❊❊❊❊❊❊❊❊

THE man who really desires divine love must so control his passion and silence his faculties as to be able to hear what God speaks in the soul. Divine love is in the conversation which the soul has with God. God loves the soul with this love and, because she return this love, she is justly loved. Christ says: "He who loveth He, heareth My Word."[1] They who refuse to hear His Word cannot love Him.

1

LOVE IS LIFE AND DEATH

The source of divine love is in the eternal Word that God utters in the soul and he who ignores this fails in the foundation of divine love. Man should, then, turn all his senses and powers towards the eternal Word in order to attain to the source of divine love. He will drink from it, become intoxicated and carried away with love.

Love becomes his whole life. He can do nothing but love. It has so penetrated him that he desires nothing else. To attribute anything else than love to him is to do him injustice, for he is all love. To take it away from him is to take away his life. Love is life and death. If he lives, he lives from love; if he dies, he dies from it. Regardless of what happens he is always one with love, and love is one with him. All that happens to love happens also to him; what interferes with love, interferes with him. To give to him is to give to love;

to take from him is to take from love. He who may wish to work closely with God brings it to completion through such God-loving men. For if these men receive a work of love then love is uppermost, and this love is the consuming fire of divine love. To feed such a man is to feed God. For when the food has been received this love draws the strength of the food and consumes it in the very source of divine love and he does not know what he has eaten. With such a man of love everything returns to the source from which it originally went forth. He is so close to this source that whatever is worked through it must pass through him. The faith and love shown to him is not likely to be lost by God. For love and faith lifted to such a height cannot be overlooked by God.

But those who truly love God are only loved by men who are worthy of His love. It is natural that they are much despised for very few are worthy of them or equal to them. As St. Paul says: "The world is not worthy of them;"[2] hence they must endure many insults.

This unworthiness, however, proves the dignity of love. Worldly honour is spurned by God-loving men and to shower it upon them is to offend them. The cross of Christ is their honour and in its love rests its dignity. St. Paul says: "Let all worthiness be far from me except through the cross of our Lord Jesus Christ."[3] But the cross of Jesus Christ not only leads to, but also is defamation, hatred, persecution and so forth. Yet it is from these that love obtains its honour. He who wants to be honoured and satisfied with a dignified worldly position proves at once that he lacks divine love. Divine love desires equality with nothing except that which it loves. To try to detract it from this equality is to make it ill. But to treat it with equal love is to fill it with joy. And this is how one knows those who possess divine love.

Real divine love springs from the fatherly Heart when God utters His eternal Word in the soul. In this conversation the love of the Holy Spirit overflows and floods the soul and all its faculties so that everything that flows from her is love. This brings the senses under the control of the inner man, silencing their powers, while the inner love burns in God. Thus the soul expands and the eternal Word, from which perfect love issues, is spoken.

He, then, who desires to attain to a perfect life should adopt an interior life and withdraw himself from exterior activity, from craving for material things, so that if he wants to perform some external work, he will possess no materials with which to execute it. When he has done this and emptied himself even of the *desire* to accomplish an external work and to have any property, he can then really live in truth and grant God full opportunity to act in him.

That is why the highest perfection of a spiritual, poor life rests in being so wholly devoted to God that one does not notice the actions and defects of creatures. Then God can complete His perfect work which grants everlasting blessedness. As Christ says: " If thou wilt be perfect, sell all that thou hast and give it to the poor."[4] Now he does not imply that all men without temporal possessions are perfect. *He simply says that through the lack of unnecessary possessions one is released from irrelevant activity and hence is able to give attention to that which God works immediately in the soul.* A spiritual, poor life leads to the highest perfection, but it is only a condition that makes it possible for one to forget creatures and attend only to God. Just as a teacher gives the first rank to his disciple and expects him to pay attention to him and not to somebody else, so spiritual poverty is the highest rank that God can give to His friends in order that they can better attend to Him.

But the poor man who preoccupies himself in outward things has a poverty far more injurious than perfect. God has called him to an interior life, and to attend to Him alone. When he attends to external interests he does not fulfil God's order and goes counter to the life of spiritual poverty. He who would serve creatures must have possessions, but he who would serve God must not turn to creatures but only to God. Hence, our Lord advised Mary Magdalene that she should discard all valuable things so that she might more easily turn away from creatures towards Him, and contemplate Him without hindrance. He also says: " She has chosen the best part "[5]— that is, she turned from the service of creatures, leaving temporal things and attended to God where the best part is to be found.

He who possesses many temporal things must attend to creatures and serve them through God, for by this order they may reach Him. And he who does not possess temporal things should have his attention directed wholly to God, and that will be his best order of reaching God. Concerning this, Seneca said: " Whosoever wisheth to have the freedom of poverty must be truly poor, or live as a poor man." But the truly free man is only he who is able to direct himself to the best part—God. And this is possible only in detachment from temporal things. Temporal things are naturally heavy and they detract the mind which is interested in them. The man who is truly detached has a mind attracted towards God, and thus, in emptiness, with no intruding obstacles, unity and freedom are established.

Now it often happens that they who are burdened with temporal things criticize freedom since they do not have it, and what one does not have one does not favour. True detached freedom consists in an interior life and in realizing God in it. One is bound by creatures if he turns to them, and this bond hinders him from returning inwardly to God. That is why it is advisable to remain much to oneself so that one may be unhindered and unfastened by creatures, so that one may always find God in the ground of the soul where His real dwelling-place is.

2

HOW DIVINE LOVE IS RECEIVED

Man should draw in his senses and attend to the inner man because man's best part is within. And it is right that one should serve the best and forgo the worst. To favour the senses is to act like a man who forsakes his best friend in favour of a foe. The enemy of the soul is sensuality. To serve the senses is to serve one's enemy and it is right that one should then receive the reward of this enemy, which is mortality.

Since the senses cause death their reward is death. No one gives what he does not have. And since the senses do not have life they cannot give it. This was the case with Eve— when she saw that the fruit was pleasing, she desired it, ate it and thus served her sensuality and death was her lot. It is still the same with all who favour their senses. Had Eve followed her reason she would have turned away from her senses and then life would have been her lot.

It is frequently said that God damns man. God damns no one. Rather man damns himself, for by wilfully turning himself towards sensuality and living in it, he chooses death and forgoes life. Were God to grant him life he could not accept it, for he has no place in which it could be received. All that is in him is death, and hence death becomes his lot. Even if God were to grant life to such sensual men, it would be like throwing one's best friend into filthy dung. All that is sensual is impure dung, as St. Paul says: " I count all things as dung."[6]

Life is the best good that God possesses. And He does not give it to any man who lives in the senses so that He may not be mocked. Let no man wonder then if he thinks that God does not give him enough grace. It is not in accordance with God's order to throw away divine goodness to men who waste themselves in sensuality. Some also say that if God would, He could give many gifts to man. This is true, and were man to turn to grace, God would give them. But if man turns to where there is no grace, God cannot be expected to throw it away.

No, if man really wants to receive grace from God he should silence his senses and direct himself inwardly to God. If he continues to live in the senses, turned away from God, then God will not give him any grace. He who wants to receive something from another must be with him from whom he would receive. And all that is in man should be inwardly with God, since that is where God is. In this way only can divine love be received.

One should draw in his senses because each time he turns to the exterior, the senses contact something impure, carry it with them and spoil the soul. He who wishes to remain pure should keep his senses within and not allow them to wander, and in this way his heart will stay at peace. Should one wander too much towards external things even for the sake of good works, he will not have true peace of heart, for this peace of God is beyond the senses.

All that is sensual is also unstable and unpeaceful. The man who wishes to attain to true peace should detach himself from the senses and penetrate the centre of his soul where there is stability; only there will he find peace and quiet. Let no one consider himself so free and perfect that he imagines that to turn to unnecessary exterior works would not harm him. No one is so saintly in time that he can remain as pure if he turned outwardly as if he remained within. This is true because if man turned outwardly without necessity he would contact creatures as they are found there. And no one can remain as pure with creatures as with God; the creature is unfruitful, whereas God is fruitful. To deny that this outward turning is injurious is to prove that one has never experienced inward purity. A very small thing may cause great pain to the eye, and one must be careful to keep it clean. But a smaller thing can infect the inner man and even greater care than that taken for the eye is required to keep the inner man pure.

All that is external is impure, and if the senses turn in this direction they acquire impurity, and in returning to the interior they carry it with them and infect the heart. It is then quite right that one should always keep himself within in order that his heart may remain pure. The interior life belongs to a spiritually poor life. To turn to the exterior is to wander from the path of true spiritual poverty, for spiritual poverty pertains to the inner man, the outer cannot contain it. Spiritual poverty is a pure simple being, and he who complicates himself with external things cannot be pure. Purity is born of God within, not of creatures without, and so it follows that he who wants to keep spiritual poverty should live within.

No one can be truly poor in spirit unless God makes him poor in spirit. And God makes no one poor in spirit unless they remain with Him within, in which case He removes all that is not Himself. He who is the most internal is also the poorest in spirit, and he who is the poorest in spirit is also the most internal. Inwardness and spiritual poverty stand on the same level. The man who has not departed from externals can hardly be said to have attained to true inwardness, which, after all, consists in an utter abandonment of oneself and all things—inwardly as well as outwardly; all must give way to true inwardness.

Thus the will enters into God's most perfect will and unites itself with God. All that God wills for the best the inner man also wills. And God's most perfect will is that one should follow Christ in His life and teachings. This was the voice of the Father to the Son when St. John baptized Him: "This is My beloved Son in whom I am well pleased; hear ye Him."[7] "In whom I am well pleased" means that all the good pleasure of the Father is alone in the Son, and hence it is the Father's highest will that they who follow Him should also follow His Son as closely as possible. He said again: "Hear ye Him," which implies that it is His will that one should follow His teachings.

Now the life and teaching of our Lord imply exterior and interior poverty, and the pure will that turns to God also desires this work. He who does not turn his will to this work proves that his will is neither internal nor yet united with the divine will. When one is inwardly occupied, when his will is united with the will of God, he will know at once what he ought or ought not to do. The will of God is that one should follow the life and teachings of Christ. He who follows Him the closest is the most internal, and he who loves most inwardly also follows Him the closest.

3

DYING IN GOD

Only the man who attains to a spiritual, poor life in this inwardness is truly poor in spirit. And it is necessary that he who desires to be really poor in spirit should be inwardly turned. Poverty without inwardness is like a king without a country, or a body without a soul, or a soul without God. And as God gives the soul life, and as the soul gives love, so inwardness makes man's life fruitful and well-pleasing to God. Christ says: "Unless the seed of corn falls into the earth and dies, it can bring forth no fruit."[8]

All things must die within us, and we must die in God. It is then that we bring forth much fruit and it is then that the life which pleases God is born in us. He who does not enter into his heart can neither inwardly die nor bring forth any fruit. External display of poverty has no value. Beggars in the street have as much, but that certainly does not make them holy. A man must die inwardly in the ground of the soul. This befits a spiritually poor life in which lies perfection.

What, then, is a dying, interior poor life? A man is dead when he forgoes all sin and acquires virtue so that virtue becomes his very being. He is internal when all that is external is painful to him. He is poor when his spirit becomes a pure instrument of God, so that God can speak His eternal Word in the ground of the soul without obstruction. These three things stand for ever on the same level in the purity of a pure being: True dying is unity, true unity is spiritual poverty, true spiritual poverty is inwardness.

Christ says: "One thing is needful."[9] The one thing needful is that God should work in the soul, that man should draw himself together in a dying, interior and pure unity. Only such a condition is receptive of God's work, and He can only perform His best in unity. He who is most united is most receptive to God. When the sky is clearest, the sun can best send out its rays. When the soul is really simplified, the divine sun can best send out its light to the soul; it enlightens the soul with divine light. To the extent that the soul lacks unity, she lacks light. Since each thing works according to its nature, its operation is in unity.

The light, which is godlike, always shines in unity and to turn oneself away from unity is to turn oneself away from the divine light. The highest perfection consists in the soul being internal and united. He who is internal and united, who always remains within, increases most in perfection. More than any other he receives the influx of the divine light which enlightens the reason to know pure truth. Right knowledge of truth moves on to unity, and no one with dissipated faculties, no one whose reason is preoccupied with the manifold, attains to that real light in which all divine truth is revealed. Since that light is simple, the ground of the soul must be simple in order to reflect its brilliance, for each thing must adapt itself according to its worth. This is why it is necessary that he who wants to have light should be internal and united. As Christ says: "If thine eye be single, thy whole body shall be light."[10] Man's eye is the reason, and when this is single, all that it understands is pure truth, and all its acts are pure virtue.

What does not spring from a simple ground is deception. Hence, if one does not wish to be deceived, he should turn from multiplicity towards unity where deception cannot be mixed. The reason man is deceived is that the imagination forms too many images and it fancies these images to be true. It is possible for the evil spirit to enclose himself in these, hold up false images and deceive a man. Since the evil spirit cannot enter a really simple and pure ground, he cannot deceive a pure and simple man. The man who attaches importance to so-called visions, who preoccupies himself with images, shows that his ground is not altogether pure and simple. For in a pure and simple ground nothing is forthcoming except God and what is godlike.

Now God is invisible, elevated above all images; hence they who wish really to see Him are deceived. That which is forthcoming in a pure ground is so delicate and simple that no one can grasp it by images, nor can they even speak of it. The man who really knows the pure truth, knows well that it is true and pays no attention to visions, especially during these times. Truth has been revealed in our Lord Jesus Christ, and to seek it outside Him and His Church is to deceive oneself and others too. They who put their trust in a person who does this are ill in faith and have more in common with Antichrist than with Christ. They who live in Christ and in whom He lives, can put their trust in nothing but Christ. Should anything else be revealed to them they regard it with suspicion. And only they remain undeceived by falsehood.

Yes, even a pure and simple man, whose heart has been captured by Christ, must often resist a pure distinction of God-imaged truth. He must do this in order that he may remain pure in his simplicity and that God may not be obstructed in His operation in him, an operation which is elevated above all the distinctions of imaged truth. Even if such a man sometimes observes a thing by distinction in order to be able to teach his neighbour about it, he loses the very image of the thing as soon as he turns away from the teaching. He must then return to Christ and leave all the rest as it is, and this returning keeps him in true purity.

Such a man performs the greatest work and bears the greatest responsibility that anyone can have in time, for he must resist all that is in time, all that is not God. He must overcome all with a persistent struggle; all that is in him must be penetrated and separated. It sometimes happens that a man who is weak by nature or still weighed down with sins, must lie down sick and say with the loving soul, "Tell it to me beloved, for I lie sick with love."[11]

4

GOD FOR GOD!

The love of the Holy Spirit pierces all of man's members and inflames them with the fire of love. This fire consumes all unlikeness, it straightens that which was bent. Man thinks that he will be completely consumed and this is called active, overwhelming love. As long as there is unlikeness in man, this love must act. When this active love has worked off all unlikeness, a sweet love springs up in man and this is called passive love. It suffers in a quiet and gentle silence *all* that God does. It no longer acts, only God acts while it endures. Finally the soul attains to an everlasting entrance into the Godhead. Here God leads her with Himself, makes her one love with Himself, and thus man becomes one love with God.

To give this poor spirit a proper name would be to give him the name of love, for he is nothing but love. He does not concern himself with visions or any singularities—only with simple divine love. And this is brought about by the simple, pure ground, out of which simple, divine love springs. The greatest joy that exists in time is found in this. It is not a natural joy, nor one contrary to truth. It is godlike, and it reveals the truth which is God. This joy should not be criticized, for it is direct from God, annihilating all natural joy that is contrary to God.

But one should not retain this love for the sake of the joy. Were one to love God for the sake of joy, he would love Him in a natural way or as creatures love. One should not love God for the sake of pleasure. One should love God, *God for God*, abandon all pleasure and cling to God alone without any why or wherefore. Then one's love will be perfect.

May God help us to love Him perfectly! Amen.

NOTES

Introduction

1 Matthew 5.3.

2 See *Vorwort, Die Predigten Taulers, Deutsche Texte der Mittelalters,* by F. Vetter. Vol. XI, 1910. See note 110.

3 Marcus von Lindau was Franciscan Superior of the Strasbourg Province. See Bishop Greith in note 105.

4 Luther himself was familiar with the book and even enthusiastic about those aspects which grant a deeper insight into personal religion. He seems, however, to have forgotten these when he came to construct his rigid theology of a "completely other God". See *Luther's Theologie,* by Köstlin, and also note 100.

5 *Geschichte der Entdeckung der deutschen Mystiker,* G. Fischer, and also note 100.

6 It should be mentioned that the references made to Eckhart by Hegel and Schopenhauer are from writings falsely attributed to him, hence it is inaccurate for them to regard him as a kindred spirit. See *Das Göttliche in der Seele,* O. Karrer, Würzburg, 1928.

7 Hugueny, P., *Sermons de Tauler,* Paris, 1927, I, p. 73. Furthermore: "A disciple of Eckhart, Tauler is, as his master, wholly penetrated with Scholasticism." F. Vernet says: "These Rhineland mystics are, after all, theologians trained in the scholastic discipline, formed by the school of St. Thomas and in complete accord with him." (*Dictionnaire de Spiritualité,* I, col. 325.) See also: E. Gilson—*La Philosophie au moyen âge,* Paris, 1922, II, pp. 142-143; X. de Hornstein —*Les Grands mystiques allemands,* Lucerne, 1922, p. 228; M. Grabmann —*Die Lehre des heiligen Thomas von Aquin der Scintilla Animae in Ihrer Bedautung für die deutsche Mystik im Predigeorden,* in *Jahrbuch für Philosophie und spekulative Theologie,* 1899, p. 413.

8 Grundmann, J., *Religiöse Bewegungen,* Berlin, 1935, p. 276.

9 IV, ii, 7.

10 *Itinerarium Mentis ad Deum,* C. VII.

11 Lehmann W., *Johann Tauler Predigten,* Vol. II, p. 235, Jena, 1913. (A translation of Vetter.)

12 Büttner, H., *Meister Eckharts Schriften und Predigten,* Vol. II, p. 196, Jena, 1912. See also Suso's *Buchlein von der Wahrheit,*

ch. VII; *Theologia Germanica,* Ch. XXV; and our author's section on "Spiritual Misdirected Freedom," I, iv, 3.

13 Sermon on the Fifth Sunday in Lent, No. 31, Frankfort Ed., 1836. See also Lehmann, *op. cit.,* Nos. 36 and 40, and his Introduction, for a good life of Tauler based on the genuine available data.

14 Lehmann, *op. cit.,* Vol. II, p. 216.

15 Jundt, A., *Les Amis de Dieu au quatorzième siècle,* Paris, 1879; E. Peterson—*Der Gottesfreund (Beiträge zur Geschichte eines religiösen Terminus),* in *Zeitschrift für Kirchengeschichte,* Gotha, 1923, V, pp. 161-202; K. Egenter—*Gottesfreundschaft,* Augsberg, 1928; M. Grabmann—*Idee der Gottesfreund (Beiträge zur Geschichte der Philosophie des Mittelalters),* II, p. 1021; B. Schoemann—*Die Rede von den XV Graden, Rheinische Gottesfreundmystik, "ein characteristik Texte",* Berlin, 1930.

16 For the use which the *Gottesfreunde* made of Psalm 138.17, see *Speculum Ecclesiae,* by Kelle, p. 94; also *Kirchengeschichte Deutschlands,* I, p. 70. Prof. Chiquot says: " In this sense referred to by Tauler, so St. Augustine, St. Bernard, St. Albert the Great, St. Thomas, St. Bonaventure were proclaimed Friends of God." (*Amis de Dieu, Dictionnaire de Spiritualité,* I, col. 493.) The Rhineland Friends of God were known to quote St. Thomas's *Caritas amicitia quaedam est hominis ad Deum,* 2. 2. qu.23, a.1.

17 Sermon on the Birth of Our Lady, No. 127, Frankfurt Ed.

18 These two books may now be had in one volume in Prof. J. M. Clark's splendid translation. (Faber and Faber, London, 1953.) *The Book of Truth* is published in English for the first time.

19 Karrer, Otto, *Meister Eckhart,* Das system seiner religiösen Lehre und seiner Lebensweisheit, Munich, 1926.

20 *The Great German Mystics, Eckhart, Tauler and Suso* (Oxford, 1949).

21 Lehmann, *op. cit.,* Vol. I, p. 71.

22 Strauch, P., *Schriften aus der Gottesfreundliteratur,* Halle, 1927. See also: A. Chiquot—*Histoire ou légende? Jean Tauler et le ' Meisters Buoch',* Strasbourg, 1922, with review in *Revue D'Histoire Ecclésiastique,* XXI, p. 428.

23 Denifle, H. S., *Die Dichtungen Gottesfreundes im Oberlande, Zeitschrift für deutsches Altertum,* 1880. Perhaps had Rufus Jones, for his *Flowering of Mysticism,* and Evelyn Underhill, for her *Mysticism,* studied this and other more current works they would not have written so favourably of Merswin.

24 IV, vii, 3.

25 Büttner, *op. cit.,* Vol. I, pp. 13-14. See also Tauler's *Eine Gute Lehre Uber Gottes Wesen,* Lehmann, *op. cit.,* Vol. II, p. 80.

26 Lehmann, *op. cit.,* Vol. I, p. 2.

27 Büttner, *op. cit.,* Vol. I, p. 170.

28 *Ibid.,* pp. 169-177.

29 Pfeiffer, F., *Meister Eckhart,* Tractate iv, Göttingen, 1924.

30 I, i, 2.

31 I, vi, 1.
32 II, iii, 1.
33 I, i, 3.
34 III, ii, 2.
35 IV, v., 1.
36 I, ix, 5.
37 IV, vii, 3.
38 IV, vii, 1.
39 IV, vii, 2.
40 I, viii, 1.
41 I, i, 2.
42 II, i, 2.
43 II, i, 1.
44 II, ii, 3.
45 I, i, 3.
46 IV, iii, 2.
47 III, i, 4.
48 II, ii, 5.
49 See St. Thomas, 2. 2. qu.82, a.3, ad.3.
50 I, iv, 3.
51 IV, iv, 4.
52 Lehmann, *op. cit.*, I, p. 3.
53 *Mystica Theologia,* I, 3.
54 St. Thomas, 2. 2. qu.82.
55 *De Servo Dei* (Ven. 1764, III, c.50).
56 III, i, 4. Here he follows Suso and Tauler; see Lehmann, *op. cit.*
Vol. II, p. 135.
57 *De causis*, Lect. 24.
58 II, ii, 3.
59 II, iii, 3.
60 I, iii, 1.
61 III, iv. 3.
62 II, ii, 3.
63 I, iii, 1.
64 I, iii, 2.
65 St. Thomas, 2. 2. qu.81, a.6, ad.1.
66 IV, iii, 3.
67 IV, iii, 3.
68 II, iii, 2.
69 I, iv, 3.
70 III, iii, 3.
71 IV, vii, 2.
72 I, vii, 3.
73 III, iii, 3.
74 I, ii, 2.
75 IV, iv, 4.
76 IV, vii, 4.
77 IV, vii, 4.

T

78 IV, iv, 2.

79 IV, vii, 1.

80 IV, ii, 7.

81 IV, vii, 4.

82 I, vi, 4.

83 *Summa Theologica,* I, qu.61, a.5.

84 *Buchlein von der Wahrheit,* Ch. IV.

85 II, ii, 2.

86 St. Thomas, I, I, 37, qu.3, a.3, ad.4.

87 Büttner, *op. cit.,* I, p. 10.

88 III, ii, 2.

89 I, i, 1.

90 Lehmann, *op. cit.,* Vol. II, p. 138.

91 *De Gen. ad Lit.,* xii, c.31. See also: *Cor.* vii, 9; *De Cir. Dei,* x, 2; *De vera Rel.,* xi and xiv. Plotinian views became known to the Rhineland School principally via St. Augustine and St. Dionysius. As Prof. F. Vernet says: "The mystics of 'l'école allemande' speculate—as, in general, all the Dominican school—and their speculation is influenced by Neoplatonism. This is not entirely new. After St. Augustine and St. Dionysius, many had speculated about union with God in the light of the Plotinian theories. St. Albert the Great, among others, and St. Thomas himself, have used Neoplatonism known through St. Augustine and St. Dionysius" (*op. cit.,* I, col. 326). Marsilius Ficinus did not make his Latin translation of the *Enneads* until 1492.

92 *Mystica Theologia,* I, 1.

93 *De Adhaerendo Deo,* Ch. VI.

94 *Buchlein von der Wahrheit,* Ch. IV.

95 Lehmann, *op. cit.,* Vol. I, p. 6. Some critics believe this sermon to be Eckhart's.

96 *The Spirit of St. François de Sales,* by Camus, p. 45 (New York, 1952. Harpers; London, 1953. Longmans). Both the saint and Camus had, of course, Tauler in mind, believing him to be the author of the book.

97 IV, iv. 3.

98 An English translation of this was made by S. Winkworth (London, 1857). Because they have not examined the research made on this question, some scholars continue to regard the biography as genuine.

99 Schmidt, C., *Bericht von der Bekehrung Taulers* (Strasbourg, 1875). C. Rieder argued against Denifle that Nicholas von Löwen, Merswin's secretary, and not Merswin was the inventor of the fictitious Gottesfreund (*Der Gottesfreund vom Oberland,* Innsbruck, 1905), but A. Chiquot says: "Il est assez difficile d'admittre la thèse de Rieder."— *Dictionnaire de Spiritualité,* I, col. 492.

100 To understand the influence which *The Book of the Poor in Spirit* has played on so many spiritual writers, it is necessary to remember that they all believed it came from Tauler's pen. Believing as they did in the famous "conversion story", many came to regard it as his

post-conversion masterpiece. Of those directly influenced by the pseudo-Tauler writings, one might mention St. François de Sales, Jean Pierre Camus, the Dominican Chardon, the Carmelite Jean de Saint-Samson, the Jesuit Surin, the Capuchin Benet de Canfield, the Benedictine Augustine Baker, Bossuet, the Dominican Bl. Venturin di Bergarne and St. Paul of the Cross in Italy, Juan dos Angos and St. John of the Cross in Spain, Abbot Blosius, the Carthusians Denis de Rijckel, Ludolph of Saxony, the Benedictine John de Castel, Cardinal Nicholas von Cues. Among the Lutherans of Germany: Johann Gerhard (*Meditationes Sacrae,* Leyde, 1627), Johann Arndt (*Von Wahern Christenthum*, Magdeburg, 1610).

The *Book of the Poor in Spirit*, along with the other genuine and pseudo-writings of Tauler, has been a part of minor doctrinal controversy. After Marcus von Lindau quoted extensively from it in his *Buch von den Zehn Gebeten*, and the appearance of many of its paragraphs in the *Mystischen Tractate*, which Bishop Greith later edited, St. Peter Canisius (d. 1597) quoted from it in his *D. Taulers Göttliche Lehren*, Cologne, 1543, and, according to Père Hugueny, did so in order to demonstrate that Tauler was not a forerunner of Luther, an argument which some pietistic Reformers tried to make (v. I, p. 47, *Sermons de Tauler*, Paris, 1927). In the preface which Surius (d. 1578) wrote to his Latin translation of Tauler's works, he also clears him of certain charges brought against his writings. These were principally concerned with pantheistic and mystical elements which not only Lutherans, but even the Catholic Johann Eck (*De purgatorio contra Lutherium*, Paris, 1548) read into Tauler. Blosius (d. 1566), the famous Abbot of Lissus, met the challenge and wrote a long *Apologia pro Doktor Joanne Taulero adversus Joan Eckium* (v. *Opera,* p. 417, Cologne ed. 1606), as well as an Appendix to his *Institutio Spiritualis,* 1551, in his defence. The entire first chapter of this appendix, written as "a defence of Tauler against the harmful attacks of Johann Eck", is taken almost word for word from *The Book of the Poor in Spirit* (v. *Ibid*. C. I, p. 403); he endorses the doctrines of spiritual poverty, p. 403, col. 1, 1s. 6-20; receiving the Holy Eucharist, p. 403, col. 2, 1s. 5-37; spiritual desolation, p. 404, col. 1, 1s. 28-49; abandonment, p. 405, col. 1, 1s. 22-39; etc.). Nicholas von Cues, in defence of the Rhineland school against Johann Wenck von Herrenberg (*De Ignota Litteratura*), wrote his *Apologia Doctae Ignorantiae* (v. *Opera,* Basle, 1565, p. 71). The genuine and pseudo-writings of Tauler, as well as the works of Ruysbroeck and Harphius, were criticized by the Jesuits in Spain in 1575 and in Belgium in 1598. Fr. Augustine Baker, the seventeenth-century English Benedictine, rendered high tribute to Tauler and even translated for his disciples many long passages from his *Sermons* and *The Book of the Poor in Spirit* (v. *Life of Fr. Augustine Baker,* by Dom McCann, O.S.B., London, 1933). Fr. Baker's references to Tauler in his *Holy Wisdom* on pages 109, 119, 183, 478, 497, 506, may be traced to *The Book of the Poor in Spirit*. In seventeenth-century France the writings of Tauler were again discredited and defended in the Quietist controversy.   Bossuet (1627–1704), though he warned Gerson of Tauler's exaggerations in style, nevertheless regarded him as "un des plus solides et des plus corrects des mystiques" (v. *Instructions sur les états d'orison,* Oeuvres, Vol. II, Traite 1, 1, n.3, p. 15).   In 1693 he also gave praise to the French translations of *Les Méditations sur la vie et la passion du Sauveur,* and our book, *De L'Imitation de la vie pauvre de Jéus-Christ* (v. *Correspondence de Bossuet,* I, p. 506).

101 A considerable number of publications have been made of this book. Aside from a reprint of the 1621 edition, it was again published in Frankfurt in 1670, 1681, 1692; at Leipzig in 1703, 1720; a modern German edition by Nicholas Casseder at Lucerne in 1820, 1821, 1823 (two printings); again at Frankfurt in 1824; then, with a new title and some changes in the divisions of paragraphs, it was published by Matthew Schlosser at Frankfurt in 1833; by Wilh. Meck at Constance in 1850, and at Regensberg in 1855.   The first Italian edition was published by Father Strozzi at Venice in 1584; the first French edition by the Oratorian Jacques Talon at Paris in 1693.   Most religious of the various countries, including England and Spain, continued to refer to the Latin translation of Surius which always accompanied Tauler's *Sermons,* etc.   Altogether the book has been published under three different titles: *The Following of the Poor Life of Christ, The Book of Spiritual Poverty,* and *The Book of the Poor in Spirit,* and it is under this last title that new editions are again contemplated in Germany and France.

102 Schmidt, *op. cit.*; also his *Johannes Tauler von Strassburg,* Hamburg, 1841; Preger, F.—*Geschichte der deutschen Mystik im Mittelalter,* 3 vols., Leipzig, 1893; furthermore, Bähring believed that *The Book of the Poor in Spirit* "was incontestably the work of Tauler", and adds that "it is the most beautiful fruit of his conversion" (*J. Tauler und die Gottesfreunde,* Hamburg, 1833, p. 89).   Böhringer shares this view in his *Die deutschen Mystiker des XIV und XV Jahrhunderts,* Zurich, 1855.

103 Denifle, H. S., *Das Buch von geistlicher Armuth* (Munich, 1877).

104 *Ibid., Einleitung,* p. 51.

105 Ritschl, A., *Untersuchungen des Buches von geistlicher Armuth,* in *Zeitschrift für Kirchengeschichte,* IV, 1881.   Like Denifle it is quite possible that Ritschl's method of criticism may have blinded him to some of the reasons in favour of the traditional opinion; at least he displays little understanding of the fourteenth-century Dominican doctrine of poverty.

After a detailed study of the entire problem, it would seem that Denifle's best arguments for *The Book of the Poor in Spirit* not being written by Tauler are primarily, if not solely, on the subject of style. But in order to substantiate further his hypothesis, he definitely exaggerates even this point as well as the other points of difference which he raises.   The method of cricitism used by Denifle, an old-guard Neoscholastic, is now regarded as unprofitable by contemporary Thomists. Furthermore, Blosius had long since defended the book's essential views on spiritual poverty, abandonment and the practice of communion. And both Augustine Baker and the cautious Bossuet supported our author's doctrine of contemplation. And, as Père Noël says, chapter and verse from the treatise itself could be quoted against each point raised by Denifle. As for the Protestant Ritschl's opinion, that the " authors " were Scotists and members of the Fraticelli, Denifle himself demonstrates how Ritschl completely failed to comprehend the writings or thought of both Tauler and our author (v. *Die deutsche Dichtungen R. Merswin*, in *Zeitschrift für deutsche Altertum*, XXV, p. 121). Lehmann believes that " die ganze Geschichte Taulers ist gegenstandlos " (*op. cit.*, p. xxix), and Siedel that " unangefochten wird die wirkliche Bekehrung Taulers bleiben müssen " (*Die Mystik Tauler*, p. 11, 1911). As recent a scholar as Prof. M. de Gandillac believes that it is unlikely that we shall ever know the true story of Tauler but insists that Denifle's grasp of the fourteenth-century Dominican notion of poverty and contemplation was very limited. No twentieth-century investigator has offered any new reasons why the author of *The Book of the Poor in Spirit* was not a Dominican and a direct disciple of Tauler, and they are almost unanimous in believing with Père Noël that " Denifle, in exaggerating his case, has done great harm to a very important guide to the Rhineland school of mysticism ".

Further evidence in support of the treatise coming from the pen of an orthodox Dominican is to be gathered from the research made by M. Seitz into the origin of the early MS. edited by Bishop Greith (*Die deutsche Mystik im Prediger Orde*, Fribourg, 1861), which is a compilation of texts taken from Eckhart, Tauler, Suso and *The Book of the Poor in Spirit* (v. *Der Traktat des unbekannten deutschen Mystikers bei Greith*, by M. Seitz, Leipzig, 1936). P. Debongnie says in his review: " Le sein jette une lumière precise sur l'histoire de la diffusion de la mystique spéculative dans les couvents de dominicaines aus XIV siècle." (*Revue D'Histoire Ecclésiastique*, Vol. 36, p. 468). In his short but excellent study of *The Great German Mystics*, Prof. Clark gives notice to the treatise in his chapter on Franciscan writings, but his information seems to be based only on Denifle's criticism.

106 See E. P. Noël, O.P.—*Imitation de la vie pauvre de N.S. Jésus Christ* (Paris, 1914); *Oeuvres complètes de Jean Tauler* (Paris, 1911, Trans. from Surius), with review by J. Paquier in *Revue D'Histoire Ecclésiastique*, XIII, p. 114. Xavier de Hornstein—*Les grands mystiques allemands du XIV*e *siècle*, Lucerne, 1922, with reviews by R. M. Martin, O.P., in *Revue D'Histoire Ecclésiastique*, XXI, p. 134; essays in *Revue Thomiste*, 1918, I, p. 224; 1919, II, p. 45. O. Karrer—*Textgeschichte der Mystik*, Munich, 1926, Vol. II. F. Vernet—*Allemande Spiritualité*, Vol. I, col. 314, Paris, 1937, published under the direction of Marcel Viller, S.J. R. Schleuszner—*Mystikertexte und Mystikerüberzetzung*, in *Der Katholik*, 1913. P. Pourrat—*Tauler*, in *Dictionnaire de Théologie Catholique*, 1946, Vol. 15, I, p. 66. J. Quint —*Deutsche Mystikertexte des Mittelalters*, Bonn, 1929. J. Koch—

Untersuchungen über Datierung, Form, Sprache und Quellen, Kritisches Verzeichnis sämtlicher Predigten, in *Deutsche Mytikertexte des Mittelalters,* Heidelberg, 1940. M. Grabmann—*Mittelalterliches Geistleben,* Munich, 1926. L. Nauman—*Untersuchungen zu Johann Taulers deutschen Predigten,* Rostock, 1911. W. Oehl—*Johann Tauler,* Munich, 1911. A. Chiquot—*Buch von geistlicher Armuth,* in *Dictionnaire de Spiritualité,* I. Col. 1976. F. W. Wentzlaff-Eggebert—*Studienz Lebenslehre Tauler,* in *Abhandlung d. preuss. Akad. der Wiss. Philos.-hist., Kl. In-4,* Berlin, 1940, with review by E. Seeberg in *Zeitschrift für Kirchengeschichte,* LIX, p. 492. P. von Loe, O.P.—*Johann Tauler,* in *Kirchenliteratur-zeitung,* XI, col. 1279. M. de Gandillac—*Tradition et development de la mystique rhénane,* in *Mélanges de Science religieuse,* 1946, III, pp. 37-82; *Les Aspects de la mystique rhénane,* in Fliche and Martin's *Histoire de L'Eglise,* 1951, XIII, p. 386.

107 Dufourq, A., *L'Avenir du Christianisme,* Vol. VI, pp. 381 and 453; G. R. Galbraith—*The Constitutions of the Dominican Order,* Ch. IV.

108 I, iv, 3.

109 First Sermon on the Feast of All Saints, Frankfurt Ed.

110 Second Sermon on the Feast of All Saints, Frankfort Ed. In Vetter's Edition, see Sermons V, p. 23, XII, p. 58, XXI, p. 87, XXXVI, p. 139, LXIII, p. 345. Nor do these quotations contradict Sermon VII, p. 36. It would seem that several Sermons in the Frankfort Edition (1826) not included in Vetter's collection must be attributed to Tauler. Some of these are quite as valid as most of the eighty-one in his collection. See P. Strauch, *Zu Taulers Predigten, Beiträge zur Geschichte des deutschen Sprache und Literatur,* vol. 44; A. L. Corin, *Zur Filiation der Taulerischen Handschriften, Revue belge de philosophie et d'histoire,* III, 1924.

111 Cf. Maldonatus, Cornelius à Lapide, Denis the Carthusian on the First Beatitude and on Matthew XIX, 16-24. Cf. also: St. Augustine—Serm. 28 de Verb. Apost; Serm. 50, n.3; Epist. 31, n.5; Epist. 157, n.24 and n.34; Quest. Evang. II, qu.31. St Jerome—Epist. 24, ad Julian; Epist. 125, n.20; Epist. 150, ad Hedib.; Advers. Vigil, n.14. St. Leo the Great—Serm. 42, n.2. St. Gregory the Great—I Homil. in Evang. 5, n.2. St. Peter Damian—Opusc. 27: *De commune vita canonicorum.* St. Anselm—*De Similitudinibus,* 84. St. Bonaventure—*Apologia Pauperum;* Quest. disp. de Perf. Evang. qu.2, art.2. St. Thomas—III a, qu.40, art.3; *Contra retrahentes,* cap. 15, in Matt. XIX; *De perfectione vitae spiritualis,* cap. x. Bussuet—*L'éminente Dignité du Pauvre.* See also: *Le Pauvre dans la Bible,* by C. Didiot, Paris, 1903; *La littérature du Pauvre dans la Bible,* by I. Leob, Paris, 1892. Concerning the thesis: " since riches are a grave danger to the spirit, therefore poverty is far to be preferred ", see the Encyclicals *Rerum Novarum* of Leo XIII, 1891, *Quadragesimo Anno,* of Pius XI, 1931, and Pius XII's Pentecost message, 1941.

112 Pfeiffer, *Die Deutsche Mystiker,* pp. 301-314.

113 Pfeiffer, *Meister Eckhart,* Tractate x.

114 2. 2. qu.182, a.2, ad.1.   See also *Contra Gentiles,* 3, c.133.

115 *Allemande Spiritualité, op. cit.,* Vol. I, col. 327.   He says further:
" L'école allemande est une grand école de mysticisme.   Elle a, d'une
manière saisissante, mis en relief la nécessité de l'abnégation, du
détachement de soi et des creatures, pour ' suivre de Christ ' et s'unir
avec Dieu.   Elle a fragé la route à saint Jean de la Croix et à sainte
Teresa.   Elle a, par ses spéculations, préparé, conjointement avec
Ruysbroeck, une métaphysique du mysticisme, sans abandonner le
domaine de l'observation psychologique."   Col. 331.

116 Wisely realizing this, Surius, in making his Latin translation, care-
fully translated Armuth as " spiritual poverty " or " poverty of spirit ".
Compare also the modern Regensberg edition of 1855.

117 Denifle, H. S., *op. cit., Einleitung,* p. 53.

118 *Buch von geistlicher Armuth, op. cit.,* I, col. 1977.

PART I

Chapter I.   True Spiritual Poverty is Detachment

1 *Confessions,* VII, 4.
2 John 17.3.
3 See *Introduction,* p. 34.
4 St. Thomas, 1. 2. qu.65, a.1; St. Bonaventure, 3, dist. 3b, qu.1;
St. Gregory, *Morals,* xxii, 1.
5 II Corinthians 12.9.
6 *Ethics* II, 65b, 17; cf. St. Augustine, *In Joannem,* II, 14.
7 *De Trinitate* VIII, 4.

Chapter II.   True Spiritual Poverty is Freedom

1 Matthew 11.12.
2 Romans 8.35.
3 John 8.34.
4 Philippians 4.13.
5 I Corinthians 6.17.
6 See *Categories* 14, 64; cf. St. Dionysius *Divine Names,* V, 3; St.
Bonaventure 2, dist. 3, pl; St. Albert *In coelest. hierarch.,* Ch. I, 10a.
7 II Corinthians 3.17.
8 Philippians 3.8.
9 Matthew 11.29.
10 I Timothy 1.9.

Chapter III.   External Works of Charity

1 Matthew 11.28.
2 Romans 14.17.
3 Luke 14.13-14.
4 Romans 12.1.
5 Matthew 5.44-45.

Chapter IV.   Misdirected Freedom

1 Homil. 34 in Evang. 2.
2 *Inter excerpta,* ed. Lips., 1170, p. 1004.
3 Luke 18.22.
4 See II Corinthians 12.7.
5 II Corinthians 11.14.

Chapter V.   True Spiritual Poverty is a Pure Action

1 Homil. 9 in Evang. 6.
2 Lib. past. curae, p.3, ad.35.   Cf. St. Bonaventure: "Nolle profi-cere deficere est."   (Epistle 254, No. 4.)
3 Cf. St. Gregory, Homil. 32 in Evang. 1.
4 Titus 1.15.
5 The theme of this entire chapter emphasizes the apostolic signifi-cance which the Rhineland School gave to spiritual poverty.   More than the active ministerial work characteristic of the Dominican Order, we find these mystics stressing the pre-eminent apostolic nature of the very internal work of pure love and contemplation.   Moreover, do we not see in their writings a concern for a return to the traditional notion of the apostolic man?   For the first twelve centuries of Christianity *vir apostolicus* was, as Rupert von Deutz explained, a man who led the life of the Apostles and their immediate successors, one who imitated the spirit of prayer and the conduct of the early Christians and thence the early Fathers and monks (v. *De vita vera Apostolica,* Migne, 170, col. 611-664).   Père P. R. Régamey, O.P., points out how poverty is essential even to the active apostolate and that there can be no apostolic effectiveness in any work if the person who performs it is not poor in spirit.   (See: *La Pauvreté,* Ch. III, Paris, 1941.)

Chapter VI.   The Work of Nature

1 Cf. St. Thomas I. qu.62, a.5.
2 This is the famous scholastic doctrine: "*Deus non destruit naturam, sed perficit eam.*"
3 Meister Eckhart: Pfeiffer, *op. cit.,* p. 513.
4 John 16.13.

Chapter VII.   The Work of Grace

1 Matthew 11.5.
2 Matthew 13.11-13.
3 Cf. Ecclesiasticus 24.11.
4 Deuteronomy 5.6-21.

Chapter VIII.   The Four Spirits that Speak in Man

1 Cf. St. Thomas, 1. 2. qu.64, a.1.
2 II Corinthians 12.7.
3 II Corinthians 12.9.
4 Matthew 7.16.
5 I Corinthians 6.17.
6 The famous "*Ama et fac quod vis*".

Chapter IX.   The Friends of God

1 Cf. *Ethics* 1166, a.31.
2 John 15.15.
3 Cf. *Ethics* 1167, a.6.
4 Cf. I Thessalonians 4.3.
5 *Confessions* I, 1.
6 Luke 11.41.
7 Cf. Psalms 49.8, 50.8.
8 Proverbs 23.26.
9 Classical logic reminds us, however, that contraries are not contradictories.
10 Luke 11.41.
11 Matthew 7.12.
12 I John 3.17.
13 Homil. 20 in Evang. 2.
14 Philippians 3.8.
15 Matthew 5.3.
16 Hebrews 12.29.
17 Galatians 5.17.
18 Apocalypse 3.1.
19 Matthew 19.21.
20 Matthew 19.27.
21 Our author implies, of course, that the actual giving up of all exterior things is only a *counsel* for those free of obligation; the *precept* is that all should become spiritually detached from material goods and even from spiritual goods.   The counsel offers the safest and easiest way to obey the precept.   St. Thomas explains how perfection is founded upon the counsels, and how all are called to perfection; but he also points out that marriage, physical handicaps, necessary obligations, etc., are not obstacles to perfection.   (v. 2.2. q.184, art. 3, *and* q.189, art. 10.   See also St. Augustine, Epist. 89, ad Hilar.)

PART II

Chapter I.   God *Is* His Work

1 Proverbs 8.31.
2 John 17.21.
3 The Church prayer: *Deus celsitudo humilium et fortitudo rectorum, qui per unigenitum Filium tuum ita mundum erudire dignatus es, ut omnis illius actio nostro fieret instructio, excita in nobis Spiritus Tui fervorem, ut quod ille verbo et exemplo salubriter docuit nos efficaciter imitari valeamus.*
4 I Peter 2.21.
5 In Cant. Sermon, 21, 2.
6 John 12.26.
7 John 10.1-10.
8 John 4.14.
9 II Corinthians 12.4.
10 Philippians 3.20.
11 Luke 17.21.
12 Philippians 1.23.
13 Romans 7.24.
14 I Corinthians 2.2.
15 Cf. Luke 24.46.
16 Cf. Canticle of Canticles 4.9.

Chapter II.   God's Intimate Speech

1 Philippians 4.13.
2 John 10.3.
3 John 10.4.
4 John 10.16.
5 Epistle 147, 1.
6 Matthew 21.13.
7 Romans 14.17.
8 Luke 11.28.
9 Cf. Cant. of Cant. 4.7.
10 John 17.1.
11 John 12.28.
12 John 17.1-4.
13 John 1.5.
14 Matthew 5.20.
15 Cf. I Thessalonians 5.22.
16 the famous scholastic maxim: *Majus est quod ex impio fiat justus, quam creare coelum et terram.*
17 John 4.14 and 7.38.
18 II Corinthians 12.4.
19 This is in accordance with Egyptian mythology.

Chapter III. The Perfect Will

1 *Confessions* XIII, 8.
2 Cf. Ecclesiasticus 24.11.
3 I Thessalonians 4.3.
4 Mark 10.21.
5 *Mystica Theologia* I, 1.
6 Matthew 10.19.
7 Psalms 93.12.
8 *Ibid.*

PART III

Chapter I. Following Christ's Life and Teaching

1 John 14.23.
2 Cf. *De diligendo Deo,* IV, 11.
3 Romans 6.19.
4 I John 3.9.
5 Luke 12.49.
6 Matthew 26.38.
7 Cf. Philippians 3.20.
8 Philippians 4.13.
9 John 14.23.
10 Cf. Luke 10.42.
11 John 15.6.
12 James 1.17.
13 Galatians 2.20.
14 Psalms 32.9.
15 Romans 1.20.
16 Cf. John 6.35.
17 It is clear from this chapter that our author never wants us to infer from the poverty of Christ a condemnation of the *right* to possess: This would be akin to the opinion held by the Fraticelli which John XXII declared erroneous in 1324. (See: The Bull *Cum inter non nullos,* Nov. 12, 1323, and the Constitution *Quia quorumden,* Nov. 10, 1324.) The heretical error is known as "the absolute poverty of Christ". Pope Nicholas III pointed out, however, that one is left free to suppose that Christ never made use of His right.

Chapter II. The Perfection of Virtue

1 Eckhart, see Pfeiffer, *op. cit.,* Tractate IV.

Chapter III. Dying to Self

1 Apocalypse 14.13
2 John 12.24-25.
3 Matthew 19.21.
4 Colossians 3.3.

5 II Timothy 4.8.
6 II Corinthians 11.14.
7 Cf. I Corinthians 4.15.
8 Matthew 11.29.
9 Romans 8.35.
10 John 3.3.
11 For the scholastic doctrine that only God can operate in the essence of the soul, see St. Thomas, 1. 37. qu.3, a.3, ad. 4. Regarding the transformation of the spirit from the soul, Richard of St. Victor says: "For this to happen in us, the vision of the Word of God is necessary; the spirit is separated from the soul and is transformed in this image of divine glory."—*De Extern.* Ch. 18.
12 Romans 6.8.

Chapter IV.   The Contemplative Way

1 Cant. of Cant. 1.2.
2 Philippians 4.13.
3 Luke 18.28.
4 Cf. John 14.23.
5 *Confessions* VII, 16.
6 Cf. II Corinthians 12.4.
7 Cf. John 17.8.
8 John 7.38.
9 John 21.22.
10 Luke 10.42.
11 Psalms 81.6.
12 Matthew 7.21.

PART IV

Chapter I.   The First Way: Detachment

1 Matthew 5.5.
2 Homil. 11 in Evang. 2.

Chapter II.   The Second Way: Through Christ to the Godhead

1 John 14.6.
2 Cf. Matthew 20.21-22.
3 I Peter 2.21.
4 I Corinthians 2.2.
5 I Corinthians 15.22.
6 John 8.12.
7 Matthew 7.15.
8 *Mystica Theologia* V, 1.

9 See what our author says regarding submission in I, ii, 2; also Suso's *Buchlein von der Wahrheit*, Ch. VII. The implication is that spiritual poverty spurs the poor spirit on to a joyous divine obedience of the commandments of Holy Church as they apply to him.

10 Matthew 13.44.

11 This, according to Denifle, is taken from St. Bonaventure.

12 Cf. II Esdras 8.10 and 5.1.

13 John 15.5.

14 Philippians 4.13.

15 St. Thomas speaks of the *synderesis* as a power of the soul which transcends the reasoning faculty (2. dist. 39, qu.3, a.1). St. Bonaventure refers to it as the apex of the mind (*Itiner.* Ch. I). In the next paragraph our author says that when God reveals Himeslf in the centre of the soul, He "draws all the faculties to Him and unites them with Himself".

16 John 12.32.

17 Cf. John 20.21 and 15.16.

18 Cant. of Cant. 2.1.

19 Luke 19.5.

20 Matthew 20.8.

Chapter III. The Third Way: The Acceptance of Suffering

1 Matthew 18.7.

2 I John 4.18.

3 John 12.32.

4 Matthew 7.1.

5 Romans 2.1.

6 I Corinthians 13.5.

7 I Corinthians 13.2.

8 Wm. of St. Thierry, *Epist. to the Cart. of Mont Dieu*, c.11.

9 Luke 18.19.

10 Luke 14.33.

11 Cf. Luke 14.26 and Matthew 10.38.

12 "Sufficiently prepared" implies, of course, not being in a state of mortal sin. St. François de Sales even addressed those whose confession he had just heard as "saints", for, considering their contrition, intention and resolves they were at that moment altogether pure. See also Blosius' defence of "Tauler": *Opera*, p. 403, col. 1, Cologne Ed., 1606. It should be remembered that our modern doctrines on the Holy Eucharist were not really inaugurated until the seventeenth century.

13 Psalms 91.15-16.

14 Cf. Ecclesiasticus 24.26.

15 Matthew 5.10-11.

16 Matthew 5.12.

17 Matthew 26.38.

18 Philippians 4.4.

Chapter IV.   How the Friend of God Suffers

1 Luke 6.23.
2 Isaias 28.19.
3 Homil. 14 in Evang. 3.
4 Cf. Acts 14.22.
5 Cf. II Timothy 3.12.
6 Wisdom 5.4-5.
7 Apocalypse 14.13.
8 See Roman Breviary, Feast of St. Martin, antiphon in Second Vespers.
9 *De Trinitate* XIII, 4.
10 Mark 4.24.
11 I Corinthians 9.22.
12 Cf. Proverbs 12.21.
13 Matthew 5.6.
14 John 12.27.
15 Matthew 7.15.
16 Matthew 10.41.
17 See *Introduction*, p. 28; cf. Dionysius, *De Div. Nom.* c.7, 3.
18 Apocalypse 21.5.
19 Ephesians 4.22-24.
20 Matthew 18.3.
21 Cf. Romans 6.19.
22 Luke 18.19.

Chapter V.   The Protecting Spirit

1 Proverbs 24.16.
2 Luke 24.36.
3 Homil. 40 in Evang. 6.
4 For the schoolmen this principle was expressed: *Remota causa, removetur effectus.*
5 *De vera religione,* XIV, 27.
6 Hebrews 12.29.
7 I John 3.9.
8 Romans 5.20.
9 Romans 8.28.

Chapter VI.   The Fourth Way: Peace of Heart

1 Cf. *Confessions* VII, 10 and I, 1.
2 *De vera religione,* XLIX, 94.
3 Cf. James 1.17.
4 Psalms 84.9.
5 Mark 16.16.
6 Matt. 7.21.
7 James 2.20.
8 See Osee 2.14.

Chapter VII.   Union with Divine Love

1 John 14.23.

2 Hebrews 11.38.

3 Galatians 6.14.

4 Matthew 19.21.

5 Luke 10.42.

6 Philippians 3.8.

7 Matthew 3.17.

8 John 12.24.

9 Luke 10.42.

10 Matthew 6.22.

11 Cant. of Cant. 2.5.

ADDENDA

It has seemed wise to remain within the limits of these few referential and explanatory notes, rather than insert many quotations from other texts. However, a few observations remain:

A. When considered *de fond en comble,* the Rhineland School is seen to contain far more than just those eloquent, metaphysical teachings by which it has become popular. In fact these are counter-balanced by much that is downright pedantic and catechetical, with a special emphasis on practical detachment and Passion Piety. (v. P. Maréchal, *Psychology of the Mystics*, II.) And it is doubtful if a real understanding of the lofty themes can be had without an appreciation of those more business-like. But the "work" of following Christ is, for these mystics, pre-eminently an act of the higher intellect and will, rather than of the imagination. Is not His Passion and life *imprimis* "a sign of spiritual poverty indicating its own ultimate decrease so that realization of the Godhead may increase?" (IV, ii, 3.) How unlike that self-extending and therefore dubious *passion-mystique* which endorses an accretion and conservation of images!

B. The author's classification of the faculties of the soul—*intellect, will, memory*—are probably direct from Rich. of St. Victor (cf. *Benj. Minor*, 3.6). But the ultimate source is St. Augustine *De Trinitate*, XII, 3). For St. Augustine and many scholastics, *mens* implied *memoria* (cf. St. Thomas, *De Veritate*, I, ad.2) Regarding the *synderesis*, however, Abbot Thomas of St. Andrew's, Vercelli (XIII Cent.) in his commentary on the *Mystica Theologia,* says: "There is another cognitive faculty which as far surpasses the intellect as the intellect surpasses the reason or the reason the imagination; and this is the *apex affectionis principalis*, and the same is the *scintilla synderesis* which alone may be united to the divine Spirit (MS. 69, ff. 131ᵇ). St. Thomas speaks of the *synderesis* as a "*virtus* inborn in our soul . . . or even a *potentia* considered as developed in us by an innate *habitus*." (In II Sent., d.27, qu.2, a.3.) It is infallible, indestructible, supra-rational, and the knowledge which proceeds from it "does not come by discursive investigation, rather it is presented all at once to the intellect". (*De Veritate*, qu.16.) St. Bonaventure calls the *synderesis* "the supreme point of the soul". For him also it is infallible, indestructible, supra-rational, but "the highest part of the will", in fact, "it is the primary impulse or *weight* of the will towards good and hence inseparable from it." (*Itinerarium*, I, 1; II Sent, 39.2, 1.)

C. Never does the author deny action nor abolish the function of external works. But he insists that the work of the poor spirit ultimately hinges on one pure act, and that the contemplative poor life is simply a series of such acts. It is one thing to subordinate the practice of the Christian life (e.g. external forms of prayer, ordinary virtues, frequent use of the Sacraments, meditation on the humanity of Christ, etc.), to this life of interior action—which he does; but it is quite another thing to disregard them altogether and in their place substitute an idle form of inaction—which he never does. As many saints have pointed out, there is a great difference between " *doing* nothing " and " not doing anything ". In stressing the need for simplicity in bringing forth the fruits of external actions, our author does not want his readers to confuse it with negative indifference. (See also: St. François de Sales, *Treatise*, IX, chapters 4 and 5.)

D. Much could be said about the relationships between Rhineland mysticism and the mysticisms of the Low Countries (e.g. *The Mirror of Simple Souls, Hedwig of Anvers,* Ruysbroeck, etc.). Though the mutual influence is obvious, they are really two schools, the latter being far more directly affected by the teachings of St. Bernard and William of St. Thierry, less by the scholasticisms of Sts. Albert, Bonaventure and Thomas. Indeed " nuptial mysticism " reached its peak in the Low Country of the XIII Century, especially among the Beguines, and it would be a mistake to think that the Rhinelanders (even Eckhart) were not indebted to them (v. P. J. Greven, *Die Anfänge der Beginen,* Munster, 1912; P. A. Mens, *Oonsprong en betekenis van de Nederlandse Begijnen,* Anvers, 1947; P. St. Axters, O.P., *Le Spiritualité de Pays-Bas,* Paris, 1948). On the other hand, the speculative and practical passion-mysticism of the Rhine found its way to the Netherlands and to Groenendael. An excellent work has recently been published (*Hadewijch d'Anvers,* par Fr. J.-B.P., *Editions du Seuil,* Paris 1954), in which the author maintains that a Beguine, Hedwig II (c. 1340?) may well be one of the " missing links " between Eckhart and Ruysbroeck (p. 47). Particularly relevant to our study is her Poem X on *The Poor in Spirit* (p. 173), for it is " *un éloge de la pauvreté, qui ne comporte pas seulement le dépouillement des biens materiels, mais celui des images et des formes, de tout ' accident', de toute opinion et de toute pensée* " (p. 54). It is not necessarily to be inferred that the author of *The Book of the Poor in Spirit* knew the writings of Hedwig II, but simply that this approach to poverty was not considered singular by the orthodox.

Nihil obstat: HUBERTUS RICHARDS, S.T.L., L.S.S.

CENSOR DEPUTATUS

Imprimatur: E. MORROGH BERNARD

VIC. GEN.

Westmonasterii, die 10a Aprilis, 1954.